DRIVING STANDARDS AGENCY

THE Driving Manual

DRIVING SKILLS

London: The Stationery Office

Published by The Stationery Office

The previous edition of this title was published by HMSO.

Published with the permission of the Driving Standards Agency on behalf of the Controller of Her Majesty's Stationery Office

ISBN 0 11 551782 0
British Library Catalogue in Publication Data
A CIP catalogue record for this book is available from the British Library

Other titles in the Driving Skills series
The Official Theory Test for Car Drivers and Motorcyclists
The Official Theory Test for Large Vehicle Drivers
The Driving Test
The Bus and Coach Driving Manual
The Goods Vehicle Driving Manual
The Motorcycling Manual
The Theory Test and Beyond (CD-ROM)

Acknowledgments

The Driving Standards Agency (DSA) would like to thank the staff of the following organisations for their contribution to the production of this publication

Department of the Environment, Transport and the Regions

Driver and Vehicle Licensing Agency

Cambridge Constabulary

Cambridge Tyre Services

Every effort has been made to ensure that the information contained in this publication is accurate at the time of going to press.
The Stationery Office cannot be held responsible for any inaccuracies. Information in this book is for guidance only.

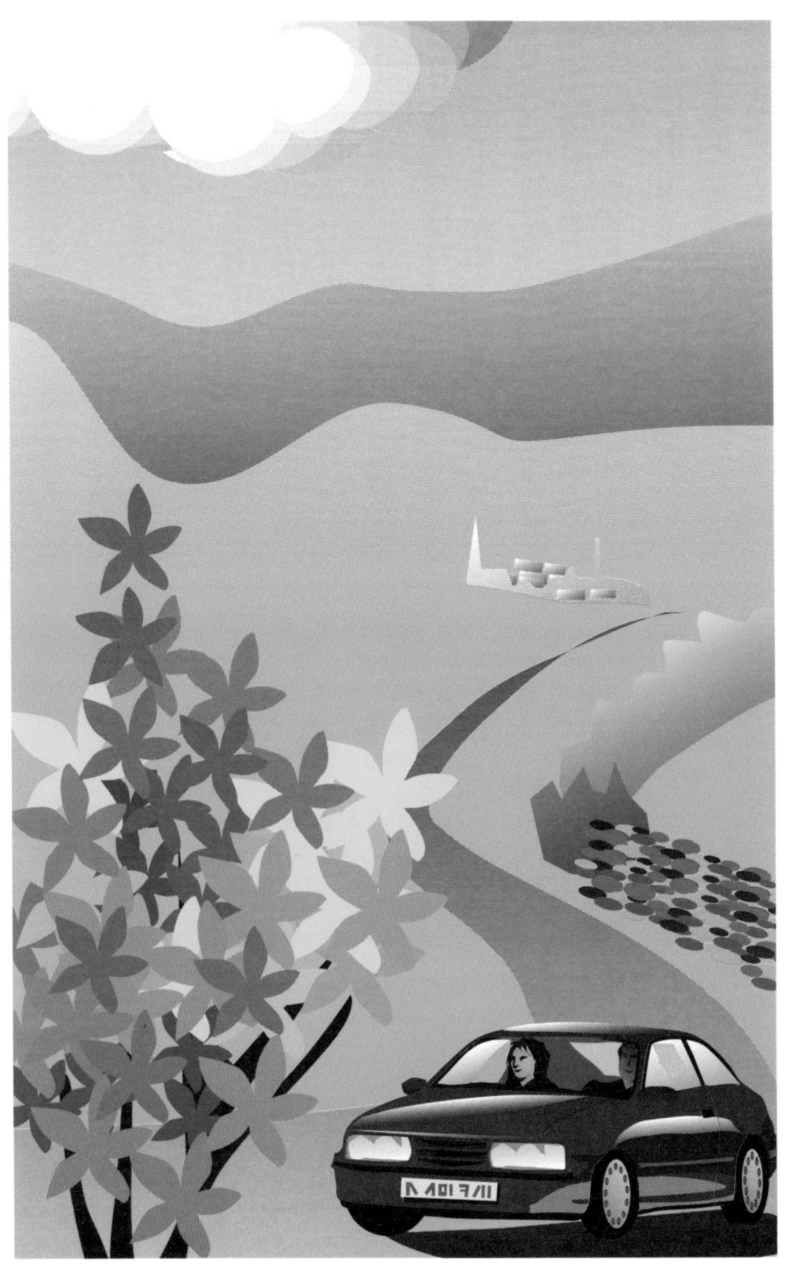

ABOUT DRIVING STANDARDS AGENCY

The Driving Standards Agency (DSA) is an Executive Agency of the Department of Environment, Transport and the Regions. You'll see its logo at test centres.

The aim of DSA is to promote road safety through the advancement of driving standards.

DSA

- conducts practical driving tests for drivers or riders of cars, motorcycles, lorries, buses and other vehicles
- plans, maintains and supervises the theory test for drivers or riders of cars, motorcycles, lorries and buses
- controls the register of Approved Driving Instructors (ADIs)
- supervises Compulsory Basic Training (CBT) courses for motorcyclists
- aims to provide a high-quality service to its customers.

CONTENTS

"Safe Driving for life"

Each year thousands of men, women and children are killed or seriously injured on roads in the UK. Unfortunately, many of these deaths and injuries are caused by the poor standard of driving that so many experienced drivers lapse into. This makes it vital that every driver understands the responsibility that driving a car brings with it and the importance of making safety their overriding priority.

Safe driving is all about developing the right attitude and approach, and combining this with a sound knowledge of defensive driving techniques. It means not only driving with courtesy and consideration for everyone else, but being prepared to make allowances for the mistakes of others.

The volume of traffic on our roads today means you'll often find yourself driving in crowded conditions on all types of road. By adopting the correct attitude and taking pride in your driving you'll ensure that this convenient means of transport remains both safe and enjoyable.

The Driving Manual has long been recognised as an essential reference book for every motorist, regardless of experience, and for instructors too. With full colour graphics this latest edition has been updated and re-styled to both improve readability and to take account of changes in legislation, roads, vehicles and driving techniques and procedures.

Read this book carefully – and put into practice the advice it gives. Above all, make sure your aim is *"Safe Driving for Life"*.

Robin Cummins
The Chief Driving Examiner
Driving Standards Agency

No matter how good, how fast, how expensive or how efficient your vehicle is, it's you, THE DRIVER, who determines whether it's a safe means of transport.

Driver skill and driver attitude are two key areas which determine your approach behind the wheel.

There is, after all, a lot of enjoyment and satisfaction to be gained from showing, not only your skill and ability, but also courtesy and consideration to those around you. Apart from the reward of a nod or smile in appreciation, you'll have the added satisfaction of knowing you are making our roads that much safer.

The right attitude and behaviour are the key factors to becoming a good driver. This section is devoted to helping you develop those qualities.

The topics covered

- Attitude
- Good habits
- Health
- Learner drivers
- New drivers
- Older drivers
- Disabled drivers

Attitude

A good driver isn't a perfect driver; It's very doubtful if such a driver exists. Nevertheless, apart from skill and experience, which only come with time, a good driver needs

- responsibility
- concentration
- anticipation
- patience
- confidence.

Together these qualities go to make up what is generally known as the driver's attitude. It is attitude which, in turn, influences driver behaviour.

Developing the right attitude and behaviour will come easier to some drivers than others, but they are so important to safe driving that it's vital for every driver to make the effort to keep working on them.

Take pride in your driving and remember that, even if you have been driving for years, there's always something to learn.

It's a fact that nearly all road accidents are caused, to some degree, by the driver. Reducing that risk is the responsibility of every driver.

What is that responsibility?

As a responsible driver, you must always be concerned for the safety

- of yourself and your passengers
- of all other road users, particularly the most vulnerable, such as
  - children
  - the elderly
  - people with disabilities
  - cyclists
  - motorcyclists
  - people in charge of animals.

Be tolerant; remember that everyone is entitled to use the road. This may mean making allowances for other road users from time to time.

Look, and plan your actions well ahead to avoid causing danger or inconvenience. In this way you can avoid the temptation to act hastily – perhaps with dire consequences.

Be responsible by recognising the limitations of yourself and others.

Remember, the responsibility for safe driving rests with you.

Concentration

To be able to drive safely in today's traffic conditions, you must have 100% concentration.

If you let your mind wander, even for a moment, the risk of making a mistake is increased enormously. Remember, mistakes frequently lead to accidents.

Avoid driving if you're

- feeling tired or unwell
- thinking about something else
- upset or annoyed
- suffering stress of any kind.

If you have to drive, make sure you allow more time to react.

Concentration is the key to anticipation and is helped by having

- good vision
- good hearing
- good health
- self discipline.

Don't

- let conversation distract you
- make or answer phone calls while driving
- use headphones of any kind
- look at road maps or guides while you are on the move
- try to tune the radio or change compact discs or cassettes on the move
- stick non-essential stickers on the windows of your vehicle; they can restrict your view
- hang objects in your vehicle (e.g. dolls, dice, football boots) where they might distract your attention and restrict your view.

Anticipation

Anticipation in driving means planning well ahead and acting promptly to deal with the changes going on around you. It should, with experience, become almost an automatic reaction. It's the hallmark of a good driver.

You need to

- continually question the actions of other road users
- fit in with what they are doing.

If you plan ahead and try to anticipate the actions of others, you can

- avoid being taken by surprise
- prevent some hazards developing
- take early evasive action for those situations that develop.

Anticipation and good planning are essential in developing defensive driving techniques (see page 193).

Patience

It's said that patience is a virtue and this is certainly never more true than when you're driving.

Sadly, incompetence, bad manners and aggression seem to be commonplace on our roads, but there are no excuses for this type of behaviour when driving.

You should not let bad driving behaviour by other motorists lead to any conflict. If you do, you're well on the way to an accident.

Be prepared to make allowances for someone else's mistakes. In everyone's interest try to turn the other cheek.

Don't

- drive in a spirit of retaliation or competition
- use aggressive language or gestures
- try to teach someone a lesson, even if another road user has caused you inconvenience.

Do

- keep calm
- show restraint
- use sound judgement.

There's no better lesson than a good example.

Be patient with learner drivers Be patient if the vehicle ahead of you is being driven by a learner.

Don't

- drive up close behind
- 'rev' the engine
- become impatient if the other vehicle is slow to move off
- overtake only to 'cut in' again sharply.

Expect a learner to make mistakes and allow for these.

Remember

Not every vehicle showing L plates (D plates in Wales) is fitted with dual controls, and the person instructing might not be a professional.

Confidence

This is all part of a driver's attitude and is closely related to

- skill
- judgement
- experience.

New drivers will naturally be unsure of themselves, but confidence will grow with experience.

A good driver will avoid being over-confident. This only leads to carelessness.

Remember

Taking risks causes accidents.

Good habits

Good habits and thoughtful behaviour can help ensure that both you and your passengers arrive safely.

If you're upset by the bad behaviour of another driver, try not to react. If necessary, slow down to cool down, even if you might feel like a more aggressive response. Stop and take a break.

While you're upset, you're vulnerable. Your powers of concentration, anticipation and observation are likely to be much reduced. An accident is much more likely.

Be prepared to make allowances for someone else's mistakes.

Relax

- Give yourself plenty of time.
- Make yourself comfortable.
- Keep your mind on your driving.

The better you feel, the easier your journey will be.

Consideration

It helps other drivers if you don't try to dominate on the road. So don't

- cut across the path of other vehicles
- rush through traffic
- change your mind at the last minute
- use aggressive language or gestures.

Irritation and anger

Irritation and anger, for whatever reason, are dangerous. They can cause mistakes, and mistakes lead to accidents.

If you're angry, take time to compose yourself before a journey. Don't jump into your vehicle when you're in a steaming rage. Wait until you've calmed down.

The chance of an accident is too great to risk driving under such pressure.

Remember

Your actions also affect the actions of other drivers. Lack of consideration can have dangerous consequences. Obey the rules set out in *The Highway Code.*

Plan your journey

- Give yourself plenty of time for your journey. Hurrying leads to mistakes, and mistakes lead to accidents.
- If it's a long journey, plan plenty of time for breaks and refreshment.
- Use road and street maps before you set out.

Getting lost can also lead to frustration and loss of concentration.

Traffic

Avoid rush hours around major cities if you can. Listen to local and national radio for news of road works and traffic congestion.

The weather

The weather is an important factor when your driving. If it's really bad, it might be best to postpone your trip, or use public transport.

Always try to avoid driving in thick fog or icy conditions. It's a much greater strain, and the risk of an accident is far higher.

Many drivers run into difficulties in very bad weather. Follow the weather forecasts and general advice to drivers through local and national media.

Animals

- Keep animals well under control.
- Don't allow animals loose in the vehicle.
- Never allow animals loose on the public road – they can cause accidents.

Driving close to home

Many accidents happen close to home on regular daily or routine journeys. If you drive to work every day, don't leave yourself the bare minimum time to get there. More haste, less speed. Don't let familiarity with your home area and surroundings lead you to start taking risks simply because you feel you know every detail. Strangers won't have the benefit of local knowledge.

Health

Your eyesight

You must be able to read in good daylight, with glasses or contact lenses if you wear them, a motor vehicle number plate from a distance of

- 20.5 metres (about 67 feet)
- with letters 79.4mm (3.1 inches) high

Fitness to drive

You must

- be medically fit to drive
- understand that some medicines should not be taken if you intend driving
- notify the DVLA Swansea if your health is liable to affect your ability to drive, either now or because of a worsening condition in future.

Don't drive if you're feeling tired or unwell. Even a cold can make you unsafe to drive.

If you find you're losing concentration or not feeling well, keep your speed down and give yourself more time to react.

Alcohol

Alcohol will reduce your ability to drive safely.
You must be aware that

- to drive with alcohol in your blood is extremely dangerous, and carries severe penalties if you drive or attempt to drive while over the legal limit. If you drink at night, you might still be over the legal limit and unfit to drive in the morning.

You must not drive if your breath alcohol level is higher than 35 microgrammes/100ml (equivalent to a blood alcohol level of 80mg/100ml)

- It's also an offence to drive while unfit through the use of any medicine or drug.

Be safe!

If you drink, don't drive!

If you drive, don't drink!

Drugs

Don't take drugs, other than those prescribed or recommended by a doctor or pharmacist.

Driving when you're under the influence of drugs is an offence. It's inexcusable and can be fatal.

Medicines

Check any medicine you're taking to see if it affects your ability to drive.

Even medicines for coughs and hay fever can make you drowsy. Check all medicines. Consult your doctor or pharmacist if you're not sure.

After a shock

A shock or bereavement can badly upset your concentration for days. In this state, avoid driving altogether.

Are you comfortable?

Make sure you're feeling comfortable. Wear sensible clothing for driving, especially on a long journey.

Shoes

Shoes are particulary important. High heels and slippery soles can be dangerous on the pedals. Shoes that are too wide, or that easily fall off, can be just as dangerous.

It's a good idea to keep a pair of shoes in your vehicle, just for driving.

Fatigue

If you're tired, pull over at a safe place to rest and refresh yourself.

If it's not possible to stop immediately, open a window for fresh air. Stop as soon as it's safe and legal to do so, and have a rest or take a few minutes light exercise, such as a short brisk walk.

On a motorway, pull in at the nearest service area or leave the motorway. DO NOT pull up on the hard shoulder just to rest.

Don't

Don't drive for too long without taking a break. Your concentration will be much better if you plan regular stops for rest and refreshments.

This is especially important at night.

The learner driver

Attitude is critical to a new driver's approach, both to their own driving and to the actions and mistakes of other road users.

If you're a novice, you need to use your sense of responsibility, patience and courtesy to develop the skills necessary to become a good driver.

A great deal of what you'll learn will depend on your instructor.

Planned tuition

A planned approach to learning is essential, particularly in the early stages.

Each lesson should be matched to your needs and abilities. There are no short cuts to becoming a good defensive driver.

Who should teach you?

The best way to learn is by having

- regular planned lessons with a good instructor
- as much practice as possible.

Once you understand the basics, it's a good idea to combine professional instruction with as much practice as you can with relatives and friends.

Approved Driving Instructor (ADI)

An Approved driving Instructor (ADI) must

- have their name entered on the Register held by the DSA
- display a green ADI identification certificate on the windscreen of the tuition vehicle
- pass a searching three-part examination to qualify
- Reach and maintain the standards required by the DSA.

How to choose an ADI

- Ask friends and relatives.
- Choose an instructor
  - who has a good reputation
  - who is reliable and punctual
  - whose vehicle suits you.

Take advice from your ADI on

- all aspects of driving
- what books to read
- when you'll be ready for the driving test
- how to practise.

Note. Some trainee instructors who have not yet completed the qualifying examination are granted a trainee licence to enable them to gain instructional experience.

This is a pink identification certificate which must be displayed on the windscreen of the tuition vehicle.

The official syllabus If you learn with an ADI, make sure he or she covers the official syllabus fully. See the book *The Driving Test* (published by The Stationery Office).

Driving with a learner

If you're driving with a learner, you should try to encourage confidence. It's also important not to put them in a situation that requires more skill than they can be expected to show.

Don't let them try to run before they can walk. Overestimating a learner's skill could lead to disturbing incidents for both the learner and other road users. This can

- setback the learners progress
- be dangerous.

Be aware that anyone supervising a learner must

- be at least 21 years of age
- have held for at least three years (and still hold) a full licence for the category of vehicle being driven.

If you pay someone for tuition, they must be an Approved Driving Instructor (ADI) or Trainee Licence holder.

Learning by example

The inexperienced

- often learn by example
- should be shown how to drive with quiet confidence
- should have examples of bad driving explained and not excused
- should be discouraged from developing bad habits and using excuses like 'Everyone else does it so why shouldn't I?'
- learn from the good examples you demonstrate.

Taking on too much

The enthusiastic learner should be very careful not to take on too much.

Over-confidence can lead to carelessness, taking risks, and sometimes tragic accidents.

The training vehicle

A vehicle being driven by a learner must display L plates (or D plates in Wales) which should be removed or covered at all other times.

If you own a car or intend to buy one, it might be best to find a driving school that uses a similar model.

At a later stage, it might also be possible to have lessons in your own car. Avoid using a different vehicle for practice in the early stages. The controls and feel of the car will be so different, it might hinder rather than assist progress.

Avoid fixing L (D) plates to the windscreen or back window; they restrict your view.

New drivers

Young and inexperienced drivers are more vulnerable on the roads. They can often be involved in accidents early in their driving careers, sometimes tragically so. Such accidents can usually be attributed to

- the natural exuberance of youth
- immaturity; inability to cope with the serious nature of driving
- showing off to friends; 'egging on' by passengers looking for excitement
- competitive behaviour, racing and so on
- lack of experience and judgement, especially when driving 'performance' cars.

Avoid

- driving too fast; speed can kill
- reckless driving; drive with consideration and care
- showing off; if you want to impress your friends, show them how *safe* a driver you are
- being 'wound up'; keep calm, learn to ignore the stupidity of others
- an aggressive attitude and behaviour; again, stay cool and safe
- loud music, which could interfere with your concentration, or with your hearing at a critical moment.
- driving beyond your capabilities; always leave yourself a safety margin
- being distracted by passengers.

  Above all, be responsible and always show courtesy and consideration to other road users.

Your life and theirs could depend on it!

Be safe, don't take risks!

False perceptions

Many younger drivers *wrongly* believe that fast reactions and the ability to handle their vehicle will make them a good and safe driver. They fail to recognise that driving skill alone will not prevent accidents.

Having the right attitude of mind and a sound knowledge of defensive driving techniques is essential.

Pass Plus

New drivers can take further training after they have passed their test.

The Pass Plus scheme has been created by DSA for new drivers who would like to improve their basic skills and safely widen their driving experience. If you take the Pass Plus course you can also be rewarded with reduced insurance premiums.

Ask your ADI for details of the scheme.

Older drivers

Although experienced, older drivers can also be vulnerable, but for different reasons. The natural and gradual deterioration in physical fitness and ability can seriously affect judgement and concentration.

So, be responsible and

- have your eyesight checked regularly, including your night vision
- don't drive if you feel unwell
- take care when judging the speed of oncoming traffic at junctions. If in doubt, wait. Don't make hasty manoeuvres. Look, assess and decide before you act
- keep concentrating on your driving – *always!*
- find a safe place to stop and rest if you feel tired
- keep up to date with the changes to rules and regulations – for example, new road markings and signs. Study the current edition of *The Highway Code* and put the advice it gives into practice
- take extra care – your reactions might not be as quick as they used to be.

Above all, recognise your own limitations. Be safe!

Disabled drivers

Advances in modern technology offer many more disabled people the chance to drive, and there's no standard production vehicle which cannot be modified for a disabled driver.

Many cars are now available with auto-matic transmission and power assisted steering to help the disabled driver.

Modifications

These can include

- hand controls to brake and accelerate
- steering and secondary control aids
- left foot accelerator conversions
- clutch conversions
- handbrake devices
- additional car mirrors
- seat-belt modifications
- harnesses
- special seating
- wheelchair stowage equipment.

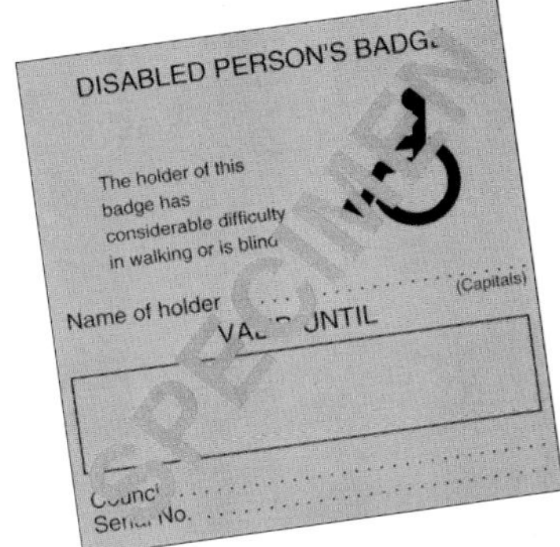

For the more severely disabled driver

- joystick and foot steering; a four way joystick can now be used to steer, accelerate and brake
- infra-red remote control systems which enable a driver to enter a vehicle and drive from a wheelchair with complete independence.

Assessment Driving assessment centres for disabled persons are available to

- test driving ability
- give advice on the sort of controls and adaptations needed to drive safely and in comfort.

A list of Disabled Driver Assessment Centres is given opposite.

Further Information
For more information contact :

The Department of Transport Mobility Advice and Vehicle Information Service (MAVIS)
The Transport Research Laboratory
CROWTHORNE
Berkshire
RG45 6AU
Tel: 01344 770456

The major motoring organisations and some motor manufacturers offer special services for disabled drivers.

Parking Concessions Severely disabled persons might qualify for parking concessions. Contact your Local Authority to apply for the 'Orange Badge' scheme.

Be considerate If you're not disabled, and don't have a disabled person with you, don't use parking facilities specifically intended for disabled drivers.

Association of Driver Educators for People with Disabilities (ADEPD)

ADEPD aims to bring together people actively involved in helping disabled persons to become safe car drivers.

ADEPD also aims to

- improve the availability and standard of advice and driving instruction given to people with disabilities
- encourage information exchange and research in this field.

Further details can be obtained from The Secretary, Banstead Mobility Centre (see below).

UK Forum of Disabled Drivers Assessment Centres

Banstead Mobility Centre
Damson Way
Orchard Hill
Queen Mary's Avenue
CARSHALTON
Surrey SM5 4NR
Tel: 0181 770 1151

Cornwall Friends' Mobility Centre
Tehidy House
RCH (Treliske)
TRURO
Cornwall TR1 3LJ
Tel: 01872 260060
Fax: 01872 260043

The Department of Transport Mobility Advice and Vehicle Information Service (MAVIS)
Transport Research Laboratory
CROWTHORNE
Berkshire. RG45 6AU
Tel: 01344 770456

Derby Disabled Driving Centre
Kingsway Hospitals
Kingsway
DERBY DE3 3LZ
Tel: 01332 371929
Fax: 01332 382377

Disabled Drivers' Voluntary Advisory Service
Woodlands View
Lancaster Moor Hospital
Quernmore Road
LANCASTER
Tel: 01524 734195

Edinburgh Driving Assessment Service
Vehicles Centre
Astley Ainsley Hospital
133 Grange Lorne
EDINBURGH EH9 2HL
Tel: 0131 5379000

Mobility Centre
Regional Rehabilitation Centre
Hunters Road
NEWCASTLE UPON TYNE
NE2 4NR
Tel: 0191 219 5694

Mobility Information Service
Unit 2a
Atcham Estate
SHREWSBURY SY4 4UG
Tel: 01743 761889
Fax: 01743 761149

Northern Ireland Council on Disability (NICD)
31 Ulsterville Ave,
BELFAST BT9 7AS
Tel: 01232 666188

Rockwood Driving Assessment Centre
Rockwood Hospital
Llandaff
CARDIFF CF5 2YN
Tel: 01222566281

Wales Disabled Drivers' Assessment Centre
18 Plas Newydd
Whitchurch
CARDIFF CF4 1NR
Tel: 01222 615276

PART TWO THE DRIVER AND THE LAW

Driving any vehicle carries with it legal requirements, and you must satisfy some of these before you begin to drive on the public road. Others apply after you start to drive.

Most of these requirements are there for your safety and for the safety of other road users. If you neglect them, you and your family could be the first to lose.

You should be aware of the penalties which the courts can impose for road traffic offences. Complying with the law may seem expensive but failing to comply could turn out to be even more so.

The topics covered

- The Driving Licence
- Insurance
- The Vehicle Registration Document
- Vehicle Excise Duty
- The Vehicle Test Certificate
- Roadworthiness
- The Highway Code
- Seat belts

The driving licence

For the category of vehicle you intend to drive, you MUST have

- a signed, valid provisional driving licence
- a signed, valid full driving licence

or, in certain circumstances

- a signed, valid International Driving Permit (IDP)
- a full driving licence issued outside the UK.

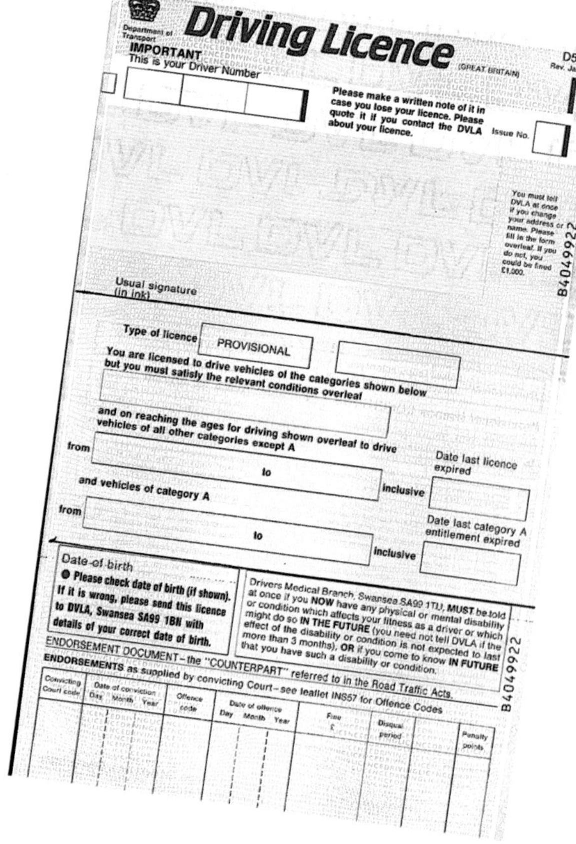

Department of Transport

Driving Licence (GREAT BRITAIN)

D51
Rev. Jan./95

IMPORTANT
This is your Driver Number

Please make a written note of it in case you lose your licence. Please quote it if you contact the DVLA about your licence.

Issue No.

You must tell DVLA at once if you change your address or name. Please fill in the form overleaf. If you do not, you could be fined £1,000.

B4049922

Usual signature (in ink)

Type of licence PROVISIONAL

You are licensed to drive vehicles of the categories shown below but you must satisfy the relevant conditions overleaf

and on reaching the ages for driving shown overleaf to drive vehicles of all other categories except A

from **to** **inclusive**

Date last licence expired

and vehicles of category A

from **to** **inclusive**

Date last category A entitlement expired

Date of birth

● **Please check date of birth (if shown). If it is wrong, please send this licence to DVLA, Swansea SA99 1BN with details of your correct date of birth.**

Drivers Medical Branch, Swansea SA99 1TU, **MUST** be told at once if you **NOW** have any physical or mental disability or condition which affects your fitness as a driver or which might do so **IN THE FUTURE** (you need not tell DVLA if the effect of the disability or condition is not expected to last more than 3 months). **OR** if you come to know **IN FUTURE** that you have such a disability or condition.

B4049922

ENDORSEMENT DOCUMENT – the "COUNTERPART" referred to in the Road Traffic Acts.
ENDORSEMENTS as supplied by convicting Court – see leaflet INS57 for Offence Codes

Convicting Court code	Date of conviction Day	Month	Year	Offence code	Date of offence Day	Month	Year	Fine £	Disqual. period	Penalty points

Your age You must be at least 17 years of age to drive a car. As an exception, if you receive a mobility allowance you're allowed to start driving at 16.

Provisional licence If you're a learner driver, you must hold a provisional driving licence for the category of vehicle being driven, and comply with the conditions listed below.

L plates (D plates) You must display L (D) plates which conform to legal specifications, and which are clearly visible from in front of the vehicle and from behind.

If the vehicle is NOT being driven by a learner driver, the L (D) plates should be removed or covered.

Your supervisor You MUST be accompanied by a supervisor who

- has held a full licence for at least three years for the kind of vehicle you're driving, and still holds that licence
- is at least 21 years old.

Motorways Learner drivers are not allowed to drive any motor vehicle on motorways.

You should also have

- a thorough knowledge of *The Highway Code* and the motoring laws
- a thorough understanding of your responsibilities as a driver.

You should also be aware of the penalties which the courts may impose for traffic offences.

New residents If you're a new UK resident, you should either take a driving test as soon as possible or, if your licence was issued by another EU member state or designated country, you may apply to the DVLA to exchange it for a full UK licence within one year.

If you don't pass the test in the first year, you'll have to

- apply for a provisional licence
- comply with the relevant conditions until after you have passed your test.

For further information, see leaflet D100 issued by the Driver and Vehicle Licensing Agency (DVLA), available at any post office.

Visitors If you're a visitor to the UK, you're allowed to drive on your current licence or permit for up to a year after your latest entry into the country.

Changes If you change your name and/or address you must complete the details on your licence and send it to: DVLA, Swansea, SA99 1BN.

Insurance

You would be *very* irresponsible to drive without insurance. It's illegal, and, should you cause injury to anyone or damage to property, it could be expensive and result in criminal prosecution.

Before you take a vehicle on public roads, get proper insurance cover. You can arrange this with

- an insurance company
- a broker
- some motor manufacturers or dealers.

Third party insurance

This is the legal minimum and the cheapest insurance cover

The third party is anyone you might injure or whose property you might damage. You're not covered for damage to your vehicle or injury to yourself.

Third party, fire and theft insurance

The same as third party, except that it also covers you against your vehicle being stolen or damaged by fire.

Comprehensive insurance

This is the best, but the most expensive. Apart from covering other persons and property from injury and damage, it also covers

- damage to your vehicle
- replacement of parts damaged in an accident
- personal injury to yourself.

Warning When you drive someone else's vehicle, check your insurance cover. You're probably only covered for third party risks. You might not be covered at all!

The cost of insurance

This varies with

- your age; the younger you are the more it will cost you, especially if you're under 25
- completion of the Pass Plus scheme
- the make of your vehicle
- the power and capacity of the engine
- where you live
- the use intended
- any court convictions.

It can also vary from one insurer to another, so it pays to shop around.

What's insured

This also varies from company to company. Read the small print and ask your insurer or broker if you're in any doubt. Otherwise you might have difficulties when you claim.

You'll often have to pay the first £50 or £100 of the cost yourself – this is called the 'excess'.

Buy the best policy you can afford. It could be the cheapest in the long run.

The certificate of insurance

A short and simple document which certifies

- who's insured
- the type of vehicle covered
- the kind of insurance cover
- the period of cover
- the main conditions.

Sometimes a broker will give you a temporary certificate or cover note while you're waiting for the certificate of insurance.

Showing your certificate Keep the certificate safe and produce it

- if the police ask you to
- when you apply to renew your Vehicle Excise Licence
- if you're involved in an accident.

The policy document This contains the full details of the contract between you and the insurance company. It's written in small print, and usually in legal language – although some companies have simplified their policies.

If you don't understand anything, ask your broker or the insurance company to explain.

Accidents

If you're involved in an accident where

- any person is injured
- any vehicle apart from your own is damaged
- certain animals not in your vehicle, including large farm animals and dogs, are injured

you must stop.

Give to anyone having reasonable cause to ask for them

- your name and address, the vehicle owner's name and address, and the registration number of the vehicle
- the name and address of your insurance company
- details of your Insurance Certificate.

If you're not able to do so at the time, you MUST report the accident to the police in person as soon as possible, and in any case within 24 hours. If there has been an injury, you must also give insurance details to the police.

If you can't produce the insurance documents when you report the accident, you have up to seven days to produce them at a police station of your choice.

This applies no matter how minor the accident, or whose fault it was.

The Vehicle Registration Document

This contains details of your vehicle make and model, including year of first registration and engine size and number.

It also gives the name and address of the registered owner or keeper.

If you buy a new vehicle

- your dealer will see that you get one of these documents.

If you buy a second-hand vehicle

- ***make sure you're given the document***
- fill in the change of ownership section and send it off to DVLA at the address given on the document.

Do this immediately, as it's an offence not to notify the DVLA at Swansea.

Warning

The Vehicle Registration Document is not proof of ownership.

Vehicle Excise Duty

This is often called road tax or vehicle licence, and must be paid either yearly or half-yearly.

The owners or operators of all road vehicles (unless exempt) must pay the duty and display the required disc on the vehicle. A disc must not be transferred to another vehicle.

Applying

If you're the registered owner, you'll normally receive the form automatically through the post. If not, you can get a Vehicle Excise Licence Application at any post office.

Most licence-issuing post offices can deal with your application, accept your payment and give you a Vehicle Excise Licence (tax disc).

You can also apply at your nearest Vehicle Registration Office.

DO NOT send the completed application to DVLA.

Documents you must present
When you apply to renew your Vehicle Excise Licence (tax disc), you'll be required to produce

- a completed application form
- a valid certificate of insurance
- a vehicle test certificate (MOT) if your vehicle is over three years old.*

*Note: Certain vehicles are covered by other requirements

The Vehicle Test Certificate

The so-called MOT test applies to all motor vehicles three years old and over.*

The purpose of the MOT test is to ensure that your vehicle's key safety and environmental systems and components meet the required minimum legal standards.

The test must be carried out every year by a Vehicle Testing Station appointed by the Vehicle Inspectorate, an executive agency of the Department of Transport.

Vehicles which must be tested

If your vehicle is more than three years old* you must have a current MOT Test Certificate. You won't be able to renew your Vehicle Excise Licence without it.

Testing time You can have your vehicle tested as much as one month before the current certificate runs out. The expiry date of the new certificate will be one year after the expiry date of the old one.

Failure

If your vehicle fails and you want to continue to use it, you must make arrangements to have the necessary repairs carried out without delay. The vehicle must pass a retest before it's used on the road except when

- driving it away from the testing station after failing the test
- driving to have the repairs carried out
- driving to an MOT test appointment booked in advance.

Even in these circumstances you can still be prosecuted if your car is not roadworthy under the various regulations governing its construction and use. In addition, check that your insurance cover remains valid.

Appeals

Details giving information on the right to appeal if you consider the vehicle has been incorrectly failed may be obtained at Vehicle Testing Stations.

***Note.** Vehicles such as

- large goods vehicles (LGVs) over 3.5 tonnes gross weight
- passenger-carrying vehicles (PCVs) with more than eight seats
- ambulances
- taxis

must be tested one year after registration and annually thereafter.

Remember

An MOT test certificate is not a guarantee that the vehicle will remain roadworthy and comply with the minimum standards of the certificate. Neither does it imply that the engine and transmission systems are in good condition – these items are not critical to safety and are not covered by the MOT test.

Fees

Ask any Vehicle Testing Station about the current test and retest fees.

Exhaust emission limits

Remember, the test now includes a strict exhaust emission test. This means your engine must be correctly tuned and adjusted.

There are prescribed emission limits for petrol-engined vehicles registered after 1975 and the MOT test will check that these limits are not exceeded.

'Roadworthiness'

You must ensure that the vehicle you intend to drive

- is legally roadworthy*
- has a current Vehicle Test (MOT) Certificate if over the prescribed age
- is properly licensed and has the correct tax disc displayed.

* See the Vehicle Inspectorate publication *How Safe is Your Car?* (published by The Stationery Office)

The braking system

Your brakes must be in good and efficient working order and correctly adjusted, including the hand or parking brake.

Tyres

All tyres on the vehicle MUST meet current requirements

Lighting (including indicators)

All lamps, including lenses and reflectors, must be in working order, even during daylight hours.

Exhaust

A silencer must be fitted which reduces noise to an acceptable level. For cars and light goods vehicles, exhaust emissions must not exceed the prescribed limits. Any MOT testing station will be able to tell you the limits for your vehicle.
For best fuel economy, have the engine tuned according to the manufacturer's recommendations.

Instruments and equipment

All instruments and equipment must be in good working order, including

- speedometer
- horn
- windscreen wipers/washers.

Appropriate mirrors must be fitted.

Disability

If your vehicle has been adapted for your disability, make sure that the modifications don't affect the safe control of the vehicle.

The Highway Code

The Highway Code contains essential advice for all road users.

A set of rules

Its purpose is to prevent accidents by ensuring that we all adopt the same rules when we use the road.

Road traffic law has developed over the years into a comprehensive set of rules. *The Highway Code* explains these rules as simply as possible and helps to make sure they are understood.

Road traffic law changes from time to time, and so do the penalties for breaking it. Make sure you keep up to date. Study and apply the contents of the current edition of *The Highway Code*.

Road signs and signals

You must know and comply with

- all traffic signs and road markings
- signals given by
  - police officers
  - traffic wardens
  - school-crossing wardens
  - any authorised person (e.g., road workers operating STOP/GO boards)
- traffic signals at
  - junctions/crossroads
  - roadworks
  - narrow bridges
  - pedestrian crossings
  - fire/ambulance stations*
  - level crossings*
  - tramway (LRT) crossings.

*usually red flashing lights

Road safety

In everyday driving, you need to follow the rules set down in *The Highway Code* for your own safety and that of all road users.

Even if you're an experienced driver, you need to know *The Highway Code* thoroughly and apply it in your everyday driving.

Although not all the rules in *The Highway Code* are legal requirements, they can be used in court to support prosecutions.

Emergency Vehicles

Move out of the way of emergency vehicles with blue flashing beacons. Do so safely and without delay.

- Police.
- Fire.
- Ambulance.
- Blood Transfusion Service.
- Bomb Disposal Team.
- Mountain/Mines Rescue.
- Coastguard.

Doctor's vehicles are permitted to show green flashing beacons. Give way to them.

Look on* The Highway Code *as an aid to safe driving.
Don't look on it as a restriction.

Seat belts.

Seat belts save lives and reduce the risk of injury. Unless you're exempt you must wear a seat belt if one is available.

The following table summarises the legal requirements for the wearing of seat belts.

Child seat restraints must be correctly fitted in accordance with the manufacturers instructions. If in doubt, seek specialist advice.

	Front seat	Rear seat	Whose responsibility
Driver	Must be worn if fitted	-	Driver
Child under 3 years old	Appropriate child restraint must be worn	Appropriate child restraint must be worn if available	Driver
Child aged 3 to 11 and under 1.5 metres (about 5 feet in height)	Appropriate child restraint must be worn if available. If not an adult seat belt must be worn	Appropriate child restraint must be worn if available. If not an adult seat belt must be worn if available	Driver
Child aged 12 or 13 or younger child 1.5 metres or more in height.	Adult seat belt must be worn if available	Adult seat belt must be worn if available	Driver
Adult passenger	Must be worn if available	Must be worn if available	Passenger

Air Bags

More and more modern vehicles are being fitted with air bags. These are designed to inflate almost instantaneously in the event of certain types of collision, and so help to prevent more serious injuries.

Warning Due to the almost explosive manner in which these air bags must inflate, drivers and front seat passengers should avoid sitting too close to the steering wheel or dashboard.

Never fit rear-facing child seats to a seat protected by an air bag. To do so could place the childs head in the path of the rapidly inflating air bag.

The controls on modern vehicles are relatively straightforward.
Each control demands a particular skill, and using them together effectively and safely takes time to learn. However, the functions of each are easy to remember.

The topics covered

- Driving position
- The hand controls
- The foot controls
- Switches
- Other controls

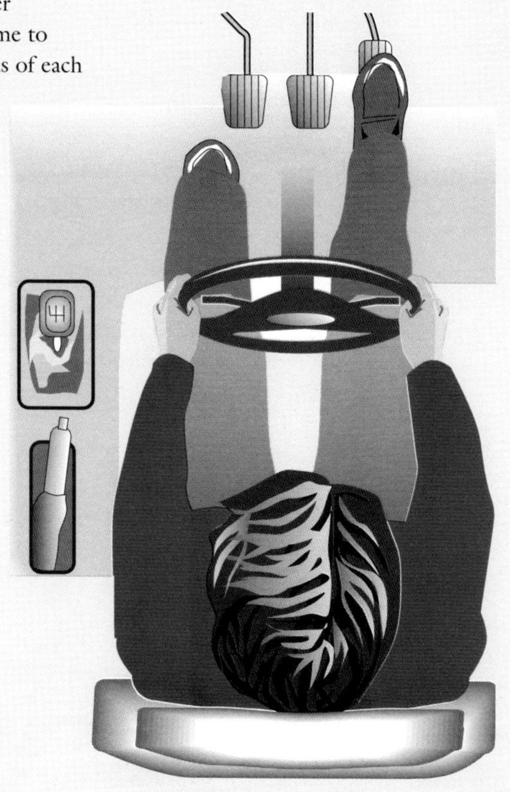

Driving position

Before you can use the controls safely, you must adopt a suitable driving position.

You must be able to

- reach and use each control easily and comfortably; for example, you should be able to operate the clutch pedal without stretching your left leg
- control the vehicle by keeping a suitable grip on the steering wheel; your arms should be relaxed and not restricted at the elbows
- see the road ahead clearly.

***Important note.** As soon as you're seated, check that the vehicle is secure by ensuring the handbrake is applied.

Steering column adjustment On some vehicles, you can adjust the angle of tilt of the steering column to suit you.

When making this adjustment, take care not to allow the steering wheel to interfere with your view of the instrument panel. Also, make sure you secure the locking mechanism after any adjustment.

Never attempt to adjust your steering column angle while the vehicle is moving.

Driving seat adjustment

You must make sure that the seat is adjusted to suit you. Most driving seats can be adjusted for

- 'rake' – the angle of the seat back
- position – the seat will move forwards or backwards.

Sometimes, especially on larger vehicles, the driving seat will also adjust for height.

If someone else has been driving the vehicle, make sure you make any adjustments **before** you start to drive.

Never adjust your seat while the vehicle is moving.

Warning After adjusting your seat, make sure it's firmly locked in position. Listen for, or feel for, the locking mechanism engaging.

An insecure driving seat is dangerous.

Head restraint adjustment

Head restraints are provided to protect against neck and spine injuries commonly referred to as whiplash.

For maximum protection correct head restraint adjustment is vital – but all too easy to overlook.

The head restraints should be adjusted so that the rigid part of the head restraint is

- at least as high as the eyes or top of the ears
- as close to the back of the head as is comfortable.

An incorrectly adjusted head restraint could offer little or no protection against whiplash injuries.

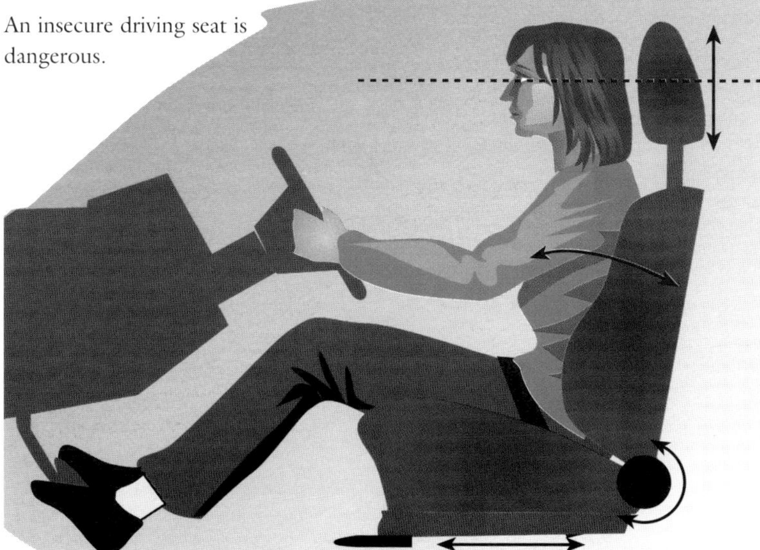

The hand controls

The main controls are in similar positions in all vehicles.

The positions of some of the minor controls, such as indicators, light switches and windscreen wipers, vary from model to model.

Before you drive a strange vehicle, you should familiarize yourself with the positions of all controls. You should never have to fumble or look down for them when you're driving.

Keep your eyes on the road.

The steering wheel

The steering wheel should normally be controlled with both hands.

Purpose To control the direction in which you want the vehicle to travel. The steering wheel controls the steering mechanism, which turns

- the front wheels in most vehicles
- all four wheels in vehicles with four-wheel steering – limited to a small number of models.

How to use the steering wheel For best control

- place your hands in the 'ten-to-two' or the 'quarter-to-three' position, whichever is the most comfortable
- avoid resting your arm on the door, which can restrict your movement
- grip the wheel lightly but firmly; when the vehicle is moving, you need very little effort to turn the wheel
- keep both hands on the wheel, unless you're
  - changing gear
  - working another control with one hand.

Return that hand to the wheel immediately you have finished the task. NEVER take BOTH hands off the wheel when the vehicle is moving.

Steering lock* This is the angle through which the front wheels turn when you turn the steering wheel: that is 'right lock' or 'left lock'.

Turning the steering wheel as far as it will go is called 'full lock'. The amount of lock varies from vehicle to vehicle.

***Note.** Not to be confused with the steering column locking mechanism which engages when the ignition key is removed on most modern vehicles as an anti-theft device.

Small cars will generally turn in a smaller circle than larger vehicles. Taxi cabs are an obvious exception, with a very small turning circle.

Turning When turning the steering wheel, avoid crossing your hands. Except at low speeds, this can reduce your control and can cause an accident. Feed the rim of the steering wheel through your hands. Vary your hand movements according to the amount of lock you want.

This is called the push – pull technique

To turn right

- Move your right hand up the wheel, but not beyond 12 o'clock.
- Pull the wheel downwards with your right hand. At the same time, slide your left hand down the wheel against the direction the wheel is turning.
- Grip and push up with your left hand while you slide your right hand up the wheel.
- Repeat the second and third steps as necessary.

To turn left

- Slide your left hand up the wheel, but not beyond 12 o'clock.
- Pull the wheel downwards with your left hand. At the same time, slide your right hand down the wheel against the direction the wheel is turning.
- Grip and push up with your right hand while you slide your left hand up the wheel.

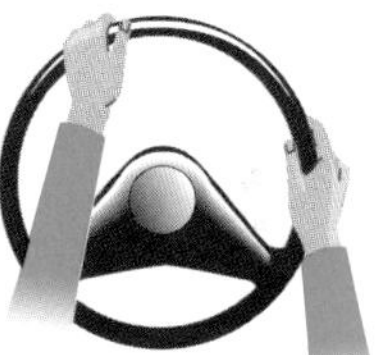

Slide left hand up

Left hand grip and PULL down, right hand slide down

Right hand grip and PUSH up, left hand slide up

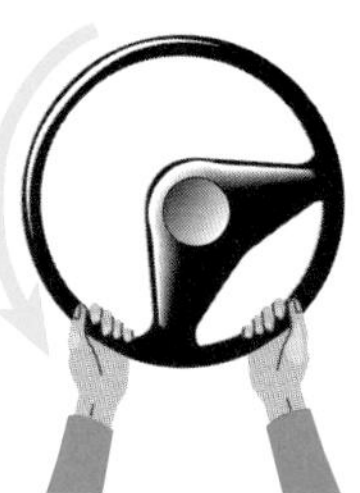

Left hand grip and PULL down, right hand slide down

- Repeat the second and third steps as necessary.

To straighten up after the turn
Feed the wheel back through your hands in the opposite direction. Try not to allow the wheel to spin back uncontrolled.

On the open road, hold the wheel at ten-to two or quarter-to-three, and turn the wheel as necessary to maintain a steady course. Looking well ahead will help you to avoid straightening up too late.

On some occasions, such as off-road activities or when manoeuvring at low speeds the 'hand-over-hand' technique can be acceptable, but should not be used for normal driving which doesn't require rapid steering movements.

Oversteer and understeer
Vehicles vary in how they behave when turning at various road speeds.

Some respond MORE than you expect in relation to the amount of turn you give the wheel (oversteer).

Some respond LESS (understeer).

You must get to know the characteristics of your vehicle, before you drive in traffic, and drive extra carefully until you're familiar with it's behaviour.

Power-assisted steering (PAS)
More and more vehicles now have power-assisted steering. This makes steering easier – particularly for drivers with weakness in their limbs.

PAS

- relieves the driver of most of the effort of steering
- senses when you start to turn the wheel
- makes the steering seem light.

The faster the vehicle is travelling, the less PAS assists, and the more stable the vehicle.

PAS is most useful at low speeds, such as manoeuvring in a tight corner or parking.

With PAS the steering feels very light and you can easily oversteer, especially if you're used to driving a vehicle not fitted with it.

Dry steering Try to avoid turning the steering wheel when the vehicle is stationary. This is known as dry steering and may cause

- damage to the tyres
- excess wear in the steering mechanism.

This applies whether you have PAS or not!

The gear lever

The gear lever is normally to the left of the driving seat, either on the floor or on a raised console.

A few cars have the gear lever protruding from the instrument panel, and a few have a gear lever on the steering column.

Function The gear lever enables you to change from one gear to another.

The gearbox The gearbox contains the gears, which control the relationship between engine speed and road speed.

First gear is the most powerful and is normally the one you use to get the vehicle moving.

As you speed up, you change up to the higher gears, each one giving you less engine power but more road speed. Top gear is the least powerful, but usually has the widest range of speeds.

Most modern cars have five forward gears while heavier vehicles often have many more.

As well as the four or five forward gears, the gearbox has a reverse gear.

In neutral, no gear is engaged.

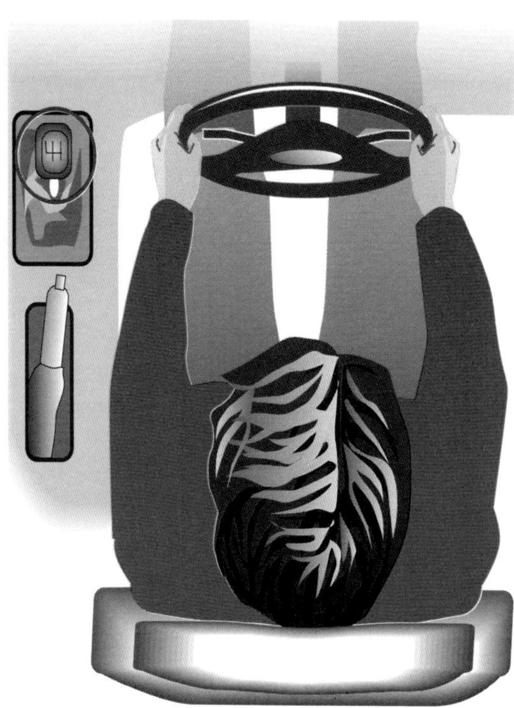

While the clutch is the link between the road wheels and the engine the gearbox links the road wheels and the clutch.

Four-wheel drive vehicles may have a double gearbox containing eight to ten gears. The lower range is normally used off road.

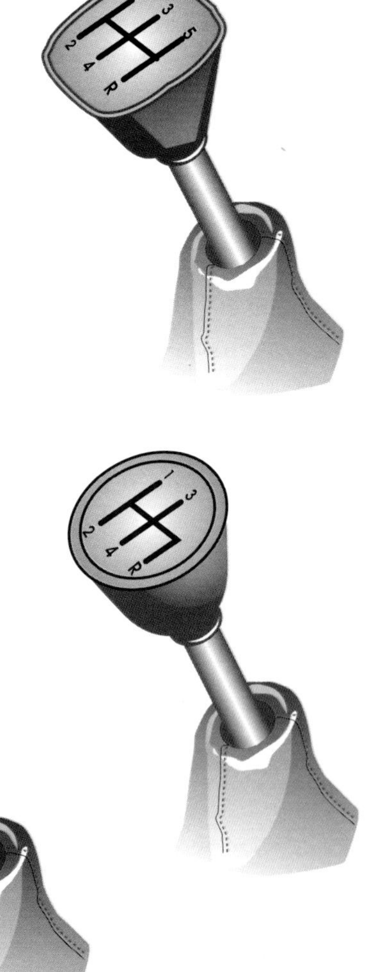

Gear positions The layouts shown on this page are popular in four and five-speed gearboxes.

The first four gears normally form an 'H', while reverse and fifth form an 'I'. Moving from fifth to reverse is frequently protected, and the gear lever automatically springs back into neutral when no gear is engaged. This lining up with particular gears is known as bias. Third and fourth gears are often lined up.

Four-speed gearboxes have the gears in an 'H', with reverse extended on the left or right.

Some gear boxes have high and low ratio ranges which effectively double the number of available gears.

Avoid looking down at the gear lever. You should have a mental picture of the gear layout. This will enable you to change gear without looking at the diagram on top of the gear lever. Your eyes should be on the road.

With practice, changing gear becomes second nature.

Automatic transmission systems

(See section 21)

The handbrake

Sometimes the handbrake is referred to as a parking brake.

Position The handbrake lever is normally floor mounted just behind the gear lever. In some vehicles, it is just under the instrument panel, while on some unusual models the parking brake is applied by operating an additional pedal.

Function The function of the handbrake is to hold the vehicle still when it has stopped.

In most cars the handbrake operates on the rear wheels only. If it's applied while the vehicle is moving, there's a real danger of locking the braked wheels and skidding.

The handbrake shouldn't be used to stop a moving vehicle, except in an emergency, such as footbrake failure – very unlikely since the introduction of dual-circuit braking systems.

Applying Press the button on top of the handbrake lever and pull the lever fully upwards. Then release the button. The handbrake will engage in the 'on' position.

Pulling the lever up without pressing the button can cause wear on the teeth of the ratchet. If it's done repeatedly over a long period it can cause the ratchet to fail and the handbrake to release without warning.

Releasing Pull the lever up slightly and press the button in to release the ratchet. Then, keeping the button in, move the lever to the 'off' position.

On some vehicles instead of pressing a button, the handbrake is released by twisting the hand grip.

Remember

When you leave your vehicle parked on a gradient, even in your own drive, always make sure that the handbrake is fully on. Many serious accidents have been caused by failure to do this.

The foot controls

To remember the order of the foot controls simply remember your **ABC**.

Accelerator – Right foot

Brake – Right foot

Clutch – Left foot

'A' The accelerator or 'gas pedal'

This is operated by the right foot and is positioned on the extreme right of the group of three pedals.

Function The accelerator controls the rate at which the mixture of fuel and air is supplied to the engine. The name 'gas pedal' comes from gasoline, the American word for petrol.

Petrol engines A carburettor mixes the fuel with air which is then drawn into the engine.

On some petrol engines, the fuel reaches the engine under pressure by 'fuel injection'. Engines of this type are often labelled 'GTi' or 'EFi'. These systems have an emergency automatic cut-off switch in case of accident.

Diesel engines A high pressure fuel injector introduces the fuel to the engine. This is known as a compression ignition engine.

In both engine types The more you press the accelerator, the more fuel goes to the engine, the more power is generated and the higher the engine speed.

Getting to know the right amount of pressure to put on the accelerator takes practice.

When moving off, you need just the right amount. Too little, and the engine stalls. Too much, and the vehicle can surge forward.

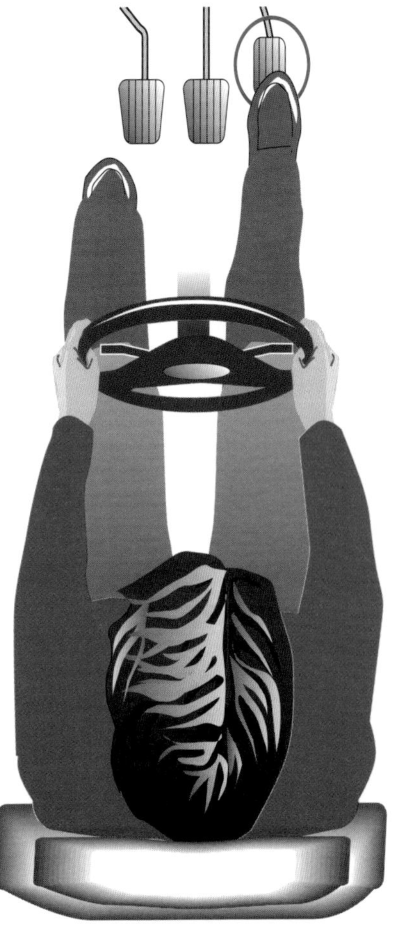

'B' The footbrake

As well as the accelerator, the right foot operates the footbrake. You shouldn't need to use both controls at the same time.

The footbrake is the middle of the group of three pedals, so the right foot can travel smoothly and quickly from one to the other.

Function The function of the footbrake is to slow down or stop the vehicle.

Using the footbrake The more pressure you put on the footbrake, the more the vehicle will slow down.

Slowing down under control isn't just a matter of slamming the footbrake on as hard as you can. As with the other foot controls, using the footbrake needs practice.

Press the footbrake with the ball of your foot. Put enough pressure to slow the wheels without allowing them to lock.

Progressive braking Always press lightly on the brake pedal to begin with, and gradually press harder as the brakes begin to act. This is known as progressive braking and will give maximum control as well as smoother stopping.

Disc brakes and dual-circuit systems Most modern vehicles have disc brakes on the front and a dual-circuit system. These reduce the risk of brake failure and give controlled braking on all four wheels of motor cars.

Anti-lock braking system (ABS)
Many modern cars are fitted with anti-lock brakes. These are designed to prevent wheels locking up in the event of excessive brake pressure being applied. Smooth, correctly timed application of the brakes is still required to prevent harsh stopping and passenger discomfort.

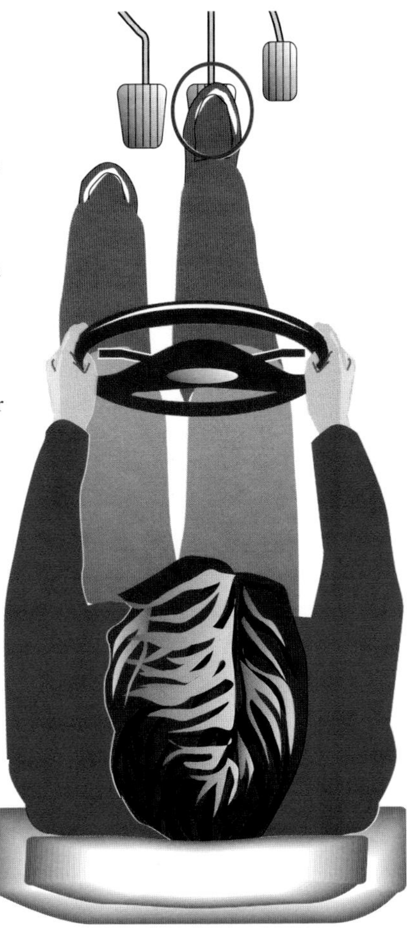

'C' The clutch

This is operated by the left foot and is on the extreme left of the group of three pedals.

Function The clutch is the connection between the engine and the road wheels. It's a connection over which the driver has control, but which requires practice in its use.

How it works In its simplest form, the clutch is made up of two plates. One is connected to the engine and rotates all the time the engine is running. The other is linked to the wheels and rotates only when it's held against the first plate by springs.

When you press the clutch pedal, you force the plates apart, breaking the drive connection.

Neutral position In neutral, both plates are touching, but the wheels do not turn because no gear is engaged. The engine is idling or ticking over.

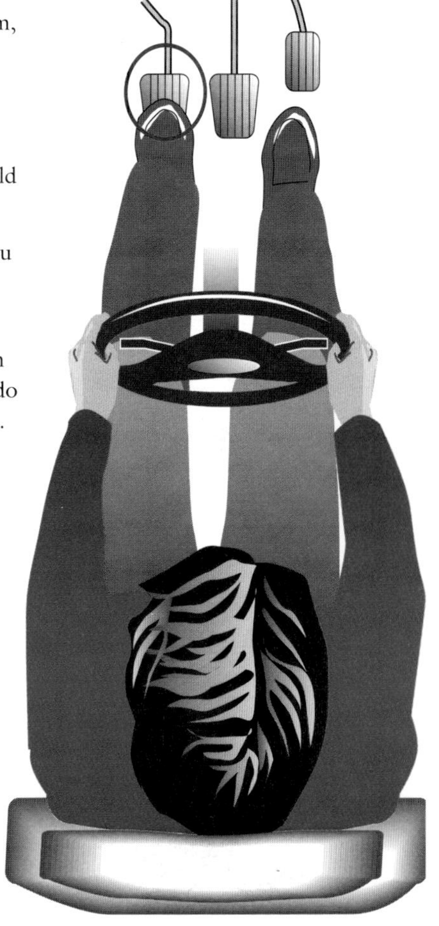

The 'biting point' The point of engagement when the two plates begin to make contact and the load on the engine increases is known as the biting point.

You'll learn with practice to judge the biting point exactly. You'll feel it and hear it, because the engine speed will drop slightly.

The feel of the clutch will vary with different vehicles. Also, as the clutch plates begin to wear, the biting point may change.

Clutch control Being able to sense the biting point is a crucial part of clutch control.

The other important part is allowing the clutch plates to engage fully and smoothly.

If the plates come together too suddenly, the engine can stall or the vehicle may jerk out of control.

Good clutch control only comes with practice, and is essential when moving off or changing gear.

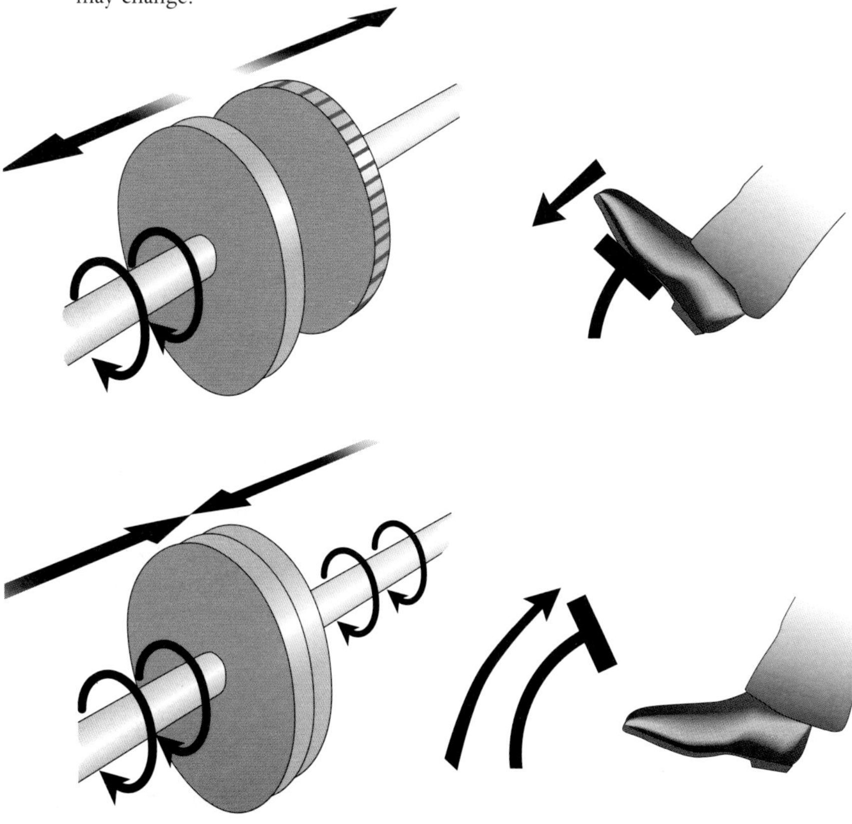

Switches

Sidelights and headlights

Position On most vehicles, the lighting controls are on a stalk at the side of the steering column.

This stalk normally has three positions

1 off
2 sidelights (or dim–dip), rear and number plate lights
3 full (main or dipped beam) and the dipping control. (On some vehicles the dipping control is a separate switch.)

Normally a warning light (usually blue) shows when the headlights are on main beam.

Some vehicles have 'dim–dip' headlights, which come on as the sidelights are switched on. It's impossible to drive these vehicles with only the sidelights switched on. The sidelights normally work without the ignition being switched on.

Use This will be covered in the section on driving at night.

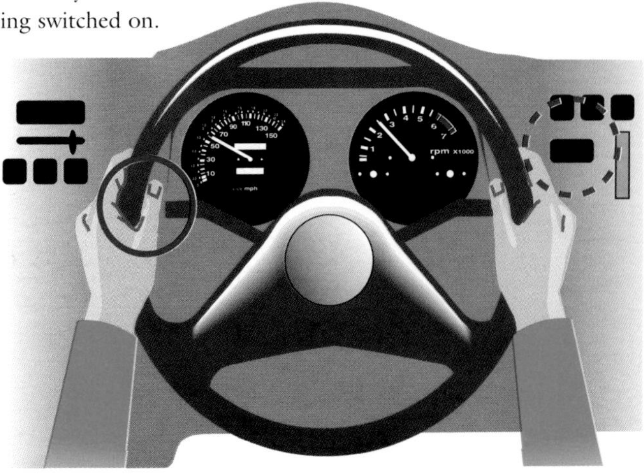

Rear fog lights switch

Rear fog lights are compulsory on all modern vehicles. They should work only when the headlights are on.

A warning light will show when they are on.

Position Since they're only used in bad weather, the rear fog lights switch is usually on the instrument panel rather than on the steering column.

Use You must only use rear fog lights when visibility is seriously reduced, to 100 metres (328 feet) or less.

You must not use either front or rear fog lights in any other circumstances because they can dazzle and distract drivers.

Direction indicator

Position The direction indicator switch is usually on a stalk which may be on either side of the steering column.

Function Its function is to enable you to use the direction indicators to show other road users which direction you intend to take. Correct use of the direction indicators is vital to safe driving.

Self-cancelling indicator switches might not cancel after a slight change of direction. Always check that the signal has been cancelled. You can do this by checking the

- repeater warning light
- audible warning, usually a ticking noise when the indicators are flashing.

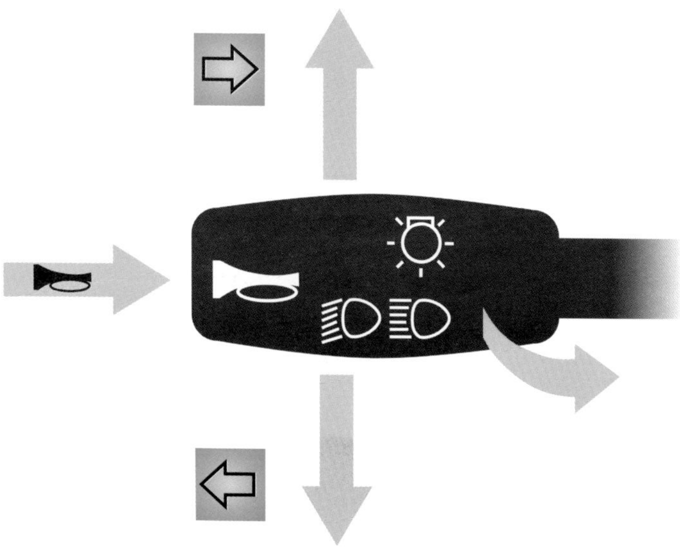

Hazard warning lights

Position The position of this switch varies. Some vehicles have it on the steering column, others on the instrument panel. It's usually

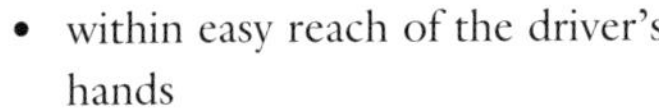

- within easy reach of the driver's hands

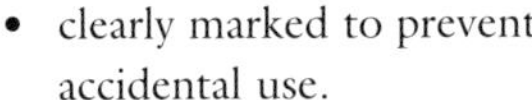

- clearly marked to prevent accidental use.

Use It should be used to warn other road users when you're temporarily obstructing traffic, for example when

- you have broken down
- you have to slow down quickly on a motorway or unrestricted dual carriageway, because of a hazard ahead. In this case, use the hazard warning lights briefly (just a few flashes) as you brake.

Don't use them to excuse stopping in a restricted area, such as on double yellow lines regardless of how brief your stop.

A warning light will flash when the hazard warning lights are in use. Don't forget to switch them off before moving away!

Remember

If another driver is unable to see both sides of your vehicle, the hazard warning lights could be mistaken for a turning signal.

Windscreen washers and wipers

Position The windscreen washer and wiper controls are usually on stalks mounted on the steering column. You should be able to find the control without taking your eyes off the road.

On most vehicles, the same stalk controls both the wipers and washers. Washers are essential in bad weather.

Where they are provided, rear wipers/washers have separate controls. Some vehicles may be fitted with miniature wipers/washers to keep the headlamps clear.

Function Their function is to keep the windscreen clear of rain, spray, snow or fog.

Use washers before wipers
Use your washers first to wet the surface before you switch on your windscreen wipers. Wiping a dry windscreen can cause scratches to the screen as well as shorten the life of the wiper blades.

Avoiding excessive dirt build up can also postpone scratches on your windscreen. Tiny bits of grit can scratch the surface and make driving at night very difficult.

Wash your windscreen regularly with a sponge and plenty of water. Wash the wiper blades as well.

Regular checks Check the fluid containers regularly, and keep them topped up.

You can use additives to prevent smearing and assist cleaning, and, especially in the winter, to prevent icing up.

Wiper blades

Wiper blades are vital to your safety.

Replace them regularly or fit 'long life' blades.

Horn

Position On most vehicles, the horn switch is either

- on the steering wheel
- on the outer end of the stalk which controls the direction indicators.

Function Its function is to warn other road users of your presence.

Use Use it to tell other drivers you're there, if this is necessary.

Aggressive sounding of the horn is dangerous. It can distract and alarm other drivers.

You must not sound your horn when

- your vehicle is stationary, unless there's danger from a moving vehicle
- in a built-up area between 11.30 pm and 7 am unless there's danger from another moving vehicle when you're stationary – otherwise flash your headlights.

Heated windscreen and rear window

Most cars have heated rear windows, and some have heated front windscreens as well.

Function Their function is to keep the windscreen and rear screen clear of

- internal condensation
- frost and ice on the outside.

Use They should be used as necessary to keep your front and rear windscreens clear, especially in wet and cold conditions.

Demister Once the engine has warmed up, you can set the controls to direct warm air to the windscreen, and on some vehicles, the front side windows.

The fan control can be set to boost the warm air flow.

Ignition switch and starter

Position Usually positioned on the steering column.

Before operating the starter, make sure that

- the handbrake is on
- the gear lever is in neutral.

In most vehicles, the ignition and starter are incorporated in the same switch. Some vehicles have a separate starter button.

On most vehicles, an anti-theft device is incorporated into the ignition switch. The mechanism locks the steering column, and slight movement may need to be applied to the steering wheel while turning the ignition key to release it.

The ignition switch and starter are operated by the ignition key.

The first position This operates some of the electrical equipment, such as the radio.

The second position This switches on the ignition, instrument panel and gauges. A red ignition warning light will usually show when the key reaches this position.

The third position This operates the starter.

The direction indicators and, on some vehicles, the headlamps will only operate when the ignition is switched on.

Use The starter is usually operated by turning the ignition key to its maximum. As soon as the engine starts, release the key. Don't operate the starter when the engine is running. This can damage the starter motor and engagement mechanism.

Warning

When the vehicle is being towed, the anti-theft device locking the steering column **must** be released by inserting the ignition key and ensuring that the steering wheel is free to move (unless a suspended tow is being used).

Choke

Position This is usually a pull control on or under the instrument panel.

Many vehicles have automatic chokes.

Function All vehicles with petrol engines have some form of choke. This reduces the amount of air in the air/fuel mixture, and helps to start the engine from cold. The smaller the amount of air in the mixture the 'richer' it is said to be.

Use With a manual choke, the further you pull the control out, the smaller the amount of air in the air/fuel mixture.

The colder the weather, the richer the mixture needs to be. The amount you need to pull the control out also depends on the type of vehicle.

Manual choke warning light

Automatic chokes These have little driver control. Look in the vehicle owner's handbook for any adjustment to the setting.

The choke engages if the engine is cold and disengages as the engine warms up.

Until the choke disengages, the engine will run too fast, making the vehicle more difficult to control.

As the engine warms up With a manual choke, you must push in the control as soon as the engine warms up, otherwise the richness of the mixture

- could damage the engine by counteracting the effects of the lubrication system
- will certainly waste petrol.

Also, the excess petrol will make the engine run too fast, and the vehicle more difficult to control.

This is particularly dangerous on vehicles with automatic transmission as it can cause the vehicle to move even when you're not pressing the accelerator (see Part Twenty One).

Diesel engines A pre-heating device is incorporated in most diesel engined vehicles.

The starter should only be operated when the indicator light goes out (where fitted).

Pre-heating warning light

Other controls

Visual aids – the instrument panel

For detailed information and guidance on this, see your vehicle owner's handbook.

The main aids

- The speedometer to tell you how quickly the vehicle is travelling in miles and kilometres per hour. It's usually a dial, with a needle showing the speed, but it's sometimes a digital display.
- Direction indicator repeater light(s).
- A fuel gauge.
- High beam indicator light (usually blue).
- On some vehicles, a 'rev counter' to tell you the engine speed in revolutions per minute (rpm).
- On diesel engines, a warming-up coil indicator lamp.
- Temperature gauge (can sometimes be a warning light).

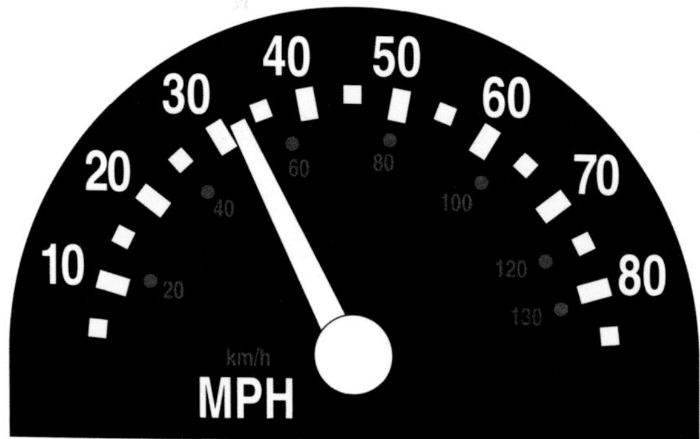

Position The visual aids are grouped on the instrument panel directly in front of the driving seat.

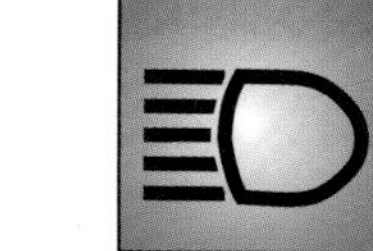

Warning lights for equipment protection

The warning lamps should light up as you turn on the ignition but should go out as the engine starts.

- Oil pressure (often amber). This shows if the oil is dangerously low or isn't circulating as it should be.
- Ignition warning light. Usually red this shows if you have a problem with the electrical charging system.

Warning lights for safety

These warning lamps come on to alert you to the respective faults.

- Brake condition warning light.
- Water temperature, if the engine is overheating (can be a gauge).
- Doors open warning light.
- Handbrake applied light.
- Four-way hazard flashers.
- Rear fog-lamp warning light.
- Rear screen heater indicator light.
- Seat-belt warning lights.
- Fog/head/side lamps indicator light.
- Boot lid unlocked warning light.

Function These lamps enable you to

- drive safely
- monitor the performance of the engine
- protect your engine and other equipment against damage
- see the functions selected.

Braking system fault

Brake lamp bulb failure

Seat belt warning light

Handbrake 'ON' warning light

Cruise control

This is usually an electronic device which enables the driver to select and maintain a safe speed on the open road.

It relieves the driver of the physical effort involved in keeping an even pressure on the accelerator pedal for long periods. It's only suitable where continuous changes of speed are unlikely to be required.

Normal control can be resumed immediately should the need arise. In most cases this happens as soon as the driver uses the accelerator or the footbrake.

Overdrive

Overdrive is a device that gives the higher gears an extra ratio. It can reduce wear and tear and improve fuel economy.

It does not necessarily make the vehicle go faster.

Although it has been in existence for many years, fewer vehicles are now fitted with overdrive since the increase in vehicles fitted with five-speed gearboxes.

It's operated by a switch on the gear lever.

PART FOUR DRIVING MIRRORS

This section explains mirrors and their use. Using the mirrors has to be part of a basic Mirror – Signal – Manoeuvre (MSM) routine. You must always know how your driving is likely to affect following traffic.

The MSM routine includes interpreting what you see in the mirror and acting appropriately. Regular and sensible use of the mirrors is an essential element of safe driving.

You should make the MSM routine an integral part of your driving.

The topics covered

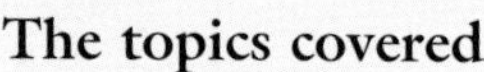

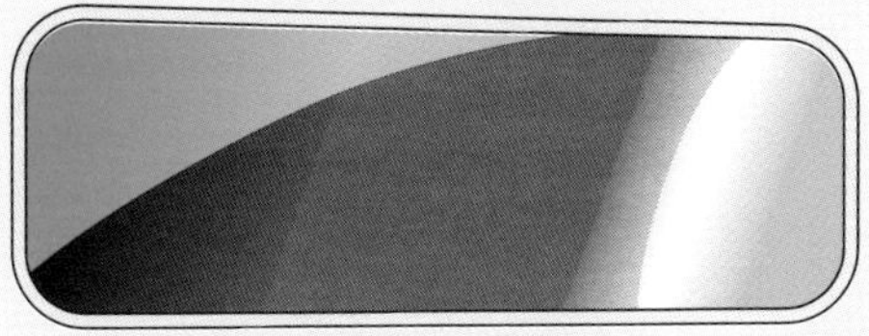

- Driving mirrors
- Adjusting mirrors
- Using mirrors
- Blind spots
- MSM routine

Defensive driving

A driving mirror is often referred to as the driver's third eye.

Mirrors are one of the keys to defensive driving. Always use them to keep up-to-date with what's behind you.

Remember, don't just look into your mirrors, **act safely and sensibly on what you see**.

Driving mirrors

Position

Many vehicles have three driving mirrors

- an interior mirror
- two exterior mirrors, one on the nearside (left-hand) door and one on the offside (right-hand) door.

Function

Driving mirrors

- give you a view of the road behind
- enable you to keep up-to-date with what's happening behind
- help you to make safe and sensible decisions, based on the position and speed of traffic behind.

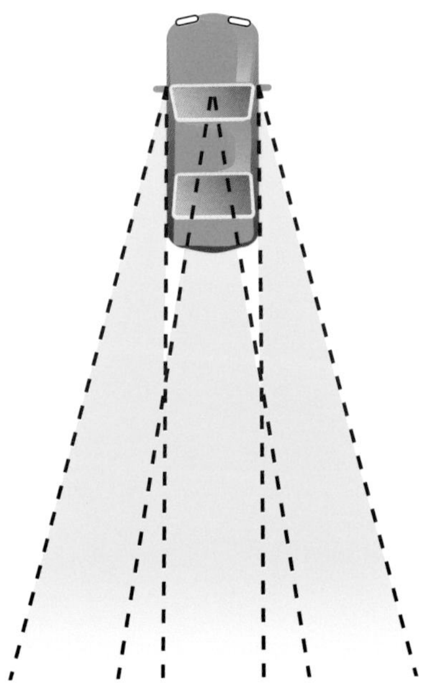

Flat mirrors

Most interior and a few exterior door mirrors have flat glass.

Flat mirrors don't distort the picture of the road behind. This makes it easier to judge the speed and distance of following traffic.

Convex mirrors

Most exterior mirrors have convex glass, which

- is slightly curved
- gives a wider field of vision.

This makes accurate judgement of speed and position of vehicles behind you more difficult.

A vehicle behind seems smaller in a convex mirror, so it could be closer than you think.

Exterior mirrors

Modern motor vehicles are required to have an offside (driver's side) mirror fitted, as well as an interior mirror.

Vans and other vehicles with a restricted view to the rear must have an exterior mirror on each side.

Towing

If you're towing a caravan or a wide trailer, fit side mirrors with extended arms to enable you to see past the caravan or trailer.

Your interior mirror can be useless when you're towing a caravan, because your view of the road behind is usually blocked.

Adjusting mirrors

Before moving off, make sure all mirrors are clean and adjusted to give you the best possible view of the road behind.

While in your normal driving position, adjust the mirrors so that you don't need to move your head to get a good view of traffic behind.

Always check your view as part of your 'cockpit drill'.

When adjusting mirrors grip them at the edge to avoid getting finger marks on the surface. Fingermarks can distort and blur the view in the mirror.

Remember to check that your exterior mirrors are still positioned correctly after you have been through a car wash.

Interior mirror

Adjust your interior mirror so that you get the best possible view through the rear window, especially to the offside, without moving your head

Exterior mirrors

Adjust your exterior mirrors

- to give the best view behind
- so that the side of the vehicle is only just visible.

Don't adjust the mirrors while you're driving. Do it before you move off, or at any time your vehicle is stationary.

Check before you get into your vehicle that they've not been knocked out of position.

Electric mirrors

Many vehicles have door mirrors which can be adjusted electrically using switches inside the vehicle.

Some of them have a heating element to keep them clear of frost and mist. Adjust your mirrors before you set out and not while you're driving.

Anti-dazzle mirrors

The interior mirror usually has an anti-dazzle position. When driving at night, you can use this to prevent dazzle or distraction from the lights of traffic behind you. You'll still be able to see the lights but the dazzle will be greatly reduced.

Remember to reset the mirror for normal use.

Using mirrors

Using your driving mirrors regularly and sensibly is vital to good driving.

Learning to judge the speed and distance of vehicles behind you takes time.

Try the following exercise when your vehicle is stationary.

- Compare the different impressions you get when you view vehicles through the interior mirror and the exterior mirror. The vehicles will seem smaller in the exterior mirror.

  Then look over your shoulder to get the real view.
- Also while you're stationary, look for blind spots. These are the areas behind that your mirrors don't always show you.

Which mirror to use

Your use of the mirrors should be linked to the manoeuvre you intend to make and the type of vehicle you're driving.

Normally you should always use the interior mirror first followed by the exterior. Your use of the exterior mirrors will depend on the manoeuvre and the situation. For example, before turning left in slow moving traffic, your nearside exterior mirror will help you to look for cyclists filtering up on your left.

When to look in your mirror

Always

- use your mirrors in good time, that is, **well before** you
  - approach a hazard
  - slow down, change lane, or begin any manoeuvre
- act sensibly on what you see
- begin the (MSM) routine EARLY.

And always use your mirrors before

- moving off
- signalling
- changing direction
  - turning left or right
  - overtaking or changing lanes
- slowing down or stopping
- opening your car door.

This is one of the few driving rules that is not subject to any exception or qualification.

What's behind you? Ask yourself

- How close is following traffic?
- How fast is it moving?
- What is it doing?
- Is the manoeuvre safe?

It's also important to use the mirrors early enough to allow other road users time to react to any signal you need to give. Use your mirrors to check their reaction.

Blind spots

Blind spots can occur when bodywork interferes with your view through the mirrors.

Vehicles with different shapes have different blind spots.

Exterior mirrors help reduce blind spots, but remember that mirrors will not show you everything behind you. Auxiliary mirrors are available to mount on the surface of exterior mirrors. These give an even wider angle of vision and go some way to reducing blind spots, but won't entirely eliminate them.

Defensive driving

Even though you have used your mirrors, ***always*** look round over your right shoulder to check the blind spot BEFORE you move off.

Checking blind spots on the move

There will be occasions when it will be necessary to check blind spots on the move. These blind spots will be just behind and to either side and should not require looking around but more a quick sideways glance.

Looking right around to check blind spots on the move would be unnecessary and dangerous, especially when driving at high speeds; in the time it takes you'll lose touch with what's happening in front.

Regular and sensible use of the mirrors will keep you up-to-date with what's happening behind. You will however, still need to know when a glance into the blind area is needed.

A quick sideways glance A quick sideways glance into the blind area might be necessary

- before changing lanes
- before joining a motorway or dual carriageway from a slip road and acceleration lane
- before manoeuvring in situations where traffic is merging from the left or right.

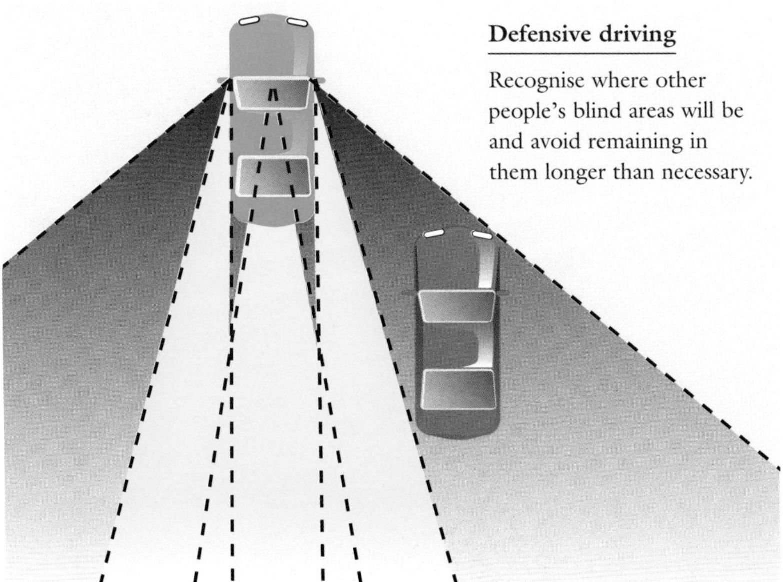

Defensive driving

Recognise where other people's blind areas will be and avoid remaining in them longer than necessary.

MSM routine

Regardless of your driving experience, you **must** make the Mirror – Signal – Manoeuvre routine an integral part of your driving.

Remember the routine

- **MIRRORS** – check the speed and position of traffic behind you
- **SIGNAL** – consider if a signal is necessary. If it is, signal your intention to change course or slow down in good time
- **MANOEUVRE** – a manoeuvre is any change of speed or position.

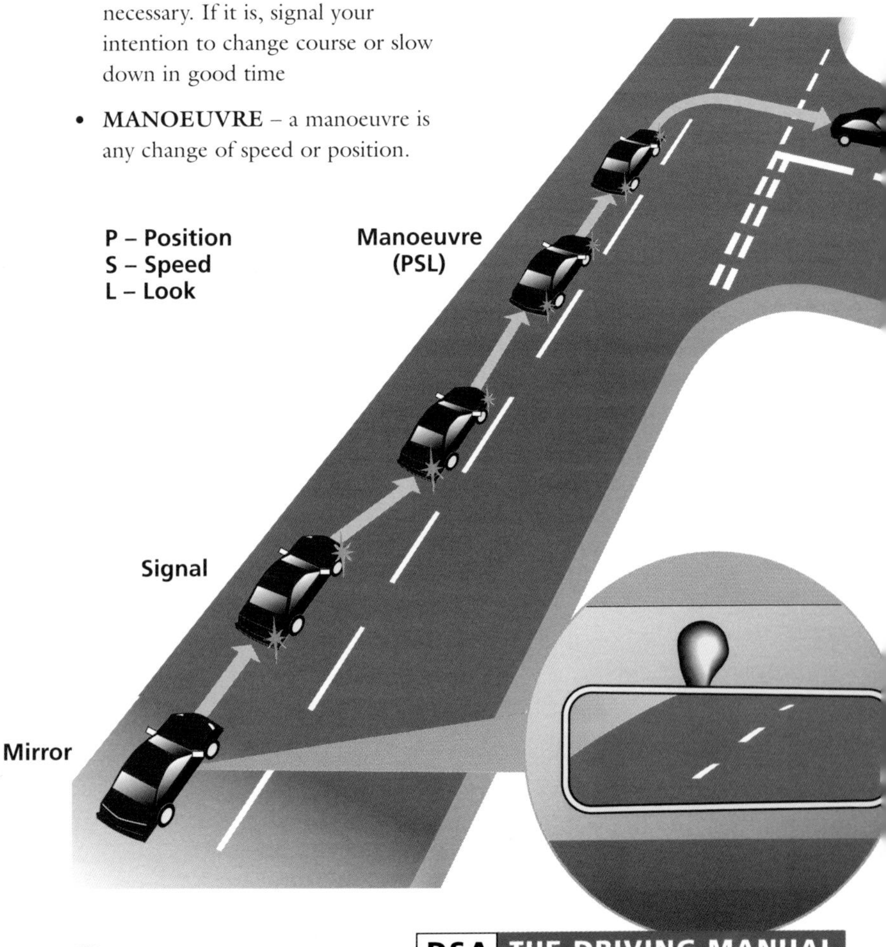

MANOEUVRE

This is broken down into

- **P – Position**
- **S – Speed**
- **L – Look**

Position

Your vehicle must always be in the correct position for the manoeuvre. When a change of direction is required, move into position in good time.

Speed

Ensure that the vehicle is travelling at the appropriate speed to complete the manoeuvre safely.

Look

Looking means **three** things

- *Assessing*.
  What **can** you see?
- *Deciding*.
  Depending on what you see.
- *Acting*.
  Either continue or wait.

Always

Use the MSM routine before

- moving off
- signalling
- changing direction
  – turning left or right
  – overtaking or changing lanes
- slowing down or stopping.

Never

- Signal without checking mirrors first.
- Rely solely on mirrors when you're reversing. Keep looking around to watch for other road users.
- Assume that, because you have signalled, you can carry out the intended manoeuvre safely. Check to be sure.

  Other road users might not
  – have seen your signal
  – understand your intention.

The mirrors and hazards

A hazard is any situation which involves you in some risk or danger.

A hazard might cause you to slow down or change course.

When approaching a hazard, you should use your mirrors and be prepared to change speed and/or direction.

Hazards include

- bends in the road
- junctions
- pedestrian crossings
- road works
- livestock on the road.

Always look in your mirror in good time to decide

- if a signal is necessary
- whether it's safe to make a move

and ***before*** you change direction.

Keeping up-to-date

Keep up-to-date with the position and speed of traffic behind you.

Good drivers should always know as much about the conditions behind as they know about the situation ahead.

Traffic positions change rapidly on some roads. Frequent glances in mirrors keep you up-to-date with what's behind. How frequently depends on road and traffic conditions.

Motorway driving

For motorway driving check your mirrors earlier than you would on ordinary roads.

The higher speeds are more difficult to judge and situations develop more quickly.

Before you drive on busy roads and in traffic, you should master the basic techniques of starting, moving off and stopping. You must have full control of your vehicle at all times and this involves

- a good working knowledge of the various controls
- being able to coordinate hand and foot controls together.

In addition you need to have

- an understanding of the rules of the road
- a respect for the needs of other road users.
- a basic knowledge to enable you to check your vehicle to make sure everything is working correctly, and the vehicle is safe before setting out.

The topics covered

Getting started

Starting to drive isn't just a matter of starting the engine and driving off. You should first of all check your vehicle to make sure it's safe and ready for the road.

Everyday checks

Make a habit of checking daily that

- the windscreen, windows and mirrors are clean
- all lights (including indicators) are working; replace any dead bulbs immediately (It's a good idea to carry spare fuses and bulbs)
- the brakes are working; don't venture out with faulty brakes.

Periodic checks

These checks are both for safety and good vehicle maintenance.
Check

- engine oil; top up if necessary
- water level in the radiator or expansion tank; top up if necessary
- brake fluid level; top up if necessary
- tyres; make sure they are
  - legal (They MUST have the correct tread depth and be free of dangerous cuts and defects.)
  - at the right pressure
- battery; top up with distilled water if necessary (Some batteries are maintenance free and don't need topping up.)
- windscreen and rear window washer bottles; top up if necessary.

How often?

How often you make the checks depends on how much you drive. Consult your vehicle owner's handbook. If you drive a lot, you may need to do these every day.

Regular servicing

Have your vehicle regularly serviced. The owner's handbook will tell you when servicing is recommended.

Cockpit drill

Make these checks for the safety of yourself, your passengers and other road users.

Every time you get into your vehicle, check that

- all doors are properly closed
- the driving seat is in the best position, and you can
  - see clearly in all directions
  - reach ALL the controls comfortably
- the mirrors are clean and correctly adjusted
- you and your passengers have seat belts on
- you have enough fuel for the journey.

Know the controls

Get to know the controls in an unfamiliar vehicle before you start the engine, especially in bad weather.

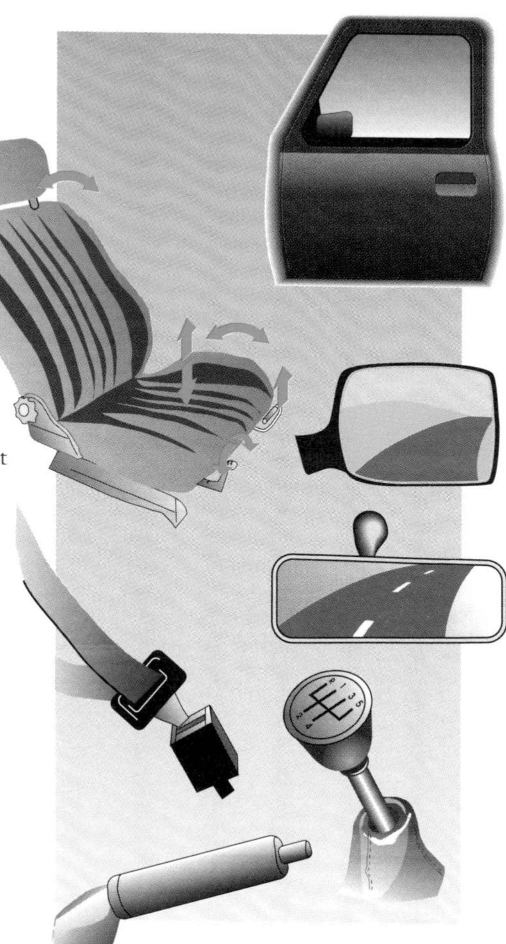

Starting the engine

After you've made the preliminary checks and you're settled comfortably in the driving seat, begin the drill for starting the engine.

- Check the handbrake is on by trying to pull it on slightly further.
- Check that the gear lever is in neutral (or P or N if driving an automatic).
- Pull the choke out if necessary. Many vehicles have an automatic choke.
- Switch on the ignition by turning the key. The ignition and oil pressure light, if fitted, will come on. Other warning lights should also come on.

  With a diesel engine you might have to wait for a glow plug lamp to go out.
- Operate the starter by turning the key further, or use the separate starter switch, if one is fitted.
- Release the starter key or switch as soon as the engine begins running, otherwise the starter could be damaged.

  Do not operate the starter if the engine is already running.

You might find it necessary to use the accelerator a little as you operate the starter. The amount will depend on the make and model of your vehicle.

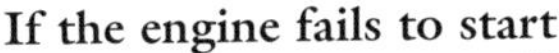

If the engine fails to start

If the engine fails to start first time

- Release the key or switch.
- Wait a moment.
- Try again. Be patient, you might flood the carburettor with too much fuel.

When the engine starts

- You may need to press the accelerator *slightly* to help the engine keep running.
- The engine should now be idling or 'ticking over'.

The ignition and oil pressure warning lamps should go out when the engine is running. If either light stays on, switch off the engine and have the fault checked.

Never drive a vehicle with the oil pressure warning light showing – it could damage the engine.

Manual choke

As the engine warms up, push in the choke.

Don't drive with the choke out any longer than necessary. This wastes fuel, causes wear to the engine, and can be dangerous, especially with automatic transmission.

Moving off

- With your left foot, press the clutch pedal fully down and hold it down.
- Move the gear lever into first gear.

  If it won't engage
  - move the gear lever to neutral
  - let out the clutch and press it down again
  - repeat the first two steps.

You should prepare to move off only if you'll be able to do so shortly.

- With your right foot, press the accelerator *slightly* and hold it steady.
- Slowly and smoothly, let up the clutch pedal until you hear the engine noise change slightly. This change means the clutch is at the biting point. With experience, you'll be able to feel the biting point.
- Hold the clutch steady in this position.
- Now make your final safety checks
  - use your mirrors
  - look over your right shoulder to check the blind spot.
- Decide if a signal is necessary. The timing of any signal is crucial. Avoid waiting unduly with the clutch at biting point.

Don't

- signal and move out regardless
- sit with the signal showing when you can't move out safely.

- If it's safe to move off, be ready to release the handbrake.
- Look round again if necessary and keep an eye on your mirrors.
- When you're sure it's safe and convenient to move off
  - release the handbrake
  - at the same time, let the clutch pedal come up a little more. The vehicle will begin to move. Tight clutch control is needed, so keep the clutch pedal just above the biting point.
- Gradually, press the accelerator for more speed and let the clutch come up smoothly, and then take your left foot off the clutch pedal.

Biting point The 'biting point' is when the clutch plates start to engage. You must be able to find this point confidently when you bring up the clutch pedal. Although you can press the pedal down quickly, you must not let it come up too fast. Practise.

Practice makes perfect Getting these steps in the right order is difficult at first. Choose a quiet level road to practise starting, moving off, and stopping.

Defensive driving

- Check all round before moving off.
- Signal if necessary.
- Don't move out into the path of oncoming traffic.
- Don't rush.

Braking

Safe and controlled braking is vital in good driving.

Try to slow down gradually and smoothly.

Anticipation and braking

If you anticipate properly, you'll seldom need to brake fiercely.

Good anticipation will give you time to brake *progressively* over a longer distance.

Late, harsh braking is a sign of poor anticipation and of reduced safety margins.

Braking and steering

Braking shifts the balance of weight of the vehicle forward. This causes the front tyres to grip the road more than the rear tyres.

The extra weight on the front suspension and the increased tyre grip makes steering more difficult.

If you have to brake hard, only do so when you're travelling in a straight line.

Remember

The harder you brake the greater the shift in weight. This in turn makes it harder to steer.

The greater your speed when you brake

- the more difficult it is to control the vehicle
- the greater the distance you need to stop the vehicle.

You should consider

- the safety and peace of mind of everyone concerned, including your passengers
- wear and tear on brakes, tyres and suspension
- following vehicles whose brakes might not be as powerful as yours.

Avoid braking on bends

Braking on a bend can have serious consequences.

The weight and momentum of the vehicle is thrown outwards as well as forwards. The front tyre on the outside of the curve will be overloaded and gripping much more than the other tyres. This extra grip acts as an anchor and the vehicle could be thrown into a severe skid.

Road surface conditions can have a big effect in these situations. Watch for uneven, loose or slippery surfaces. Where possible, brake while travelling in a straight line.

Think ahead

Think well ahead to avoid the need for harsh, uncontrolled braking.

You should never drive too fast or too close to the vehicle in front. Other drivers might be affected by your actions.

Always use your mirrors before braking and give yourself plenty of space.

Consider

- your own speed of reaction
- the mechanical condition of your vehicles – brakes, steering and suspension
- the type, condition and pressure of your tyres
- the size and weight of your vehicle and its load
- the gradient of the road
- whether the road has a camber or bend
- the weather and visibility
- the road surface. Is it rough, smooth, loose, wet, muddy, covered with wet leaves, ice or snow.

Five rules for good braking

- Anticipate. Think and look well ahead.
- Know your own limitations and those of your vehicle.
- Take note of the state of the road and its surface.
- Give yourself plenty of time and distance to brake progressively.
- Avoid the risk of skidding, rather than trying to control it.

Defensive driving

If the vehicle behind is too close, slow down gradually to increase your distance from the vehicle ahead so that you can avoid having to brake suddenly.

Stopping

The drill for stopping is always the same, except in an emergency. You must learn it thoroughly from the beginning.

The amount of pressure you need to apply to the foot-brake depends on

- your speed
- how quickly you need to stop.

Drill for stopping

- Use the mirrors.
- Decide whether you need to signal your intention to stop.
- Signal if necessary.
- Take your foot off the accelerator. The engine will slow down.
- Push down the brake pedal lightly with your right foot, then more firmly (see Progressive braking).
- Just before the vehicle stops, press the clutch pedal right down with the left foot. This disengages the engine from the driving wheels and prevents stalling. Don't do it too soon: the engine helps with braking.
- Ease the pressure off the foot-brake just as the vehicle stops.
- Apply the hand-brake.
- Put the gear lever into neutral.
- Take both feet off the pedals.

Changing down before you stop It's seldom necessary to change down when you're stopping normally. However, your vehicle should always be in the right gear for the road speed and conditions.

Progressive braking

This is a safe driving technique, which

- allows other drivers time to react
- prevents locked wheels
- prevents skidding
- saves wear and tear on brakes, tyres and suspension
- saves fuel
- is more comfortable for your passengers.

To brake progressively

- put light pressure on the brake at first
- gradually increase the pressure as required to stop the vehicle
- when the vehicle has almost stopped, ease off the pressure so that the vehicle stops smoothly. There should be little or no pressure as the vehicle actually stops.

Practice Choose a particular point at which you would like to stop.

See how near to it you can get. It's better to stop short of the mark rather than overshoot it.

You can always ease off the brakes and run forward a bit more.

Stopping at the kerb needs practice too. Aim to stop reasonably close to the kerb without hitting it.

Both hands should be on the steering wheel.

Stopping in an emergency

In normal conditions, a good driver should not need to brake really hard.

However, emergencies can happen – for instance, when a child runs into the road in front of you – so you must know how to stop quickly under control. Stopping in an emergency increases the risk of skidding.

Remember, even when stopping quickly, follow the rule of progressive braking – pushing the brake pedal harder as the vehicle slows down.

A *quick reaction* is crucial in an emergency. The sooner you start braking, the sooner you should stop!

Practise the following

- **Keep both hands on the steering wheel.** You need as much control as possible.
- **Avoid braking so hard that you lock any of the wheels.** A skid sideways or a wheel sliding along may cause serious loss of control.
- **Don't touch the clutch pedal until just before you stop.** This helps with your braking and stability.
- **Don't touch the handbrake.** Most handbrakes work on the back wheels only. Extra braking here can cause skidding.

Unless you're moving off again straight away, put the handbrake on and the gear lever into neutral.

Practise braking to judge the correct pressure and remember to take into account road and weather conditions.

If the road is dry, you should apply firm pressure, but on a wet road or loose surface, you should avoid using too much. This means you'll need to reduce speed and increase your separation distance from the vehicle in front.

When braking in an emergency

- Don't signal – you need both hands to control the steering.
- Don't make a special point of looking in the mirror – you should know what's behind anyway.
- Stop as quickly and safely as possible, keeping your vehicle under full control.
- Look all round before moving off again.

Defensive driving

- Try to avoid the emergency arising
  - look well ahead
  - watch for children playing
  - remember school times
  - look out for pedestrians
  - look for clues, such as reflections.
- Always drive at such a speed that you can stop safely in the distance you can **see** to be **clear**. If it's not clear, **slow down**.
- Anticipation means being prepared for the unexpected.

Cadence braking

This is a special braking technique for car control in very slippery conditions. It works on the principle that maximum braking effort is achieved at the point just before the wheels start to lock up.

In an emergency the technique is to

- brake using maximum pressure to the point where the wheels are about to lock
- then momentarily release the brake pressure
- quickly apply it again.

Apply and release the pressure until the vehicle has stopped or the need for braking has passed.

Cadence braking is an advanced technique to be aware of but it is not a substitute for proper care and anticipation. It should only be used in certain emergency situations to avoid skidding.

Anti-lock braking systems (ABS)

Anti-lock brakes are becoming an option on many vehicles, and are a requirement on some categories of large goods vehicles and their trailers.

They work in a very similar manner to cadence braking and can be mechanically or electronically operated.

Just as the wheels are about to lock, the sensor control releases the brake and immediately applies it again.

ABS also allows you to apply the brakes and steer at the same time. This can be very useful in an emergency.

Refer to the owners handbook for details of the manufacturers recommended method of use.

ABS has limitations

Knowing ABS will help you to stop safely should not encourage you to drive less carefully. If you drive too fast or don't concentrate ABS may not be able to save you. Safety is your responsibility.

ABS cannot overcome the laws of physics; it's still possible for one or more of the tyres to skid because of

- poor road contact
- surface water
- loose road surface.

ABS will enhance your skills, NOT replace them.

The handbrake

You should normally apply the handbrake whenever the vehicle is stationary.

Apply the handbrake and put the gear lever into neutral when you're stopped at traffic lights or queuing behind other vehicles, unless the wait is likely to be very short.

Your foot could easily slip off the footbrake if, for example, your shoes are wet, or if you're bumped from behind. You could then be pushed into another vehicle or a pedestrian.

Always leave a safe gap between yourself and the vehicle in front while queuing, especially on a hill.
This will give you room to manoeuvre should the vehicle in front roll back or should a driver behind come up too quickly.

Always keep an eye on the mirrors.

The use of the handbrake is even more important in vehicles fitted with automatic transmission. The handbrake will help avoid

- the possibility of 'creep'
- the vehicle surging forward if the accelerator is pressed accidentally while in **D** (Drive).

Steering

Practise steering your vehicle, at low speed at first, keeping about 1 metre (3 feet) from the kerb.

Look well ahead, not just at the front of your vehicle.

Keep your movements steady and smooth. Never make a sudden or jerky action while steering.

Push – pull technique

Don't cross your hands on the steering wheel when turning. Use the 'push – pull' technique described earlier.

Steering with one hand

When you can steer a straight course with both hands on the steering wheel, try steering with only one hand.

The reason for practising steering with one hand isn't so that you can drive like that. It's because there are times when you'll only have one hand free for steering. For example, when you're changing gear or working a switch.

Stiffen your arm slightly to help you steer a straight course without pulling the wheel down or swerving. Practise with each hand.

Changing gear

To drive safely, you should combine knowing

- how to change gear

with knowing

- when to change gear

and

- which gear to select.

These are skills which take time to acquire.

The gear positions

You need to know the various positions of the gear lever without having to look down.

You can practise and get to know the gear position with the clutch disengaged and the engine switched off.

A light but firm touch should be all you need to move from one gear to another. Never force the gear lever.

On some gear boxes you might require slight pressure to overcome the sprung bias on the pull or push movements when you're moving.

First to second You might need to put a little pressure to the left on the gear lever when you change up from first to second gear. This is to prevent the lever slipping into fourth while passing through neutral.

Third to fourth Similarly, you might need to put a little pressure to the right when you change from third to fourth gear.

Again, you might need to put slight pressure

- to the left when you change down from third or second to first
- to the right changing down from fifth or fourth to third.

Changing down to first gear You need to be able to change down easily into first gear, without having to stop your vehicle. However this should only be when your road speed is suitable for this gear.

Don't force the gear lever If you feel resistance, don't force the gear lever into any position.

Never

- rush gear changes
- take your eyes off the road when you change gear
- coast with the clutch pedal pressed in, or the gear lever in neutral
- hold the gear lever longer than necessary.

Changing up

When to change up You need to change gear in order to match the engine speed and load to the speed of the vehicle.

This will vary with the vehicle you're driving and whether you're moving on the level, uphill or downhill.

As a general rule, change up as the road speed increases.

Listening to the engine helps to determine when to change up.

- Left hand on gear lever.
- Press the clutch pedal right down at the same time as you ease off the accelerator pedal. Don't take your foot off the accelerator.
- Move the gear lever to the next highest position required.
- Let the clutch pedal come up smoothly, and, at the same time, press the accelerator gradually. Put your left hand back on the steering wheel.

Matching engine and road speed Releasing the accelerator when changing up lets the engine speed drop to match the higher gear to give you a smooth gear change.

Judging when it's time to change up comes with experience.

Changing down

When to change down You'll need to change down to a lower gear

- if you have slowed down and the gear you're in doesn't provide enough power for driving at the lower speed
- if you're going uphill in too high a gear and your engine labours or struggles to give enough power
- to increase the effect of the engine braking, for example, when on a long downhill gradient.

Driving in a high gear at low speed makes engine performance sluggish, and is bad driving practice.

Unless you intend to stop, you'll need to change to a lower gear once you've slowed down.

As a general rule, use the brakes to reduce speed before changing down to the most suitable gear for the lower speed.

It might be necessary to keep a light pressure on the foot-brake while you're changing down to stop the vehicle gathering speed on a downhill slope.

Note. In the early stages of learning to drive it may help you become familiar with the gearbox by changing down through each of the gears in turn. Be guided by your instructor.

When changing down, you might need to either

- raise the engine speed to get a smooth change
- keep a light pressure on the foot-brake to stop the vehicle gathering speed.

The procedure for changing down is as follows.

- Left hand on gear lever.
- Press the clutch pedal right down and at the same time either keep a little pressure on
  – the accelerator pedal,
  or
  – the foot-brake
  whichever is appropriate to the road and traffic conditions.
- Move the gear lever to the most suitable lower gear for the speed.
- Let the clutch pedal come up smoothly. Return to the accelerator or continue braking as necessary.
- Put your left hand back on the steering wheel.

Never rush gear changes Smooth, even movements are best.

Matching engine and road speed How much pressure is needed on the accelerator or foot-brake when changing down will depend on

- the road and traffic conditions
- the speed of your vehicle at the time the clutch pedal is released.

The sound of the engine will help you judge this.

Finding the right gear

To change gear, you need to anticipate and assess the situation well in advance. Ask yourself if the gear you're in is correct for that particular situation.

For example

- you should consider changing to a lower gear to overtake. A lower gear can give you the extra acceleration to pass safely.
  Try to avoid changing gear while you're actually overtaking. It's preferable to keep both hands on the wheel during the manoeuvre. A lower gear will give you extra engine flexibility and therefore more vehicle control
- when descending a steep hill, a lower gear gives more engine braking and control, particularly on a bend.

As a general rule

- change down to accelerate more quickly
- change down if your speed drops.

Smooth gear changing

Smooth, easy gear changes are essential to good driving. Take your time and think ahead. Assess the situation, and act accordingly.

Intermediate gears

The efficiency of modern gearboxes and braking systems make it unnecessary to change down through each of the gears in turn.

As a general rule, it's preferable, and just as safe, to brake first and then engage the most suitable gear for the lower speed. It might be necessary to maintain a light pressure on the foot-brake while changing down.

Missing out the intermediate gears will not only give you more time to concentrate on the road ahead, but also allow you to keep both hands on the steering wheel longer.

How many gears you can miss out will depend on the engine and gearbox in your particular vehicle. Fifth to third, fourth to second or third to first are the most common examples.

Accelerating in low gear

Don't accelerate too fiercely or for too long in the lower gears. This

- uses much more fuel
- could damage your engine
- could cause wheel-spin and loss of control.

Coasting

Coasting means that although the vehicle is moving it's not being driven by the engine, either when

- the clutch pedal is held down

or

- the gear lever is in the 'neutral' position.

Any form of coasting is wrong because it

- reduces the driver's control of the vehicle, particularly steering and braking
- could prove difficult to engage a gear if something unexpected happened
- would almost certainly lead to the vehicle gathering speed when travelling downhill. It would mean harder braking and removes the assistance of engine braking in low gear.

Each time you change gear you coast a little. This is unavoidable but should be kept to a minimum.

Over-run

If there is only light pressure on the accelerator pedal when the vehicle is travelling at speed, the engine may not appear to be 'driving' the vehicle.

This is known as travelling on the over-run and should not be confused with coasting. There is no loss of control, because the vehicle is still in gear and either engine braking or acceleration are available immediately.

Slipping the clutch

This is holding the clutch pedal partially down so that the clutch is not fully engaged. This allows the engine to spin faster than if it was fully engaged.

Slipping the clutch to compensate for being in a high gear at a low speed is bad driving practice and should be avoided. This is not only bad driving technique, but can result in excessive wear of the clutch.

Judgement

As you become more proficient, you'll be able to judge exactly the gear you need for the speed you intend and the manoeuvre you're planning.

Signalling

Signals are normally given by direction indicators and/or brake lights.

There are occasions when an arm signal can be helpful.

It's important that you use the correct signal.

Purpose

Use signals

- to let others know what you intend to do
- to help all other road users, including pedestrians
- in good time and for long enough to allow other road users to see the signal and act upon it.

When to signal

Signal in good time, particularly before

- turning right or left
- overtaking another moving vehicle
- moving from one lane to another.

Signalling too soon can confuse rather than help. For example, when there are several side roads very close together.

Signalling too late can cause following vehicles to brake hard or swerve.

Watch out for situations which call for special timing in signalling.

Unnecessary signals

A signal might not be necessary where there is no-one to benefit from it, or where the signal could confuse other road users.

- Moving off.
- Pulling up.
- Passing stationary vehicles, when you can position early and maintain a steady course.

Never

- signal carelessly
- wave pedestrians across the road
- fail to check that the signal is cancelled after your movement is completed
- mislead other road users. Always use the correct signal.

For example, when you signal to pull up on the left, make sure there isn't a junction just before the place you intend to stop. If you signal left too soon, a driver waiting at that junction might think you intend to turn left. Delay signaling until you're in a position where your signal can't be misunderstood.

Remember

- **Mirror(s)**
- **Signal**
- **Manoeuvre**

Arm signals

Nowadays, arm signals are seldom used. However, there are occasions when you might need to use one.

Approaching Zebra crossings When yours is the leading vehicle, using an arm signal when slowing down or stopping can be helpful.

This not only tells following traffic that you intend to stop, but also approaching traffic and waiting pedestrians, who can't see your brake lights.

Turning right Use an arm signal when necessary

- to emphasize a difficult right turn on a road carrying fast-moving traffic
- to turn right just after moving out to pass a stationary vehicle.

Stopping Use the 'slowing down' arm signal where any confusion to other road users might be caused by a 'left turn' indicator signal.

Defensive driving

Brake in good time. If necessary, lightly press the brake pedal early, or more than once to show your brake lights to following traffic.

Using the horn

If you're driving safely, and anticipating correctly, you'll seldom need to use the horn.

Only use it if you think other road users haven't seen you or cannot see you.

On a blind bend or narrow winding road, the horn might help pedestrians and other drivers who cannot see you coming.

Warning others of your presence does not relieve you of the responsibility to drive safely. Always drive with caution.

Don't sound your horn

- to reprimand other drivers
- aggressively
- in a built-up area between 11.30 pm and 7.00 am
- while you're stationary, unless a moving vehicle creates a danger.

Flashing the headlights

Flashing the headlights can be used in much the same way as the horn to warn other road users that you're there.

If you think a warning is necessary, flashing headlights can be particularly useful in situations where the horn might not be heard.

Avoid flashing your headlights to

- instruct other drivers
- reprimand another road user
- intimidate a driver ahead.

Other drivers flashing their headlights

Some drivers flash there headlights for a variety of reasons including

- inviting you to pass before them
- thanking you for your courtesy
- warning you of some fault with your vehicle
- telling you your headlights are dazzling them.

When other drivers flash, don't rely on what you *think* they mean. The signal

- might not mean what you think
- might not be intended for you.

Make sure you know their intention before you act on the signal.

Defensive driving

Remember: flashing of headlights might not be an invitation.

The other driver might

- have flashed someone else
- have flashed accidentally.

Moving off at an angle

Use the same drill as for moving off straight ahead covered under 'Moving off from rest'

When making the routine safety checks and at biting point ask yourself

- At what angle should I move out?

and

- How far will this take me into the road?

Your decision will depend on

- how close you are to the vehicle or object in front
- how wide the vehicle is ahead
- oncoming traffic. Your window pillar can obstruct your view ahead. Make sure there's nothing in the area hidden by this obstruction.

Watch out for other vehicles behind and decide whether you need to signal your intention to move out.

When you're sure it's safe and convenient to move off.

- Look over your right shoulder again.
- Release the handbrake as you ease the clutch pedal up a little more. The vehicle will begin to move. Tight clutch control is needed, so keep the clutch pedal at or just above the biting point.

  Give yourself time to complete the amount of steering you need to clear the vehicle in front.
- Release the clutch pedal smoothly only when your vehicle is clear of the obstruction.

  Allow room for someone to open a door, if you're steering around a vehicle.
- Check your mirrors.
- Move out slowly, straighten up, and be ready to brake – a pedestrian might step out from in front of the parked vehicle.

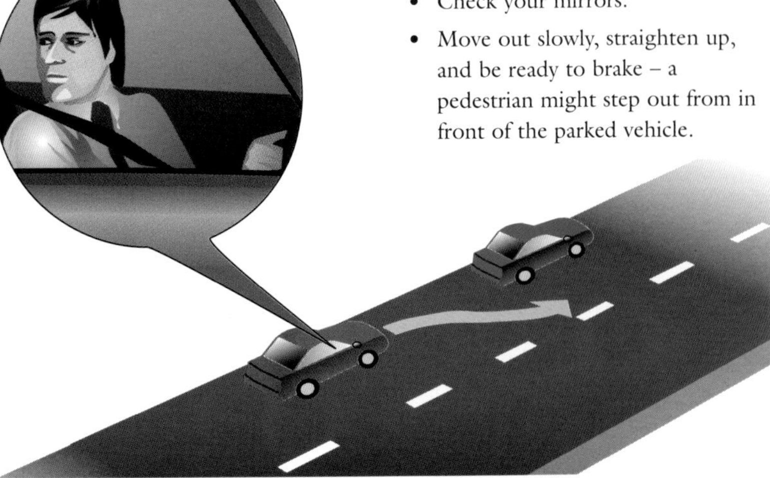

Moving off uphill

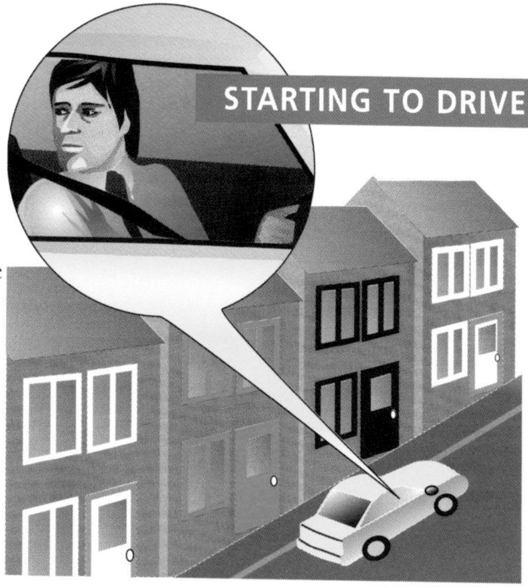

Your vehicle will tend to roll back. To avoid this, you must use the accelerator, clutch and handbrake together.

Much of the drill for moving off uphill is the same as for moving off on the level.

- With your left foot, press the clutch pedal down and hold it down.
- Move the gear lever into first.
- With your right foot, press the accelerator further than you would when starting on the level, and hold it perfectly steady. The amount will depend on how steep the hill is.
- Bring the clutch pedal up to the biting point which will be slightly higher than when you're moving off on the level.
- Make your safety checks
  - use your mirrors
  - look round over your right shoulder to check the blind spot. Remember to allow a safe gap in any traffic because your vehicle will be slower pulling away and building up speed.
- Decide whether you need to signal your intention to move off.
- Signal if necessary.
- Look round again if necessary.
- Lift the handbrake and release the button while you press the accelerator a little more. How much acceleration you need depends on the steepness of the hill.
- Let the clutch up a little more, until you feel and hear the engine trying to move the vehicle.
- Release the handbrake smoothly.
- Gradually press the accelerator as the vehicle begins to move and bring up the clutch pedal smoothly.

Controlling the handbrake and clutch

This requires good timing. If you release the handbrake too soon, the vehicle will roll back.

The vehicle will stall if

- you hold the handbrake too long
- you bring up the clutch too quickly or too far
- you don't use enough acceleration.

Practise the steps until you've mastered the technique.

Then practise moving off uphill without rolling backwards, from behind a parked vehicle, at an angle.

Moving off downhill

The routine is simpler than moving off uphill because the weight of the vehicle helps you to move away.

The aim is to prevent the vehicle from rolling forward down the hill by holding the footbrake on before releasing the handbrake.

- Press in the clutch pedal fully.
- Engage the appropriate gear for the severity of the slope (this could be second gear).
- Apply the footbrake.
- Release the handbrake, keeping the footbrake applied.
- Check mirrors. Look round just before you move off to cover the blind spots.
- Signal if necessary.
- Only move away when you're sure it's safe to do so.

  Look round again if necessary.
- Release the footbrake and release the clutch pedal *smoothly* as the vehicle starts to move.

Remember

Going uphill

You should co-ordinate the use of accelerator, clutch and handbrake as described earlier.

- Don't cut across or block traffic coming uphill. Use the MSM routine. Avoid hasty action.
- You need a larger gap in traffic before you pull away because your vehicle will not gain speed as quickly as on the level.

Going downhill

- Be careful to use the right gear for the steepness of the slope to give you more control.
- Don't forget that drivers coming downhill will need more time to slow down or stop. Again, leave a large enough gap before pulling away.

Once you've mastered the driving controls and how to get your vehicle moving, you need to know how to deal safely and effectively with various road and traffic situations.

This section covers the

- awareness and anticipation you need to drive safely on the public road
- methods of safely dealing with traffic, hills, and other problems and hazards.

The topics covered

- Awareness and anticipation
- Road positioning
- Stopping distance
- Separation distance
- Overtaking
- Obstructions
- Pedestrian Crossings
- Hills
- Supertrams or Light Rapid Transit (LRT) Systems

Awareness and anticipation

In any traffic situation there are some things that are obviously going to happen, as well as some things that *might* happen.

To anticipate is to take action when you expect something will or might happen.

You can *anticipate* what might happen by making early use of the available information on the road.

Ask yourself

- What am I likely to find?
- What are they trying to do?
- Should I speed up or slow down?
- Do I need to stop?

Changing conditions

Traffic conditions change constantly and you need to

- check and re-check what's going on around you
- be alert all the time to changes in conditions and think ahead.

The degree to which you need to anticipate varies according to those conditions.

Difficult conditions

You'll find it more difficult to decide what might happen when

- the light or the weather is poor
- the traffic is heavy
- the route is unfamiliar.

Types of road

Similarly, types of road will affect how much you can anticipate.

It's easier in light traffic to anticipate what other drivers might do, than it is on a busy single carriageway, dual carriageway or motorway, where their options are greater.

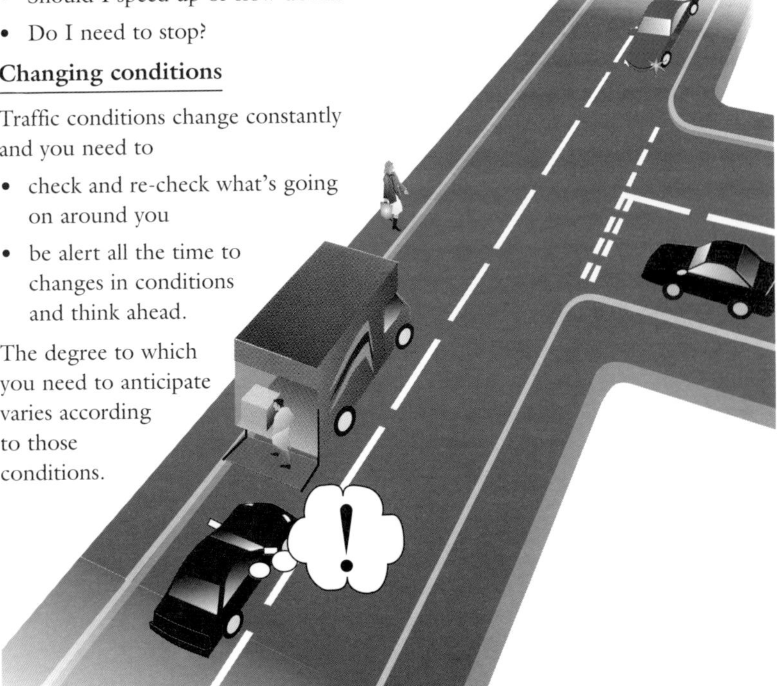

Driving ahead

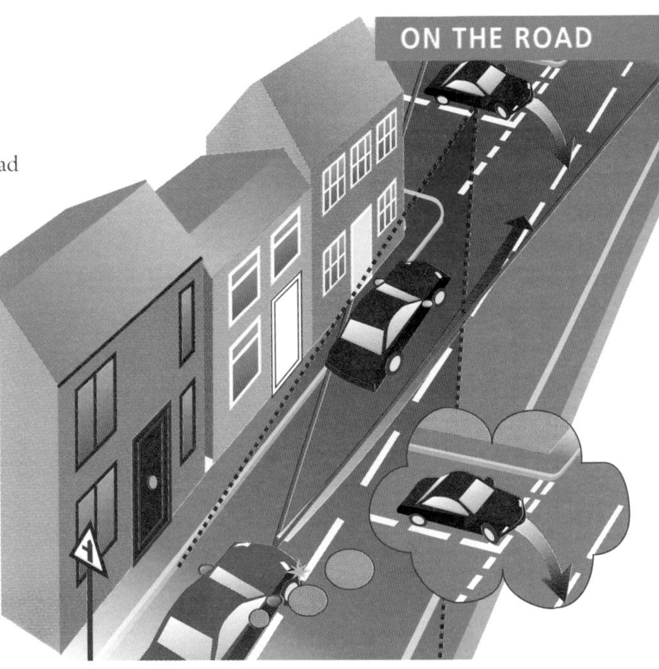

Read the road ahead to anticipate what might happen.

You need to be alert and observant at all times.

Assess the movement of all other road users, including pedestrians, on the whole stretch of road you're travelling on.

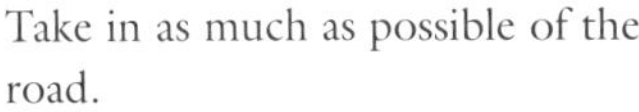

Take in as much as possible of the road.

- Ahead.
- Behind.
- To each side.

You should keep your eyes moving, and

- be able to observe the middle distance and far distance as well as the area immediately in front
- glance frequently in the mirror to see what's happening in the area you've just passed
- scan the area in your view.

Observation

If you're a new driver, you'll tend to give most of your attention to controlling the vehicle.

Practise reading the road. You don't have to be driving to do this. You can do it as a passenger in a car or bus.

Look out for

- other vehicles and pedestrians
- signals given by other drivers
- road signs and markings
- the type and condition of the road surface
- movements of vehicles well ahead of you, as well as the one immediately in front
- side roads or hills ahead. The building line may show these
- buses signalling to move out from bus stops.

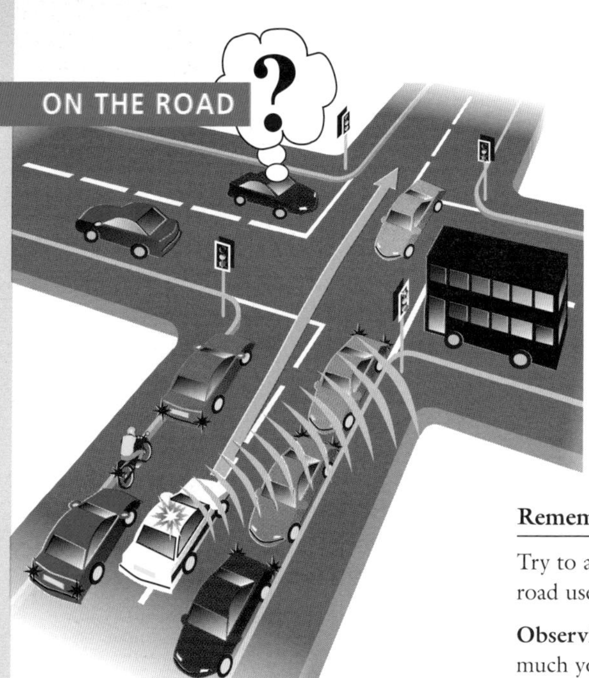

Clues

Look out for clues to help you to act safely and sensibly on what you see.

Watch smaller details in built-up areas where traffic conditions change rapidly. Observe other road users' actions and reactions.

Reflections in shop windows can often give important information

- where vision is restricted
- when reversing into a parking space.

A pedestrian approaching a zebra crossing might step out into the road sooner than you think.

Take care approaching parked vehicles, especially if someone is in the driving seat.

Watch out for a driver stopping to set down or pick up a passenger. You may find they move off without warning or without checking in the mirrors or looking around.

When following a bus, watch for passengers standing up inside: the bus will probably stop shortly.

Remember

Try to anticipate the actions of other road users.

Observing is not just seeing How much you can see depends on how well you can see.

Your eyesight can change without you being aware of it.

Have regular eyesight checks.

Your ears can also warn of what's happening around you.

Works entrances and schools can warn of an increase in pedestrians, cyclists and vehicles.

Watch for vehicles picking up and setting down at school times – buses as well as cars.

Emergency vehicles The sirens and blue flashing lights of emergency vehicles can give early warning of changes in traffic conditions. Keep out of their way

Ask yourself where it's coming from: behind (mirrors), ahead or, more importantly, across your path.

Road Positioning

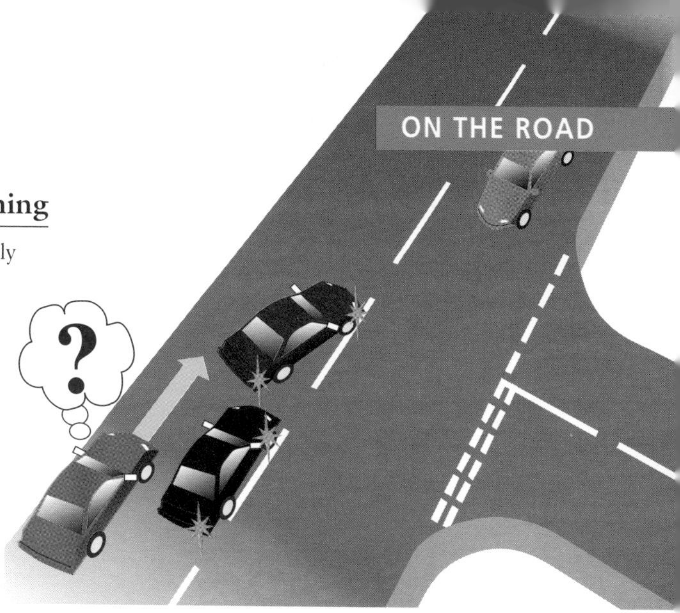

You should normally drive keeping well to the left.

Keep clear of parked vehicles, leaving room for

- doors opening
- vehicles moving off
- children running out.

Don't

- drive too close to the kerb, particularly in streets crowded with pedestrians
- weave in and out between parked vehicles. It's unnecessary and confusing to other drivers.

When necessary ease over to the left to

- help the flow of traffic
- let a faster vehicle overtake.

The correct position You should always be in the correct position for the route you're going to take.

- Keep to the left if you're going straight ahead or turning left.
- Keep as close to the centre of the road as is safe when you're turning right.

Your position is important not only for safety but to allow free flow of traffic. A badly positioned vehicle can hold up traffic in either direction.

One-way streets Position your vehicle according to whether you intend to go ahead turn left or turn right.

- To turn left keep to the left hand lane.
- To turn right keep to the right hand lane provided there are no obstructions or parked vehicles on the right hand side of the road you are in.
- To go ahead be guided by the road markings. If there is no specific lane for ahead, select a lane in good time. Follow the road markings and get into lane as soon as possible and stay in it. Watch for drivers who may change lane suddenly.

Traffic in one-way streets often flows freely. Watch out for vehicles coming past on either side of you.

Lane discipline

You should always follow lane markings, which are there for two reasons.

- They make the best possible use of road space.
- They guide the traffic.

Keeping to the lane markings is vital.

Position yourself in good time If you find you're in the wrong lane, don't try to change by cutting across other drivers at the last moment. Carry on in your lane and find another way back to your route.

Changing lanes Position your vehicle according to your route. Always check your mirrors and signal in good time before you change lanes.

- Never weave from lane to lane.
- Never straddle two lanes.
- Never change lanes at the last minute.
- Always stay in the middle of your lane until you need to change.

Heavy and slow-moving traffic Don't

- change lanes suddenly
- keep changing lanes
- straddle lanes or lane markings
- weave in and out
- obstruct 'Keep Clear' markings. Watch out for these in congested, slow-moving traffic, especially at exits for emergency vehicles.

Allow for

- pedestrians crossing
- cyclists moving up the nearside
- doors opening.

Driving ahead Keep to the left-hand lane wherever possible.

Don't use the right-hand lane just because you're travelling at speed.

On a carriageway with four or more lanes don't use the lanes on the right unless signs or markings allow you to do so. Peak hour 'tidal flow' systems might permit or forbid use of these lanes depending on the time of the day.

Bus lanes A bus lane is a separate lane shown by signs and road markings.

Details of which vehicles can use the bus lane and the times of operation are shown on the sign.

Outside those periods, all vehicles can use the bus lane.

Where no times are shown the bus lane is in operation 24 hours a day.

Don't park or drive in bus lanes when they are in operation.

In some one-way streets buses are permitted to travel against the normal flow of the traffic. These are known as contra-flow bus lanes.

Approaching a road junction

Look well ahead for signs and markings.

If you have two lanes in each direction and

- you intend to turn left stay in the left hand lane
- you intend to go straight ahead, stay in the left-hand lane unless otherwise indicated

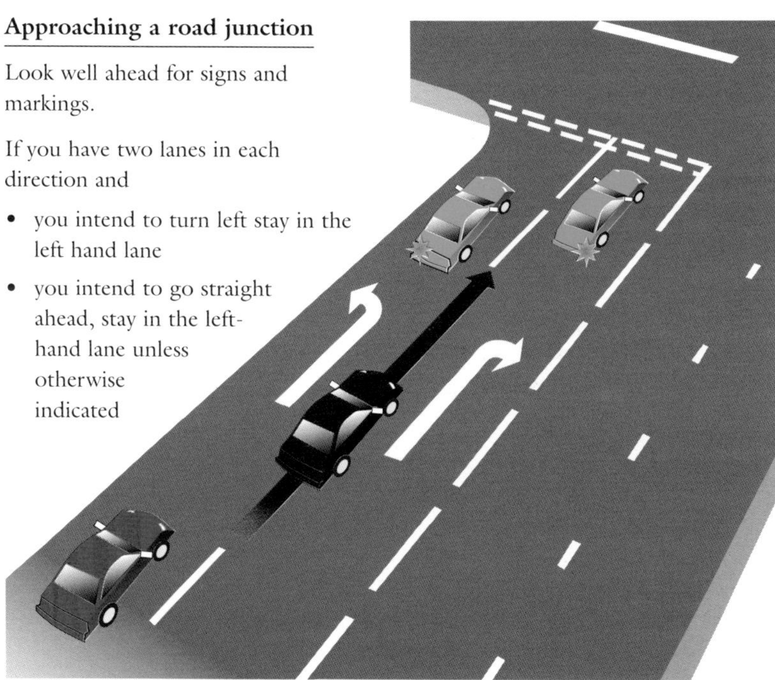

- you intend to turn right, move to the right hand lane in good time.

Don't try to gain an advantage by using an incorrect lane. Trying to change back to the proper lane at, or near, the junction is a risky business.

If you have three lanes in each direction and you intend to

- turn left, stay in the left hand lane
- go straight ahead, take the left hand lane (unless there are left filter signs) or the middle lane or be guided by road markings
- turn right, take the right hand lane.

Deceleration lane

Some junctions also have a deceleration lane.

Get into the left-hand lane in good time before entering the deceleration lane. You'll be able to slow down to turn left without holding up other traffic.

Stopping distance

This is the distance your vehicle travels

- from the moment you realise you must brake
- to the moment the vehicle stops.

You need to leave enough space between you and the vehicle in front so that you can pull up safely if it slows down or stops suddenly.

To do this you must be able to judge your overall stopping distance.

Practice judging distance while you're walking. Pick out something ahead and see how far away it is. One good stride roughly equals a metre (or yard). Check your estimate and try it out with other objects.

Stopping distance depends on

- how fast you're going
- whether you're travelling on the level uphill or downhill
- the weather and the state of the road
- the condition of your brakes and tyres
- your ability as a driver especially your reaction times when applying the brakes.

Stopping distance divides into

- **thinking distance**
- **braking distance.**

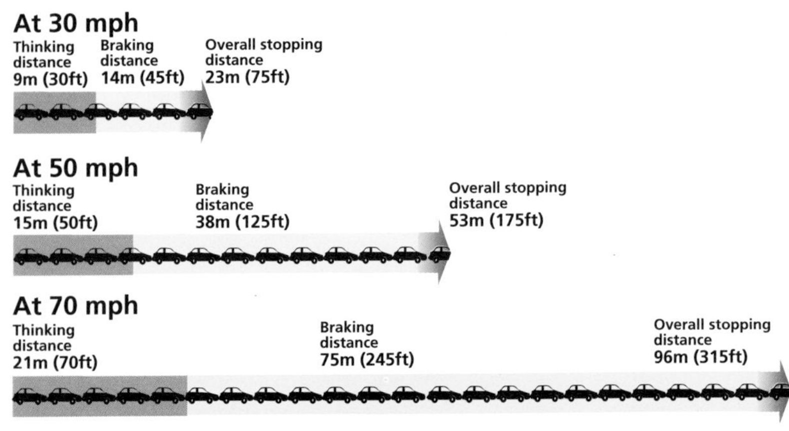

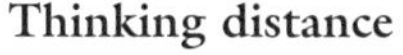

Thinking distance

This depends how quickly you react. It takes well over half a second for most people to react.

If you're tired or unwell, it will take longer.

If you're driving at 20 mph you'll travel about 6 metres (20 feet) before your brakes even begin to act

- at 30 mph, 9 metres (30 feet)
- at 40 mph, 12 metres (40 feet)

and so on.

The braking distance at 40 mph is more than 4 times the braking distance at 20 mph

Braking distance

This depends greatly on your speed and the size and weight of your vehicle.

It has even more effect on the overall stopping distance.

- At 20 mph good brakes will stop your vehicle in about 6 metres (20 feet) on a dry road.
- At 40 mph (twice the speed) they will take 24 metres (80 feet) – ***FOUR times the distance.***

Allow much more time and room to brake in bad weather.

Your tyres won't grip the road surface so well in wet weather or on loose road surfaces.

Separation distance

Far too many road accidents are caused by drivers getting too close to the vehicle in front.

It's essential that every driver is able to judge a safe separation distance in all road, traffic and weather conditions.

The safety of you and your passengers depends on it!

How far should you keep from the vehicle in front? Ideally, you should be no closer than the overall stopping distance that corresponds to your speed.

In heavy, slow-moving urban traffic that might not be practicable, without a lot of waste of valuable road space. However, even then, the gap should never be less than your thinking distance and much more if the road is wet and slippery.

Remember that your overall stopping distance is the only really safe gap and anything less is taking a risk.

A reasonable rule to apply in good dry conditions is a gap of one metre (one yard) for each mph of your speed. For example, at 55 mph a gap of 55 metres (55 yards).

In bad conditions leave at least double the distance.

A useful technique for judging one yard or metre per mph is to use the 'two-second rule'.

The two-second rule

In good dry conditions an alert driver, who is driving a vehicle with first class tyres and brakes needs to be at least two seconds behind the vehicle in front.

In bad conditions, double the safety gap to **at least** four seconds or even more.

How to measure

Choose an obvious stationary reference point ahead, such as a bridge, a tree or a road sign.

When the vehicle ahead passes the object say to yourself, 'only a fool breaks the two-second rule'.

If you reach the object *before* you finish saying it you're *too close.*

Remember

Multiple collisions often happen because the drivers involved were

- driving too close
- unable to brake in time.

You can avoid such accidents by looking well ahead and keeping your distance.

Give yourself time to react.

Defensive driving

When a vehicle behind is driving too close to you, ease off very gradually and increase the gap between you and the vehicle in front.

This will give you more time to react if the driver ahead should slow down or stop suddenly.

Overtaking

Because overtaking can put you on a collision course with traffic from the opposite direction, it's one of the major causes of accidents.

Overtaking at the wrong time or in the wrong place is extremely dangerous.

It's vital to choose your time and place carefully.

Before overtaking you must be certain you can return to your side of the road safely, without getting in the way of

- vehicles coming towards you
- vehicles you're overtaking.

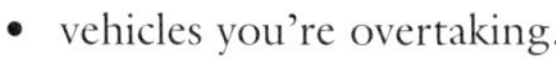

Overtaking a moving vehicle

Don't overtake unless it's necessary. For example, don't rush to get past someone only to turn off shortly afterwards.

Ask yourself if it's really necessary. If you decide it is, you need to find a suitable place.

Some places are never suitable. For example, DON'T overtake

- if your view ahead is blocked
- if other drivers might not be able to see you
- if there's too little room
- if the road narrows
- if you're approaching a junction
- if you're within the zigzag area of a pedestrian crossing
- if there's a 'No Overtaking' sign
- if there's 'dead ground', that is a dip in the road which might hide an oncoming vehicle.

Judging speed and distance when overtaking

The speed of the vehicle you're overtaking is very important.

When you're closing up behind a moving vehicle, it will cover quite a distance before you can actually pass it. It could take you quite a long time to overtake. For example, it could take a quarter of a mile just to catch up with a vehicle 200 yards ahead travelling at 15 mph, if you're doing 30 mph.

On the other hand, if you're travelling at 55 mph and an oncoming vehicle is doing the same, you're approaching each other at 110 mph, or 160 feet per second.

Overtaking takes time. The smaller the difference between your speed and the speed of the vehicle you're overtaking, the longer the stretch of clear road you'll need.

Remember, if in doubt, don't overtake.

Defensive driving

Never accelerate when someone is overtaking you. Be prepared to ease off, if necessary, to help them pass you.

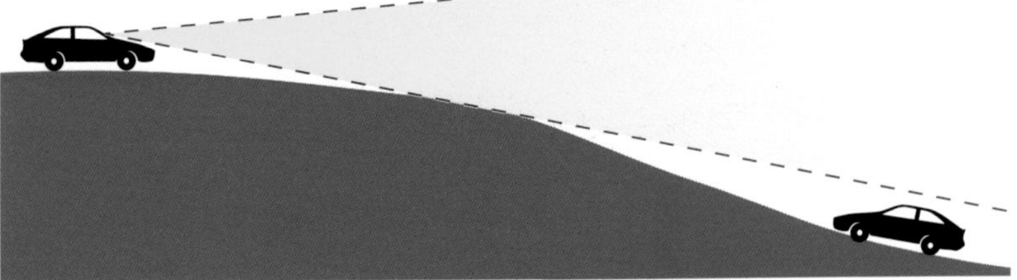

Overtaking large vehicles

You need to keep well back to get the best view of the road ahead so that you're ready to overtake.

Leave a good space while waiting to overtake. If another car fills the gap, drop back again.

If you're thinking of overtaking, note if the vehicle you intend to overtake is loaded or unloaded. The speed of large vehicles varies greatly when they're going up and down hills.

A loaded vehicle might crawl slowly uphill and then pick up speed very quickly on the downhill run.

Always remember the possible changes in speed when you're thinking of overtaking a large vehicle.

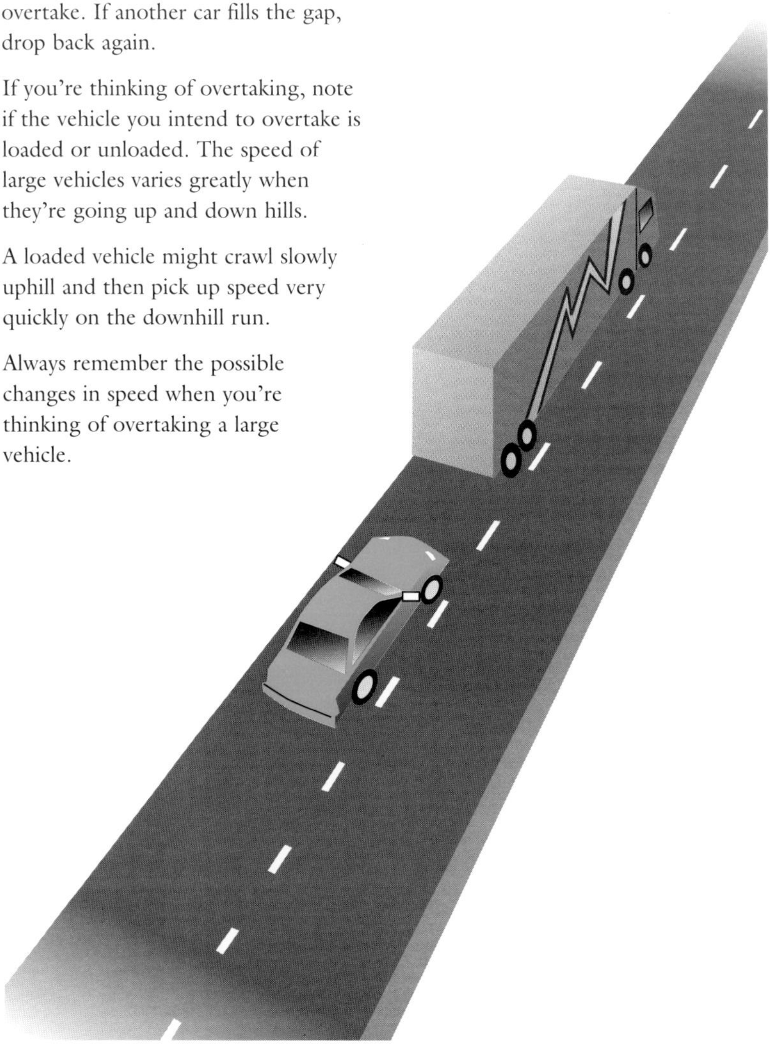

Overtaking a moving vehicle on a hill

Uphill If you're overtaking uphill give yourself time and room to return to your side of the road well before the brow of the hill.

Your zone of vision will get shorter as you approach the brow of the hill. Don't forget that oncoming vehicles will be travelling faster and could be on top of you very quickly.

Downhill It's more difficult to slow down when going downhill. Brake earlier than usual.

Overtaking on long hills On some long hills double white lines divide the road so that there are two lanes for traffic going uphill, but only one downhill.

If the line is broken on the downhill side, this means you can overtake if it's safe to do so, but uphill traffic has priority.

Some roads are divided into three lanes, where the middle lane can be used for overtaking in either direction. These roads can be particularly dangerous. Before overtaking, you must make sure the road is clear far enough ahead.

If in doubt, WAIT.

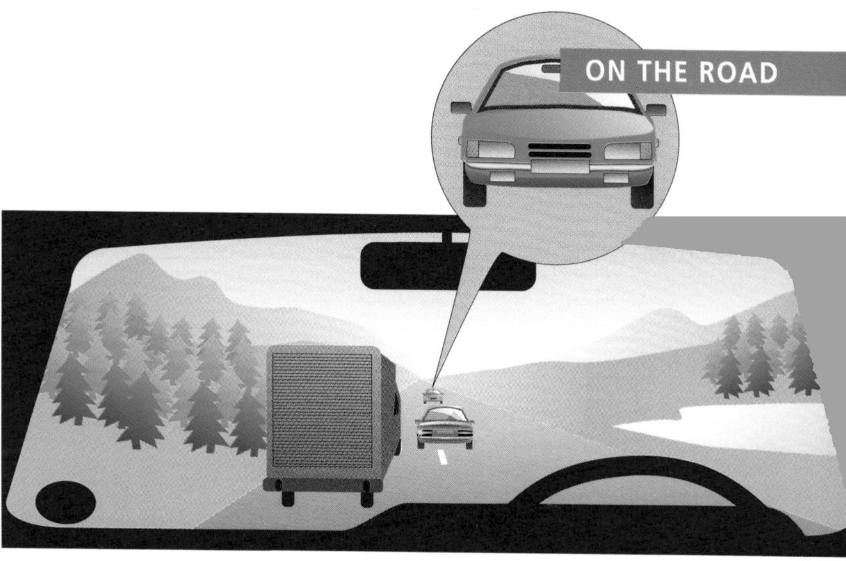

Before overtaking

Many danger spots are marked with double white lines along the road. Look out for arrows warning you to move over to the left as you are approaching these areas.

On three-lane roads, junction signs and hatch markings in the middle of the road are warnings not to overtake. Be ready to hold back in case traffic is waiting to turn right or slowing to turn left.

Watch the vehicle in front Before overtaking, decide what the driver in front is likely to do by watching both them and the road ahead for a while.

They might decide to overtake. They might continue to drive at the speed of the vehicle ahead of them. The driver could be intending to turn off soon or might have seen something ahead which you haven't.

Following through Never automatically follow an overtaking vehicle without being able to see for yourself that the way is clear.

Always make your own decisions about overtaking based on

- what YOU see
- what YOU know.

Be patient. If in doubt, hold back.

There might not be enough time for both of you to overtake at once.

Defensive driving

Keep well back from any vehicle which is too close to the vehicle in front and swinging in and out. Be patient, in case they do something hasty.

Steps to overtaking

To overtake, you might have to use some or all of these steps several times before the right moment arrives.

For example, if someone overtakes you just as you're about to overtake, you'll need to start all over again.

Mirrors Always check in your mirrors to assess the speed and position of traffic behind.

Position Be near enough to the vehicle ahead to overtake smoothly when you're ready, but not so close that you can't get a good view of the road ahead.

Speed Be fast enough to keep up with the vehicle in front and with enough reserve power to pass it briskly.

Consider changing down to get extra acceleration when you're ready to start overtaking.

Look Assess the whole situation

- the state of the road
- what the driver ahead is doing or might be about to do
- any hazards
- the speed and position of oncoming vehicles
- speed difference between you and oncoming vehicles.

Mirrors Check behind again to re-assess the situation.

Never begin to overtake if another vehicle is overtaking you or is about to do so.

Overtake only when you are sure it's safe to do so.

Signal
Always give a signal. This helps

- drivers behind
- the driver you are overtaking
- drivers coming towards you.

Manoeuvre

- Make a final check in front and behind. If it's safe, pull out on a smooth easy line.
- Overtake as quickly as you can.
- Check your mirrors to see that you're clear of the vehicle you've overtaken.
- Move back to the left again on a smooth easy line but avoid cutting in.

Remember

When overtaking cyclists, motorcyclists or people on horseback, give them plenty of room.

Never attempt to overtake them just before you turn left.

Overtaking on the left

You should never overtake on the left unless

- the vehicle in front is signalling an intention to turn right, and you can safely overtake on the left.

  TAKE CARE if there is a road to the left. Oncoming traffic turning right into it may be hidden by the vehicle you're overtaking
- traffic is moving slowly in queues, and vehicles in the lane on your right are moving more slowly than you are.

In addition you can go past on the inside of slower traffic when

- you're in a one-way street (but not a dual carriageway) where vehicles are allowed to pass on either side
- you're in the correct lane to turn left at a junction.

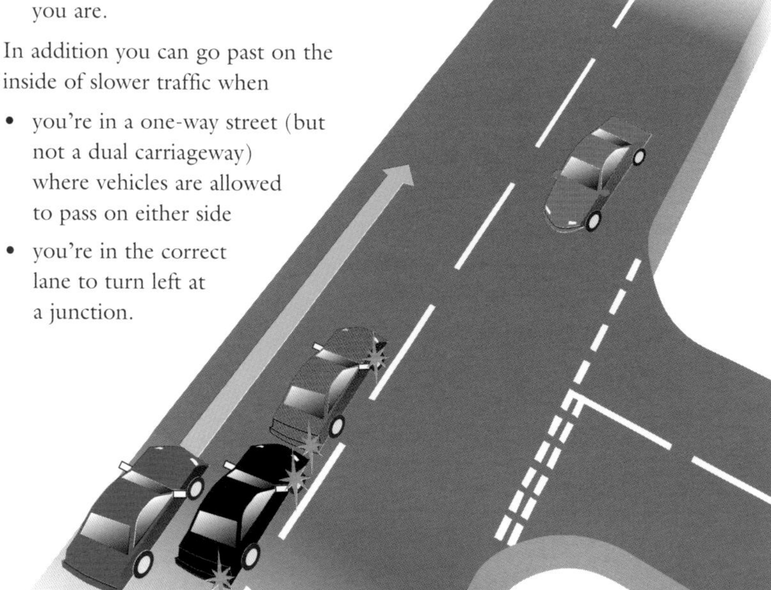

Overtaking on dual carriageways

Overtake only if you're sure you can do so safely.

Plan well ahead and use the appropriate parts of the MSM – PSL routine. For example

- **Mirrors** Look behind to assess the speed and position of following traffic. On a high speed dual carriageway, start the mirror checks much earlier.
- **Position** Keep well back from the vehicle you're going to overtake. You should change lanes gradually without any sudden movement.
- **Speed** Make sure you have enough speed in reserve to overtake briskly without breaking any speed limits.
- **Look** Look ahead and assess
  - – the condition of the road
  - – what the vehicle ahead is doing
  - – any hazards.
- **Mirrors** Check behind again to re-assess the situation.

  Don't begin to overtake if another vehicle is about to overtake you.
- **Signal** Always give a signal even when there's no one behind. This can help the driver you're overtaking and other drivers further ahead.
- **Manoeuvre** Make a final check ahead and behind. If it's safe, change lanes gradually on a smooth easy line.

  Overtake briskly, then check your mirrors again. Make sure you're well clear of the vehicle you've overtaken before moving back to the left.

  Don't cut in.

Overtaking on the left You must not overtake on the left unless

- the traffic is slow moving in queues, and the queue on your right is moving slower than you.

Never move to a lane on your left to overtake.

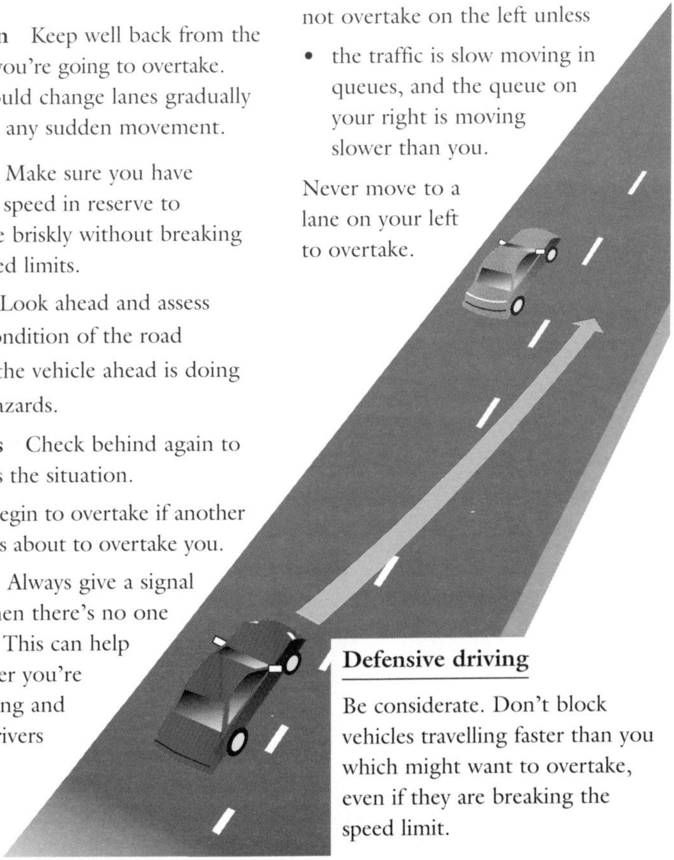

Defensive driving

Be considerate. Don't block vehicles travelling faster than you which might want to overtake, even if they are breaking the speed limit.

Obstructions

The secret of dealing with any obstruction lies in looking and planning well ahead, combined with early and sensible use of the MSM – PSL routine.

The decision to wait or go on will depend on

- the type and width of road
- whether the obstruction is on
  - your side of the road
  - the other side of the road
  - both sides of the road
- whether there is approaching traffic
- the room available.

As a general rule, if the obstruction is on your side of the road the approaching traffic will have priority.

Don't *assume* that you have priority if the obstruction is on the other side of the road. Always be prepared to give way.

Procedure

Look well ahead to identify the obstruction in good time before using the MSM – PSL routine.

- Check your mirrors to assess the speed and position of following traffic.
- Signal if necessary.
- Decide on your position. Avoid keeping too far into the left so that you have to steer past the obstruction at the last minute. A gradual change of course is required. If you have to stop and wait keep well back from the obstruction in a position that not only keeps your zone of vision open, but also doesn't impede the approaching traffic.
- Adjust your speed as necessary. This will clearly depend on the situation but aim to regulate your speed to take a smooth and steady course without stopping.
- Finally, look and assess the situation before you decide whether it's
  - necessary to wait
  - safe to proceed.

Obstructions on hills need special care. Give yourself an extra safety margin and brake earlier when necessary.

If you're travelling downhill and the obstruction is on the other side of the road don't take your priority for granted. If it's safe, be prepared to let other traffic, especially heavy vehicles, coming uphill have a clear run.

Your consideration will be appreciated.

Defensive driving

Don't follow through behind the vehicle in front without being able to see for yourself that the way is clear ahead.

Keep a safe distance from the obstruction and the approaching traffic. Where space is limited, reduce speed and take extra care. The smaller the gap the lower the speed needs to be.

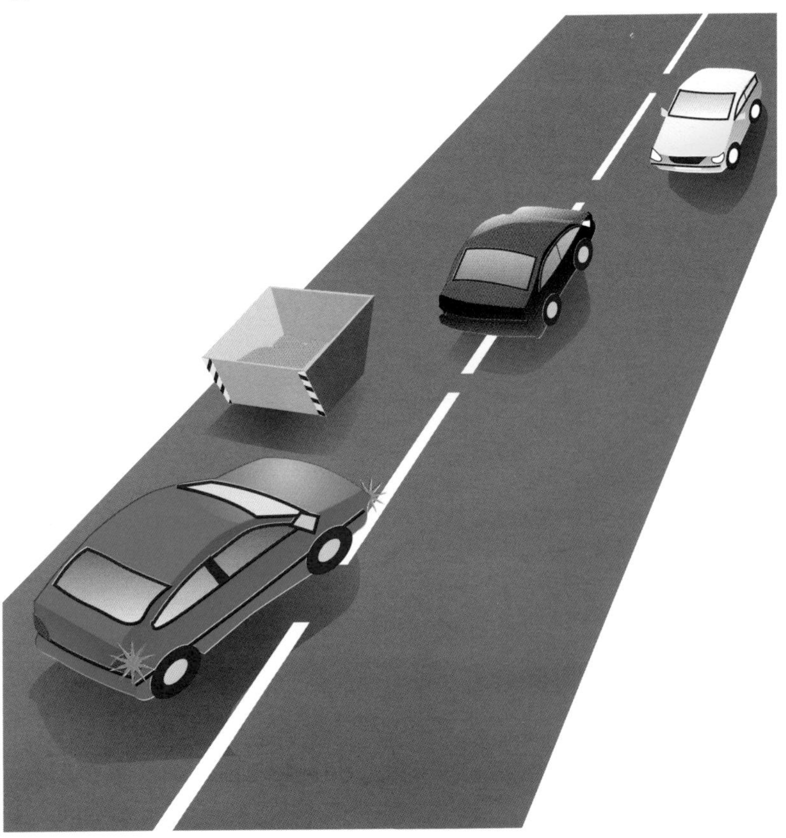

Pedestrian crossings

People on foot have certain rights of way at pedestrians crossings, but are safe only if drivers stick to the rules and do the right thing.

Zebra crossings

These have

- flashing yellow beacons on both sides of the road
- black and white stripes on the crossing
- white zigzag markings both sides of the crossing
- a give-way line about a yard from the crossing marking the place for drivers to stop.

You must not park

- on the crossing so blocking the way for pedestrians
- within the area marked by the zigzag lines. Parking here would obstruct both pedestrians and drivers view of the approach to and the crossing itself.

You must not overtake

- the moving motor vehicle nearest the crossing
- the leading vehicle which has stopped to give way to a pedestrian.

Even if there are no zigzag markings, never overtake just before a crossing. Some zebra crossings are divided by a central island. Each half is a separate crossing.

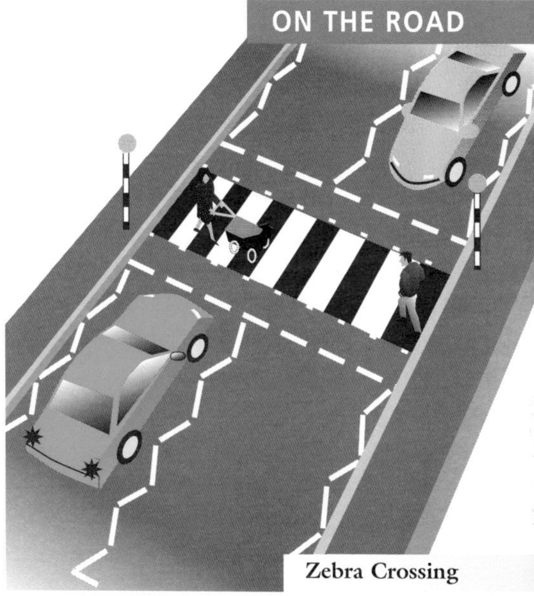

Zebra Crossing

Waiting pedestrians Where pedestrians are waiting on the pavement at a zebra crossing and obviously want to cross, slow down and be ready to stop.
You must give way to anyone who

- is already crossing
- has stepped onto the crossing.

Courtesy It's courteous to stop if you can do so safely, especially

- if anyone is waiting on the pavement with a pram or pushchair
- if children or the elderly are hesitating to cross because of heavy traffic.

Don't wave people across. There could be another vehicle coming.

Pelican crossing

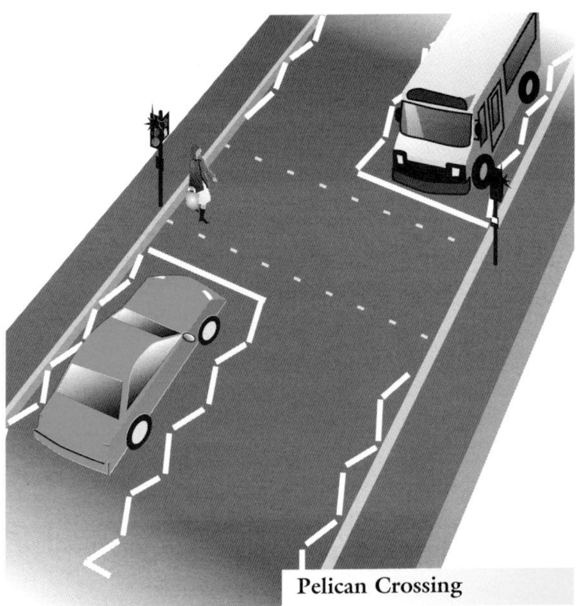
Pelican Crossing

These are light-controlled crossings where pedestrians use push-button controls to change the signals.

They have no red-and-amber before the green. Instead, they have a flashing amber light which means you must give way to pedestrians on the crossing but, if it's clear, you can go on.

While pedestrians are crossing, don't

- edge forward
- rev your engine.

They also have zigzag markings either side of the crossing.
You must not overtake or park in the area marked by the zigzag lines.

Straight pelican crossings
Remember that a pelican crossing which goes straight across the road is **one** crossing, even if there is a central refuge.

You must wait for people coming from the further side of the refuge.

Staggered pelican crossings If the pelican crossings on each side of the central refuge are not in line, the crossings are separate.

Toucan crossings

These are crossings shared by cyclists and pedestrians. They operate in the same way as Puffin crossings except

- cyclists are permitted to ride across
- pedestrian and cyclists get the green signal together.

The signals are push-button operated and there is no flashing amber phase

Toucan Crossing

Puffin crossing

Puffin stands for pedestrian user-friendly intelligent crossing. These improve road safety by reducing unnecessary delays to traffic flow.

Electronic devices automatically detect when pedestrians are on the crossing. This will delay the green light until the pedestrian has reached a position of safety.

If the pedestrians cross quickly, the pedestrian phase is shortened.

If the pedestrians have crossed the road before the phase starts, it will automatically be cancelled.

Because the signals are controlled in this way, there is no flashing amber in the sequence.

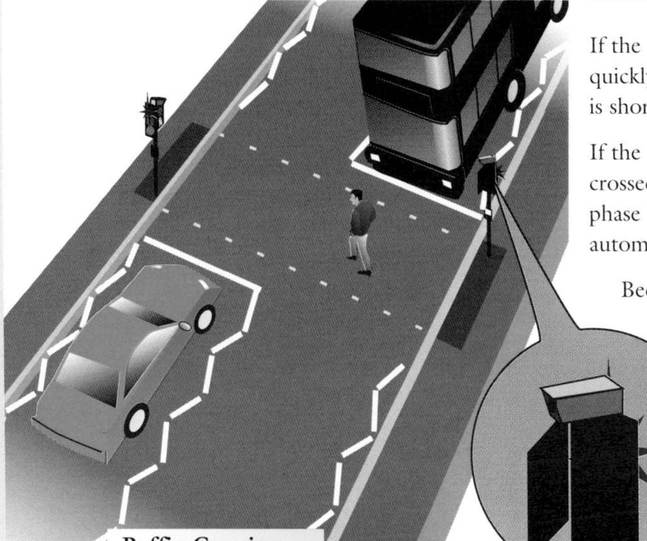

Puffin Crossing

Controlled crossings

At traffic signals or crossings controlled by police or traffic wardens, you should give way to pedestrians still crossing when you get the signal to move.

Don't stop on the crossing All pedestrian crossings should be left free during traffic hold-ups. Stop before the crossing if you can see you won't be able to clear it.

Wherever there are pedestrians

- give yourself more time to stop if the road is icy or wet
- remember that some people have hearing difficulties and might not hear your vehicle approach
- give visually handicapped or infirm pedestrians time to cross
- watch out for pedestrians who try to rush across at the last minute
- don't signal to pedestrians to cross because you can't be sure what other drivers might do
- keep to the rules, so everyone knows what to expect.

School crossing patrols

Watch out for the patrols and obey their signals.

At particularly dangerous locations, two flashing amber signals give advance warning of the crossing point.

Avoid overtaking when you're approaching pedestrian crossings.

Always keep your speed well in hand so you're ready to slow down or stop for pedestrians, if necessary.

Defensive driving Always look well ahead to identify pedestrian crossings early. Look for the flashing yellow beacons, traffic lights, zigzag markings, etc. Use the MSM routine and keep your speed well down.

Remember that if you're the leading vehicle you should consider using an arm signal when you're slowing or stopping.

The arm signal warns

- pedestrians
- oncoming traffic
- traffic behind

of your intention to stop.

Brake lights cannot be seen by the pedestrians at the crossings or oncoming traffic.

Hills

You need to understand how driving uphill and downhill can affect your control of the vehicle.

- Going uphill, your engine has to use more power to pull the vehicle up the hill.
- Going downhill, your engine is helped by the weight of the vehicle.
- In each case, the effect of the controls is different to driving on the level.

Going uphill

- You'll find it more difficult to maintain or increase speed. The engine has to work harder to make the vehicle go faster.
- Your brakes will slow the vehicle down sooner.
- You might need to change to a lower gear to maintain your speed.

  If you release the accelerator or declutch, your speed will drop more quickly than it would on the level.

  Changing to a lower gear should be done without hesitation, so you don't lose too much speed.
- When stopping, remember to apply the handbrake before you release the footbrake. You might roll back otherwise.

Look for signs You'll see warning signs telling you how steep the slope upwards is. The figures measure the gradient in percentage terms: 25% (1:4) means for every four feet along (horizontal) the road rises one foot (vertical).

The higher the percentage or the lower the second figure, the steeper the hill.

You may see another rectangular sign telling you the length of the hill and further information.

Watch out for slow-moving heavy vehicles.

Assess the hill If the hill is very steep, think ahead and consider changing to a lower gear.

Change down in good time, if any change is necessary.

If the road turns, you'll find it easier on the engine to change down *before* any bend.

Remember, turning and climbing at the same time is hard work for the engine and traffic tends to slow on hills, especially at turns.

Speed Don't stay in high gear to try to keep your speed up. Your vehicle will climb better in a low gear.

Separation distance Keep well back from the vehicle ahead.

- If you don't hold back and the vehicle ahead suddenly slows or stops, you may have to brake harshly.
- Holding back may enable you to keep going gently while the vehicle ahead regains speed. This is not only safer, but it can also help to avoid congestion.

Overtaking It's sometimes more difficult to overtake uphill. You'll find oncoming traffic is travelling at a greater speed and less able to slow or stop quickly, if necessary.

On a dual carriageway, it's easier. Here you should keep a lookout for others who can overtake with ease. Don't block their progress.

Going downhill

- You'll find it more difficult to slow down and the brakes have less effect.
- It's harder for the engine to hold the vehicle back. In higher gears it won't do so at all.
- If you declutch, the vehicle runs faster.
- Avoid braking on a bend.
- Get into a lower gear in good time, particularly if there's a bend ahead.
- Use the correct combination of lower gear and careful use of the footbrake to keep control of your speed.

Note. Avoid the danger of increasing speed caused by coasting, either out of gear or with the clutch pedal depressed.

Look for signs The steep hill (downwards) warning sign will again give you the gradient of the downward slope. Show respect for this sign.

You might also see a rectangular sign advising about using a low gear.

Assess the hill Use the sign to help you think ahead. If your route is unfamiliar, or a bend limits your view of the road, change down *before* you begin to descend.

Change smoothly and without hesitation.

Separation distance Always keep the correct separation distance from vehicle ahead.

If you don't hold back and the vehicle ahead suddenly slows or stops, you'll have to brake very hard. The driver behind will get very little warning.

If you leave a good gap, you'll have time to reduce your speed more gently.

Adjust your speed

On steep hills, you'll normally need to reduce speed. Change down to a lower gear to give yourself more braking power and control.

By selecting a lower gear, you should be able to avoid using your brakes too much. Excessive braking on hills can result in 'brake fade' and loss of control. Brake fade is a loss of braking power caused by the heat generated by continuous use of the brakes.

Look for 'escape lanes'.

Obey signs telling you to stay in low gear. The steeper the hill, the lower the gear.

Overtaking

It's only safe to overtake downhill where

- there are no bends or junctions
- your view of the road ahead is clear.

You should be absolutely *certain* that you can overtake without causing oncoming traffic to slow down or change course.

Remember that the vehicle you're overtaking may build up speed, and you'll find it more difficult to slow down for oncoming traffic. They'll find it more difficult to get out of your way.

Look out for road markings, especially continuous white lines down the centre of the road.

Junctions on hills

Using all this information, you should be able to anticipate and carefully consider all these points as you approach a junction on a hill.

Downhill junctions

- Getting into the correct position at a safe speed is essential when you're approaching a downhill junction.
- Make early use of mirrors, signals, brakes, gears and steering to get into position.
- Use the junction routine PSL. Choose a point with a good all round view before you *look*, assess, and decide to go or wait if necessary.
- Oncoming traffic will be climbing more slowly. If you need to cross their path, don't move from your *look* position until your way is clear.
- Don't block oncoming traffic and cause a hold-up.

Uphill junctions

Judge your *position* and *speed* accurately when climbing towards a junction. Your position is particularly important to drivers following you.

- If you intend to turn right, keep as close to the centre as is safe.
- If you stop in the wrong position you could force drivers behind to stop unnecessarily.

Joining a hill at a junction

You can judge the speed of vehicles coming uphill quite easily.

Turning left at a T-junction into a road where you'll be driving uphill is reasonably easy.

You don't have to cross traffic and it's easier to judge the flow of traffic coming uphill.

Turning right at a T-junction into a road where you'll be driving uphill is more difficult.

You have to cross fast-moving traffic coming downhill. At the same time, you have to fit into the flow of traffic coming up from the left without blocking them.

Hills in towns

Take particular care in towns where the elderly and the very young are crossing at junctions on hills.

Traffic speeds are generally lower and vehicles closer together. As a result your zone of vision will often be that much poorer.

Pay attention to the type of vehicle ahead of you and the distance between you.

You'll find traffic lights, school crossing patrols and pedestrian crossings stop traffic on hills from time to time.

This adds to the importance of

- using your mirrors
- recognising the sort of vehicle ahead
- leaving a suitable gap when you stop
- using your handbrake effectively
- making sure you're in the right gear for the situation.

You'll be doing these things in towns already, but on hills they have additional importance.

Parking on hills

If you park your vehicle on a slope remember the following.

Parking facing uphill

- Stop your vehicle as close as you can to the nearside kerb, if there is one.
- Leave your steering wheel turned to the right. If the vehicle rolls backwards, the front wheels will be stopped by the kerb.
- If there is no kerb, leave your steering wheel turned to the left. If the vehicle rolls back it won't roll across the road.
- Leave the vehicle in first gear with the handbrake firmly applied.

Parking facing downhill

- Leave your steering wheel turned to the left. The kerb should stop any forward movement.
- Leave your vehicle in reverse gear with the handbrake firmly applied.

Leaving a gap

Parking on a slope is more difficult than on the flat and can take more room. You should leave a bigger gap to allow extra space for manoeuvring.

A larger gap will help both you and others.

Parking with automatic transmission

Facing uphill or downhill

Make sure your vehicle is stationary and the handbrake is firmly applied *before* using the selector setting **P** – (Park).

If your vehicle has no **P** setting

- turn your front wheels to the kerb
- make sure your handbrake is firmly applied.

Supertrams or Light Rapid Transit (LRT) systems

LRTs, or 'Metros' are being introduced in large towns and in cities to provide

- a more efficient public transport system
- a more 'environmentally friendly' form of transport by using electric power.

You'll find these are modern versions of the former 'tramcars'. Many European cities use similar systems.

Extra care

Take extra care when you first encounter the trams until you're accustomed to dealing with a different traffic system.

Crossing points

Deal with these in exactly the same way as normal railway crossings.

Bear in mind the speed and silent approach of these modern 'supertrams'.

Reserved areas

Drivers must not enter 'reserved areas' for the tramway which are marked with white line markings or a different type of surface, or both.

The reserved areas are usually one way but may sometimes be two way.

Hazards

The lines present the same hazards to riders and drivers as the old tram rails did.

The steel rails can be slippery whether it's wet or dry.

Take extra care when braking or turning on them.

Take care also where

- the tracks run close to the kerb to pick up or set down passengers
- the lines move from one side of the road to the other.

Warning signs/signals

Obey all warning signs or signals controlling traffic.

Diamond shaped signs give instructions to tram drivers only. Where there are no signals, always give way to trams.

Warning of trams crossing ahead

Don't

- try to race a modern tram where there isn't enough road space for both vehicles side by side.

  When you decide to overtake remember that these vehicles may be up to 60m (about 200 feet) long. Look out for stops instead, and overtake there if you're allowed to
- drive between platforms at tramway stations. Follow the direction signs
- park so that your vehicle obstructs the trams or would force other drivers to do so.

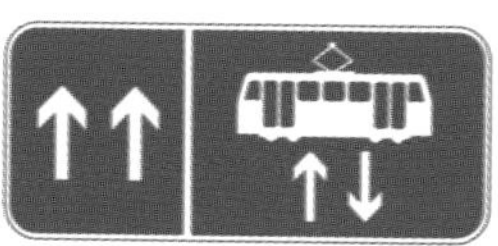

Trams travel in both directions. All other traffic obeys one-way signs.

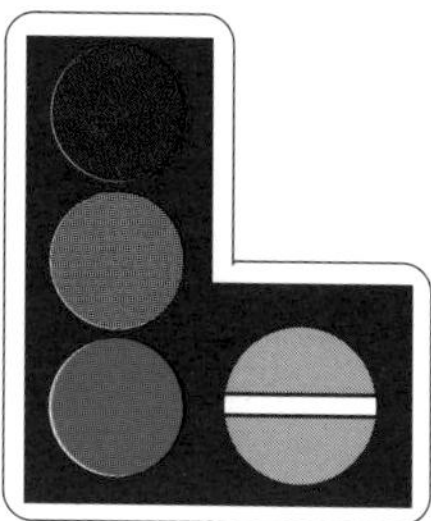

The signal mounted to the right gives instructions to tram drivers, which may not be the same as those given to drivers of other vehicles

Do

- watch out for additional pedestrian crossings where passengers will be getting on and off the trams. You must stop for these
- make allowance for other road users' mistakes until all drivers are more accustomed to the new system
- be especially aware of the problems of cyclists, motorcyclists and moped riders. Their narrow tyres can put them at risk when they come in contact with the rails.

Route for trams only

Signs are an essential part of any traffic system.

They tell you about the rules you must obey and warn you about the hazards you can meet on the road ahead.

Signs can be in the form of words or symbols on panels, road markings, beacons, bollards or traffic lights.

This section deals with the various types of traffic signs and their meaning.

The topics covered

- The purpose of traffic signs
- Signs giving warning
- Signs giving orders
- Signs giving directions and other information
- Waiting restrictions
- Road markings
- Traffic lights
- Level crossings

The purpose of traffic signs

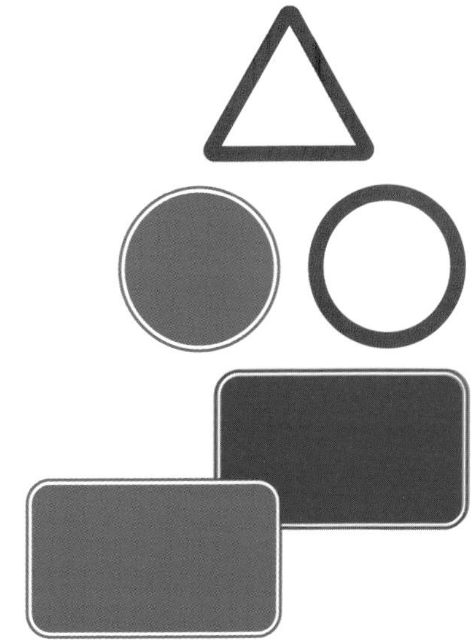

To do its job, a sign must give its message clearly and early enough for you to

- see it
- understand it
- act safely on it.

Symbols

Symbols are used as much as possible because they're

- more easily recognised and understood
- mainly standard, particularly throughout Europe.

Recognising signs – the basic rules

You'll recognise traffic signs easier if you understand some basic rules. The shape and colour of the main groups are

- circular signs, which give orders
- triangular signs, which warn
- rectangular signs, which inform and give directions
- road markings, which can do any of these three things
- traffic lights.

Signs giving warning

Usually a red triangle pointing upwards with a symbol or words on a white background.

These warn you of a hazard you might not otherwise be able to recognise in time, for example a bend, hill or hump-back bridge.

The sign will make clear what the hazard is. You must decide what to do about it.

Examples of warning signs

Narrowing roads

These tell you which side the road is narrowing from (sometimes both sides), and should warn you against overtaking until you have had a chance to assess the hazard.

Children and schools

The warning here is: watch out for children dashing out into the road, especially during school arrival and leaving times. Look out for school crossing patrols.

Low bridge sign

14'-6"

Even if your vehicle is low, watch out. An oncoming vehicle might have to use the centre of the road to make use of any extra headroom there.

Junctions

These tell you what type of junction is ahead: T-junction, crossroads, roundabout, staggered junction and so on. The priority through the junction is indicated by the broader line.

Sharp change of direction chevrons

These are used

- wherever the road changes direction sharply enough to create a hazard
- to reinforce a bend warning sign where stronger emphasis is needed.

Other hazards

If there's no special sign for a particular hazard, a general hazard warning sign is used: a red triangle with an exclamation mark on a white background.

It will have a plate underneath telling you what the hazard is, e.g., tree cutting.

Signs giving orders

Signs which give orders can be

- mandatory signs; these tell you what you *must* do
- prohibitory signs; these tell you what you *must not* do.

Mandatory signs

Mostly circular signs with white symbols and borders on a blue background.

For example

- mini roundabout
- keep left
- turn left.

In addition

- STOP – CHILDREN sign (lollipop) carried by school crossing patrol. This is circular with black lettering on a yellow background
- STOP in white on a red background, often manually controlled at roadworks
- STOP and GIVE WAY signs appear at junctions and are very important for everyone's guidance and safety.

STOP signs

- Octagonal, with white lettering on a red background.

Usually at a junction with a limited zone of vision. Always accompanied by a stop line marked on the road. The line tells you how far forward you should go before stopping at the position from which you look, assess and decide if it is safe to proceed (PSL).

What you must do at stop signs

- Stop (even if you can see the road is clear).
- Wait until you can enter the major road without causing other drivers to change speed or direction.

Prohibitory signs

These tell you what you *must not* do.

They are easy to recognise by their circular shape and red border.

Exceptions

- NO ENTRY sign: circular with white border and red background
- Bus Lane sign.

The message is given by symbols, words or figures inside a red border, or a combination of these.

GIVE WAY signs

- A red triangle pointing downwards.
- Black lettering on a white background.

Always accompanied by road markings.

GIVE WAY signs and/or road markings show you that traffic on the road you want to enter has priority.

The double broken lines across the road show you where to stop, if necessary, to take your final look.

Some junctions only have the 'give way' lines. This is usually where there's relatively little traffic.

What you must do at GIVE WAY signs

- Give way to traffic already on the major road.
- Delay entering the major road until you can do so without causing any traffic already on the major road to change speed or direction.

Remember

- Look.
- Assess.
- Decide.
- Act.

Speed limit signs

A red circle with a number on a white background shows the speed limit.

A white disc with a black diagonal line cancels the previous speed limit but you must not exceed the national speed limit for the type of road you're on.

Small repeaters of this sign are put on lamp posts where the normal 30 mph speed limit does not apply.

Repeaters of the 40 mph and 50 mph sign may also be fixed to lamp posts.

Where there are lamp posts but none of these signs are showing, you should assume that the 30 mph speed limit normally applies.

Signs giving directions and other information

These help you find and follow the road you want. They also direct you to the nearest railway station, car park, and so on.

The colours of these signs vary with the type or road.

For example

- motorways: white letters on a blue background with white border
- primary routes, except motorways: white letters on a green background and yellow route numbers with white border
- other routes: black letters on a white background
- local places: black letters on a white background with a blue border
- tourist signs: brown with white letters.

Types of signs giving directions on primary routes

Advance direction signs You will see these before you reach the junction. They enable you to decide which direction to take and to prepare yourself.

Direction signs at the junction These show you the way to take as you reach the junction.

Route confirmatory signs

Positioned after the junction, these confirm that you're on the road you wanted to take.

These signs also tell you distances and places on your route. If the route number is in brackets, it means that the road leads to that route.

Information signs

These tell you

- where to find parking places, telephones, camping sites, etc.
- about no through roads, etc.

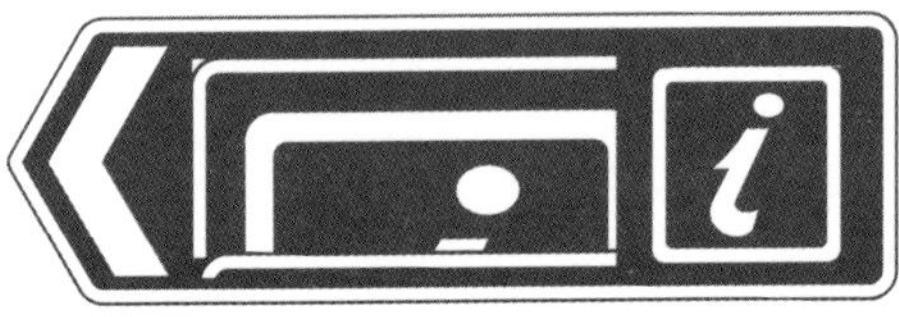

Waiting restrictions

These are indicated by signs and road markings. Yellow lines along the road parallel to the kerb indicate the restrictions are in force.

Small yellow plates are also mounted on posts or lamp posts nearby. These give more precise details of the restriction that applies.

In controlled waiting zones, the times of operation of the zone will be shown on the entry signs. The yellow plates are not normally provided in these zones.

Blue plates show that the period of waiting is limited.

In addition to yellow lines and the plates, the No Waiting sign may sometimes be provided.

Some areas and main roads are designated as No Stopping zones or Clearways. This means no stopping on the main carriageway at any time, not even to pick up or set down passengers.

Road markings

As a general rule, the more paint, the more important the message.

Markings on the road give information, orders or warnings. They can be used with signs on posts or on their own.

Their advantages are

- they can often be seen when other signs are hidden by traffic
- they can give a continuing message as you drive along the road.

For example

- a single broken line at the entrance to a roundabout tells you that traffic coming from your immediate right has priority and approaching traffic must give way.

  In exceptional circumstances, traffic on the roundabout is required to give way to those joining.

  In these cases, there will be a double broken white line across the road together with give way signs.

Single Stop lines

A single continuous line across your half of the road shows where you must stop

- at junctions with STOP signs
- at junctions controlled by police or traffic lights
- at level crossings
- at swing bridges or ferries.

Lines along the road

The most important of these are double white lines and they have rules for

- overtaking
- parking.

Overtaking When the line nearest you is continuous, you must not cross or straddle it except when it is safe and you want to

- enter or leave a side road or entrance on the opposite side of the road
- pass a stationary vehicle
- pass a road maintenance vehicle, pedal cycle or horse moving at 10 mph or less.

If there's a broken white line on your side and a continuous white line on the other, you may cross both lines to overtake. Make sure you can complete the manoeuvre before reaching a solid line on your side.

Arrows on the road often warn that there's a double white line coming up. Don't begin to overtake when you see them.

Parking On a road marked with double white lines you must not stop or park, even if one of the lines is broken. You may however, stop for a moment to pick up or drop off passengers.

Hatched markings There are dangerous areas where it is necessary to separate the streams of traffic completely, such as a sharp bend or hump, or where traffic turning right needs protection. These areas are painted with white chevrons or diagonal stripes. Remember

- where the chevrons are edged with a solid white line you should NOT enter
- where the edge is broken you may enter if you can see that it is safe to do so.

Single broken lines Watch out for places where the single broken line down the centre of the road gets longer. This shows a danger ahead.

Bus lane A continuous single white line is used to mark the edge of both bus and cycle lanes.

Reflective studs or cat's eyes

These are

- red on the left-hand side of the road
- white on the lane or centre-of-road lines.

Some dual carriageways and motorways also have

- amber cat's eyes marking the right-hand edge of the carriageway
- green cat's eyes separating deceleration/acceleration lanes from the carriageway.

At road works fluorescent green/yellow studs are used to help identify the lanes in operation.

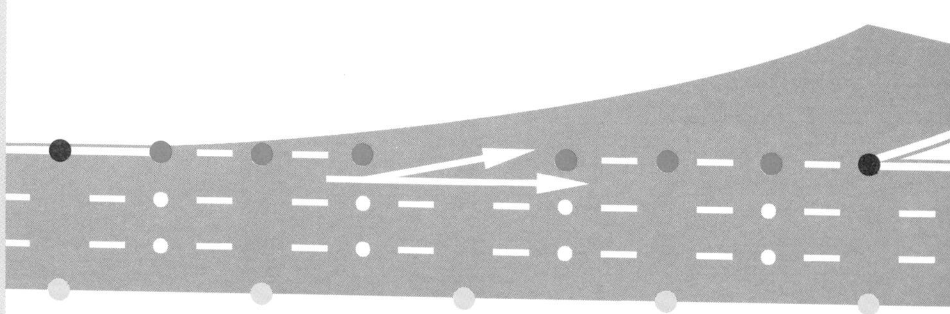

Box junctions markings

Yellow crisscross lines mark a box junction.

Their purpose is to keep the junction clear by preventing traffic from stopping in the path of crossing traffic.

You must not enter a box junction unless your exit road from it is clear. But you can enter the box when you want to turn right and you're only prevented from doing so by oncoming traffic.

If there's a vehicle already on the junction waiting to turn right, you're free to enter behind it and wait to turn right – providing that you won't block any oncoming traffic wanting to turn right.

If there are a number of vehicles waiting to turn, it's unlikely you'll be able to proceed before the traffic signals change.

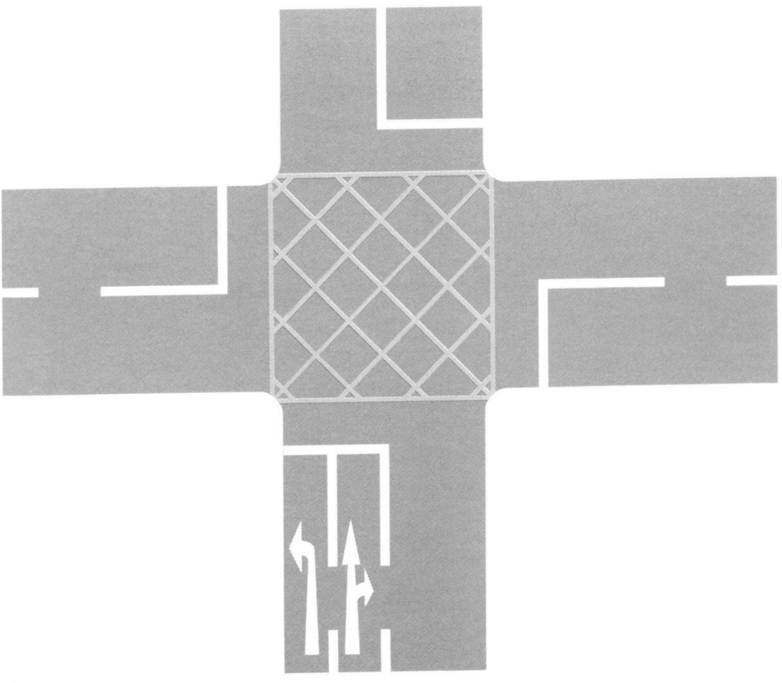

Words on the road

Words on the road surface usually have a clear meaning. They include STOP, SLOW, KEEP CLEAR and so on.

When they show a part of the road is reserved for certain vehicles, for example, buses and taxis, or ambulances, don't park there.

Destination markings

Near a busy junction, lanes sometimes have destination markings or road numbers on the road surface.

These enable drivers to get into the correct lane early, even if advance direction road signs are obscured by large vehicles.

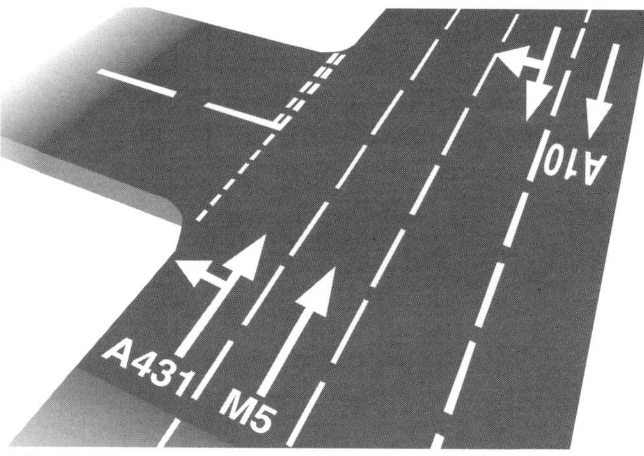

Schools

Yellow zigzag markings on the road outside school along with the words SCHOOL – KEEP CLEAR. You must not stop (even to set down or pick up children) or park there. The markings are to make sure that

- drivers passing
- children crossing

have a clear, unrestricted view of the crossing area.

Lane arrows

These tell you which lane to take for the direction you want.

Where the road is wide enough, you can find one arrow pointing in each direction

- left in the left-hand lane
- straight ahead in the centre lane
- right in the right-hand lane.

Some arrows might be combined, depending on how busy the junction is. If the road is only wide enough for two lanes, arrows might have two directions combined

- straight ahead and left in the left-hand lane
- straight ahead and right in the right-hand lane.

Left and right turn arrows are placed well before a junction to help you get into the correct lane in good time. They don't indicate the exact point at which you should turn. It's especially important to remember this at right turns.

Speed reduction lines

Approaching a number of roundabouts from some dual-carriageways and motorway exit roads, raised yellow lines are painted **across** the carriageway. The purpose of these lines is to make drivers aware of their speed after a period of driving at higher speeds. Reduce speed in good time.

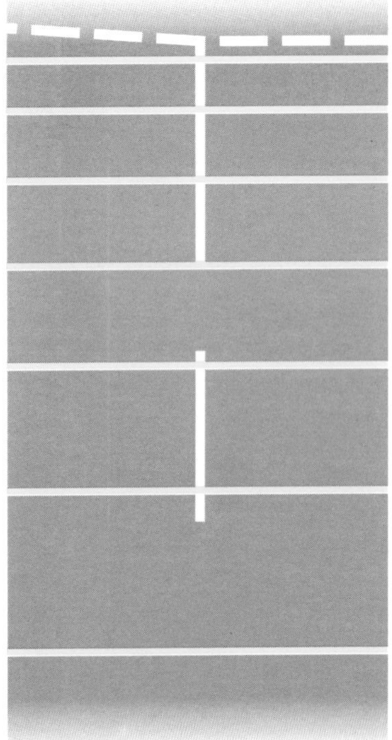

Traffic lights

Traffic lights have three lights which change in a set cycle

- red
- red and amber
- green
- amber
- red.

What the colours mean

- Red: stop and wait at the stop line.
- Red and amber: stop and wait.

Don't go until green shows.

- Green: go if the way is clear.
- Amber: stop, unless
  - you've already crossed the line
  - you're so close to it that pulling up might cause an accident.

Approaching green traffic lights

Approach traffic lights as you would any other junction. Keep your speed down.

Don't speed up to 'beat the lights'. Be ready to stop, especially if the lights have been green for some time.

Green filter arrow

A green arrow in a traffic light means you can filter in the direction the arrow is pointing, even if the main light is not showing green.

When turning left or right at traffic lights take special care, and give way to pedestrians already crossing.

MSM routine

Use the MSM and PSL routines as you approach the lights.

Pay attention to lane markings and get into the correct lane in good time. Be prepared to stop.

Special traffic lights

These are often used to control traffic where low flying aircraft pass over the road or at swing or lifting bridges, or other special sites such as fire stations. They can be either normal traffic lights, that is red, amber and green or double red flashing lights. They must always be obeyed.

Always stop at flashing red lights.

If traffic lights fail If the traffic lights fail, proceed with caution. Treat the situation as you would an *unmarked* junction.

School crossing warning

Two amber lights flashing alternatively warn traffic of a school crossing point ahead at some busy locations.

Level crossings

At a level crossing, the road crosses railway lines. Approach and cross with care.

Never

- drive onto the crossing unless the road is clear on the other side
- drive over it 'nose-to-tail'
- stop on or just after the crossing
- park close to the crossing.

Most crossings have full or half barriers.

Open crossings have no gates or barriers.

Either type may be controlled by a steady amber light followed by twin flashing red lights which warn of an approaching train. A warning alarm will also sound once the lights show. You must obey the lights signals.

Don't

- move onto the crossing after the lights show
- stop on the crossing if the amber light or audible alarm starts to operate – KEEP GOING if you're already on the crossing
- zigzag round half barriers.

If the train goes by and the red lights continue to flash, or the audible alarm changes tone, you must wait because another train is approaching.

Railway telephones

You must use the railway telephone (where provided) to contact the signal operator to obtain permission to cross if you're

- driving a large or slow-moving vehicle, or one with limited ground clearance
- herding animals.

Remember to telephone the signal operator again once you're clear of the crossing.

Accidents or breakdowns

If your vehicle breaks down, or you're involved in an accident on the crossing

- get everyone out of the vehicle and clear of the crossing
- if there's a railway telephone, use it *immediately* to inform the signal operator: FOLLOW ANY INSTRUCTIONS YOU'RE GIVEN
- if it's possible *and there's time* before a train arrives, move the vehicle clear of the crossing
- if the alarm sounds, or the amber light comes on GET CLEAR OF THE CROSSING AT ONCE – THE TRAIN WILL NOT BE ABLE TO STOP.

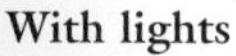
With lights

Without lights

Crossings without signals

At crossings with no lights, STOP when the gates or barriers begin to close.

Unattended crossings with signals

Some unattended crossings with gates or barriers have STOP signs and small red and green lights. Do not cross when the red light is on because a train is approaching. Cross only when the green is on.

Open the gates or barriers on BOTH sides of the crossing. Check the green light is still on and cross promptly.

Close the gates or barriers when you're clear of the crossing.

Unattended crossings without signals

Some crossings have gates but no attendant or signals. At these crossings

- stop
- look both ways
- listen and make sure that no train is approaching.

If there's a railway telephone contact the signal operator to make sure it's safe to cross.

Open the gates on both sides of the crossing and check again that no train is coming before crossing promptly.

Once you've cleared the crossing

- close both gates
- inform the signal operator, if there's a telephone.

Always give way to trains – they can't stop easily.

Open crossings

At an open crossing with no gates, barriers, attendant or traffic signals, there will be a GIVE WAY sign.

Look both ways, listen and make sure there's no train coming before you cross.

Tram crossings (LRTs)

Look for traffic signs which show where trams cross the road.

Treat them the same as normal railway crossings.

Remember

These modern versions of the tram are very silent. Take extra care and look both ways before crossing.

Modern roads present a huge variety of bends, corners and junctions – points where the road changes direction.

These are often major hazards, and accident statistics show that no driver can afford to venture out without a thorough knowledge of how to deal with them. They must be treated with great care.

The whole of this section is devoted to dealing with bends, corners and junctions safely.

The topics covered

- Bends
- Junctions
- Turning
- Emerging
- Lanes at junctions
- Types of junctions
- Dual carriageways

Bends

Dealing effectively and safely with bends demands that you look well ahead and try to assess accurately how severe the bend is and at what speed you need to be travelling to negotiate it under control.

You should exercise sound judgement and a defensive approach. Where vision is restricted, be prepared to meet

- oncoming vehicles
- obstructions such as broken down or slow moving vehicles
- pedestrians walking on your side of the road.

You should

- use the footbrake to control your speed on approach
- choose the right gear for the road speed
- use the accelerator carefully
- steer to hold the right line through the bend.

Remember

A bend could feel like a sharp corner to a driver who approaches it too fast – with disastrous results.

Speed

Judging the correct road speed as you approach bends and corners takes practice and experience.

The correct speed is the one which takes your vehicle around the bend under full control with the greatest safety for you, your passengers and other road users.

That speed will depend on the type and condition of the road, the sharpness of the bend, the camber of the road and other traffic.

Banking When rounding a bend, a vehicle is forced outwards. The higher the speed, the greater the danger of losing control.

On a few bends this can be partly counteracted by banking.

It's why racing circuits are often sloped inwards.

Camber The camber of a road is the angle at which the road normally slopes away from the centre to help drainage.

Adverse camber If the road slopes towards the outer edge of a bend, this is called adverse camber. Take extra care: if your speed is too high, the forces acting on your vehicle could cause it to leave the road.

Adjusting your speed

Don't go into a bend too fast. Reduce speed before you enter the bend.

You can reduce your speed by taking your foot off the accelerator, and

- allowing the road speed to fall
- using the footbrake progressively and, if necessary, changing to a lower gear.

Your speed should be at its lowest as you begin to turn.

Brake lights Releasing the accelerator gives no warning to drivers behind you that you're slowing down.

Your brake lights will warn following traffic. So, if there's traffic behind you, it's a good idea to press the brake pedal just enough to show your brake lights, even if you don't intend to brake.

Braking on a bend Avoid braking on the bend. This can make your vehicle unstable.

The sharper the bend the more drastic the effects of braking and the more likely the vehicle is to skid.

Brake before the bend, if any braking is necessary.

Acceleration

Don't confuse 'using the accelerator' with 'accelerating' which means going faster. When dealing with bends it also means using the accelerator just enough to drive the vehicle around the bend.

The correct speed at a corner or bend will depend on

- how sharp it is
- whether there is other traffic about, etc.

There are no hard and fast rules and you will have to judge

- the proper speed for the corner or bend
- the gear most suitable for that speed
- the correct position.

The secret of dealing with bends is to make sure that

- your speed is at its lowest before you start the turn
- you use the accelerator so that the engine is doing just enough work to drive the vehicle round the bend, without going faster.

Too much acceleration can cause the wheels, particularly on rear-wheel drive vehicles, to lose their grip and skid, resulting in the vehicle swinging off course.

Only increase your speed after you have straightened as you leave the bend.

Gears

Make sure you select the correct gear before you enter the bend. You need both hands on the steering wheel as you're turning.

Steering

Every vehicle 'handles' differently. It's very important that you get to know how the vehicle you are driving behaves when you're steering round a bend.

Some vehicles 'understeer'. They respond less than you expect in relation to the amount of steering you use.

Others 'oversteer'. They respond more than you expect in relation to the amount of steering you use.

To be able to negotiate a bend, corner or junction safely, you must be able to judge how much steering to use.

What affects steering?

Load and tyre pressures can dramatically affect steering.

Load Any change in the centre of gravity or weight the vehicle is carrying will affect its handling on bends.

A roof rack or load, including extra passengers, will cause a vehicle to behave quite differently on bends, compared to when it's lightly loaded.

Tyre pressures Incorrect tyre pressures can also affect steering.

Low pressure produces a heavier feel, and can cause the tyres to overheat. It can also affect both road holding and tyre wear due to the side walls flexing.

Excess pressure not only increases tyre wear, but also affects road holding on bends and increases the risk of skidding.

When carrying heavier loads, or setting out on long motorway journeys, tyre pressures might need to be increased according to the manufacturer's recommendations.

Correctly inflated

Under inflated

Approaching bends

Look ahead Look well ahead for any indications such as road signs, warnings and road markings which will tell you

- the type of bend
- the direction the road takes
- how sharp the bend is
- whether the bend is one of a series.

Assess the situation Ask yourself

- How dangerous does it seem? Remember, the word SLOW is usually painted on the road for good reason.
- Are there likely to be obstructions on the bend? For example, slow moving vehicles or parked cars.
- Are there likely to be pedestrians on your side of the road? Is there a footpath?
- What's the camber like?

Always drive so you can stop safely within the limit of your vision.

Approach with care

- As you approach, follow the MSM/PSL routine.
- Before you reach the bend
  - Take up the best approach position for the type of bend
  - Adjust your speed, if necessary, and select the most suitable gear.

Entering the bend As you enter the bend, press the accelerator just enough to keep

- the wheels gripping
- the vehicle under full control.

After you begin to turn Avoid braking, except in an emergency.

As you round the bend Keep watching for hazards as the road unfolds and your view improves.

Stopping on a bend Avoid stopping on bends, except in an emergency.

If you have to stop, do so where following traffic can see you. This is especially important on left-hand bends where vision can be more limited.

If you can, park clear of a continuous centre line and give clear warning of any obstruction to approaching traffic. Use hazard warning lights and an advance warning triangle, if you have one.

Positioning on bends

Left-hand bend

- Use the safe approach routine.
- Road position
  - keep to the centre of your lane as you approach
  - don't move to the centre of the road to improve your view. (This could put you too close to oncoming traffic and a vehicle coming the other way might be taking the bend wide.)
- Where your view is restricted, drive at a speed which will allow you to stop safely within the limits of your vision.

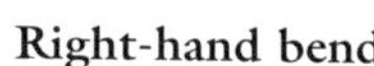

Right-hand bend

- Use the safe approach routine, including MSM/PSL.
- Road position. Keep to the left to improve your view of the road, but don't let a clear view tempt you to enter the bend at too great a speed.
- Remember that adverse camber could make your vehicle veer to the left. Look well ahead – it's too late to find out in the middle of the bend when your brakes can't help you.

Double bend

Negotiating a series of bends

Double and multiple bends are almost always signed. Take note of

- road signs
- double white lines
- arrows warning you to move to the left.

For example, if the second bend followed closely after the first and you haven't taken notice of the road sign or markings, you could find yourself speeding up when you should be slowing down. This can result is hasty re-planning and loss of control.

So, on a winding road, use your gears sensibly and select the appropriate gear for the speed. This will enable you to drive at a safe speed while keeping the right amount of load on the engine and the right amount of grip on the road.

Bends in series often swing in alternate directions. As soon as you have negotiated one you have to prepare for the next. Look well ahead for changes in the camber of the road which could affect your control.

Negotiating bends at night At night, the lights of oncoming traffic make cornering a little easier to predict. However, negotiating bends at night has its own hazards. Drive with extra care.

- Be prepared for hazards around the bend.
- Be prepared to be affected by the lights of oncoming traffic, especially on right-hand bends. Don't be taken by surprise.
- Dip your headlights in advance for oncoming traffic approaching the bend, especially on left-hand bends.

Drive defensively

Always be on the lookout for other vehicles creating dangerous situations. Stay well back from trouble. For example

- a vehicle overtaking too close to a bend
- a vehicle approaching a bend too fast
- oncoming vehicles straddling the centre lines
- oncoming vehicles skidding in bad weather
- a vehicle waiting to turn into a concealed entrance.

Junctions

A junction is a point where two or more roads meet.

Junctions are hazards with a higher risk of accident. Treat them with great care, no matter how easy they look.

Types of junction

There are five main types.

- T-junctions.
- Y-junctions.
- Staggered junctions.
- Crossroads.
- Roundabouts.

Advance information

Look for information about the junction ahead and the level of difficulty, such as

- the amount of traffic
- warning signs
- road markings
- Direction signs
- GIVE WAY and STOP signs
- traffic lights (see Part Seven)
- a break in the line of buildings
- changes in road surface.

Zones of vision

A zone of vision is what a driver can see from the vehicle. Zone of vision is determined by

- buildings and hedges
- bends in the road or contours in the land
- moving and parked vehicles
- available light and weather.

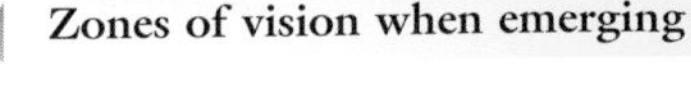

Zones of vision when emerging

As you approach a junction, your zone of vision onto the other road usually improves. The last few feet are critical.

Making eye contact with other road users helps you to tell whether they have seen you.

Vehicles with high driving positions, such as buses and large goods vehicles, often have better zones of vision than smaller vehicles, such as cars and motorcycles.

Sometimes parked vehicles interfere with your zone of vision so that you have to inch carefully forward to see more. If another vehicle or a pedestrian is not in your zone of vision, you're not usually in theirs.

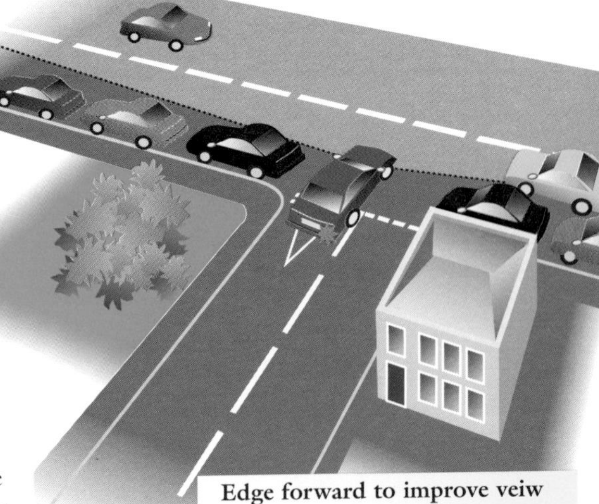

Edge forward to improve veiw

Options at junctions

How you approach a junction depends on what you intend to do. You might want to

- cross a major road going ahead
- emerge into a major road by turning right
- emerge into a major road by turning left
- leave a major road by turning right or left into a minor road
- stay on a major road and pass the junction.

A major road is one with priority over another at a junction.

Priority

Usually, road signs and markings indicate priority. Where no priority is shown at a junction, take extra care.

The junction routine

At every junction use the MSM/PSL routine.

- M – check in your mirrors to assess the speed and position of vehicles behind.
- S – signal clearly and in good time.
- M – manoeuvre – use PSL.
- Position your vehicle correctly and in good time. Early positioning lets other road users know what you are going to do.

If the road has no lane markings

When turning left keep well to the left, your nearside about 1 metre (3 feet) from the kerb.

When turning right keep as close to the centre of the road as is safe. Take into account any parked vehicles or obstructions on the right-hand side of the road.

In a one-way street move to the right-hand side of the road as early as you can before turning right.

If the road has lane markings

Use the correct lane for the direction you intend to take, and move into it as soon as you can.

- Speed – adjust your speed as necessary.
- Look – for other traffic when you reach a point from which you can see.
- Assess – the situation.
- Decide – go or wait.
- Act – accordingly.

Defensive driving

Take extra care if your path crosses or joins the path of other road users.

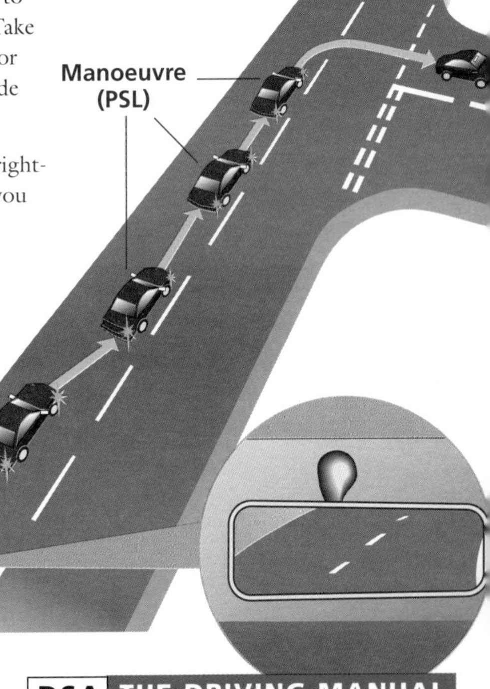

Turning

Turning left

Use the MSM routine on approach.

Road position

Your road position should be well to the left, the nearside of your vehicle about 1 metre (3 feet) from the kerb.

Speed

Left turns into minor roads are often sharper than right turns.

Make sure you slow down sufficiently, or you could swing wide of the corner and finish up on the wrong side of the road.

Parked vehicles

Watch out for vehicles

- stopping to park, or parked, just before a left-hand junction
- parked just around the corner
- approaching in the side road.

Pedestrians and cyclists

You should

- give way to pedestrians already crossing when you turn – they have priority
- keep a special lookout for cyclists coming up on your left
- take special care when crossing a bicycle track or bus lane
- don't cut in on a cyclist you have just overtaken.

Avoid steering too early or too sharply: a rear wheel might mount the kerb.

After the turn

- Check in your mirrors so you know what's following you in the new road.
- If it's safe to do so, speed up as you leave the junction.
- Make sure your signal has cancelled.

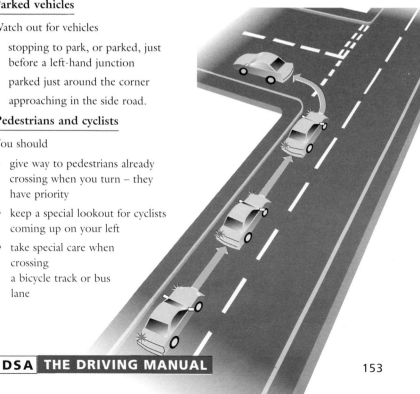

Turning right

Use the MSM routine on approach.

Road position

- Move into position early when turning right. It helps other drivers.
- Position yourself as close to the centre of the road as is safe, so that vehicles can pass on your left if there's room.
- In a one-way street keep to the right-hand side of the road.

Speed of approach

- Adjust your speed as necessary. Approach at a safe speed.

Oncoming traffic

- Watch out for oncoming traffic, especially motorcycles and bicycles which are less easily seen.
- Watch particularly for vehicles overtaking oncoming traffic.
- Stop before you turn if you have any doubt about being able to cross safely.

Emerging vehicles

- Watch for vehicles waiting to emerge from the minor road.

Pedestrians

- Make sure pedestrians are clear of your path before you turn. They have priority.

Obstructions

- Look carefully for anything that could prevent you entering the minor road safely and leave you exposed on the wrong side of the road, risking a serious accident.
- You MUST NOT cross to the other side of the centre line in the road until you are sure you can enter the minor road safely.

Turning

- Don't cut the corner.
- Don't accelerate fiercely. Your engine should be just pulling as you turn.

Emerging

'Emerging' is when a vehicle leaves one road and joins, crosses or turns into another.

You'll have to judge the speed and distance of any traffic on the road you intend to emerge into, and only continue when it's safe to do so.

This needs care and sometimes patience as well.

When to 'go'

You have to decide when to wait and when it's safe to go. That decision depends largely on your zone of vision

You can only decide to wait or go on when you have put yourself in a position where you can see clearly.

Looking means that you need to assess the situation, decide whether it's safe and act accordingly.

Remember

An approaching vehicle, particularly a bus or a truck, can easily mask another moving vehicle which may be overtaking.

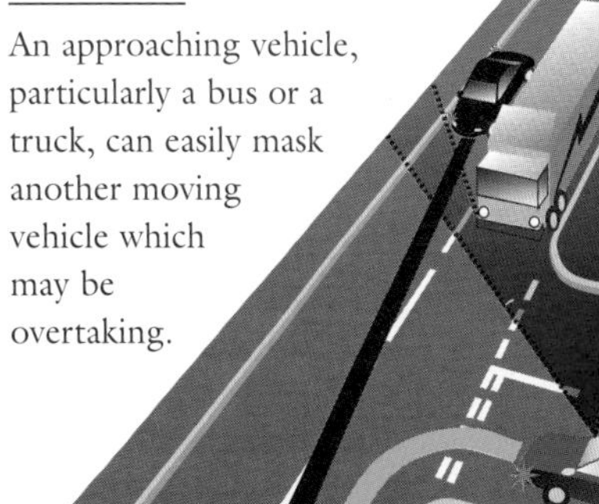

GIVE WAY sign or lines

A GIVE WAY sign means that you must give way to traffic which is already on the road you intend to enter.

If you can emerge without causing drivers or riders on that road to alter speed or course, you can do so without stopping.

Otherwise, you must stop.

STOP sign

You MUST always stop at a STOP sign no matter what traffic is like on the road you intend to enter.

Move off only when

- you have a clear view
- you're sure it's safe.

Junctions without signs or road markings

Treat these with great care.

Don't assume you have priority at an unmarked junction

Other traffic

Bends and hills will make it more difficult to judge the speed of oncoming traffic.

If the vehicle approaching from your right is signalling to turn left into your road, wait until you're sure the vehicle is turning and not just pulling up on the left beyond your road.

Emerging left into a major road

Assess the junction. Check road signs and markings and use the MSM/PSL routine.

M – Look in your mirrors to assess what's behind.

S – Signal left in good time.

M – Manoeuvre – use PSL.

P – Keep well to the left, about 1 m (3 feet) from the kerb.

S – Reduce speed. Be prepared to stop: you must give way to traffic on a major road.

L – Look in all directions at the earliest point from which you can see clearly.

Keep looking as you slow down or stop, if necessary, until you're sure it's safe to enter the major road.

Emerging right into a major road

Assess the junction. Check road signs and markings and use the MSM/PSL routine.

M – Look in your mirrors to assess what's behind.

S – Signal right in good time.

M – Manoeuvre – use PSL.

P – When turning right, it's important to take up your position early.

Position yourself as close to the centre of the road as is safe.

In a one-way street, position yourself on the right-hand side of the road.

S – Reduce speed. Be prepared to stop: you must give way to traffic on a major road.

L – Look in all directions at the earliest point from which you can see clearly. Keep looking as you slow down. Stop, if necessary, and wait until you are sure it's safe to turn.

Defensive driving

Always remember A vehicle could be overtaking at the approach to a junction and might not see you until it's too late. You could easily emerge into its path.

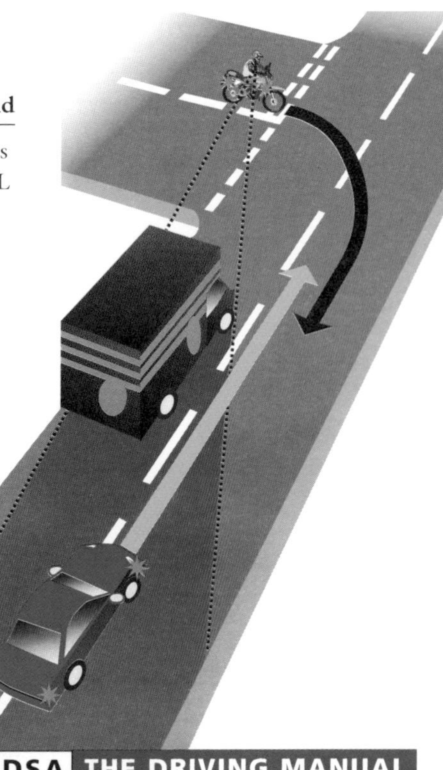

After emerging left or right

- Use your mirrors to check the speed and position of traffic behind.
- Make sure your indicator is cancelled.
- Speed up to a safe speed for the road and conditions as soon as possible.
- Keep a safe distance from the vehicle in front.
- Don’t attempt to overtake until you've had time to assess the new road.

Remember

When turning right, even though there might be little traffic approaching from the right, don’t be tempted to move out and drive down the centre of the road hoping to fit into a gap in the traffic. If the road narrows, or if there are junctions or bollards, you will have nowhere to go.

Defensive driving

When turning left or right into a major road, it takes time to complete the steering manoeuvre safely.

You need to accurately assess the speed of approaching traffic.

If in doubt, wait!

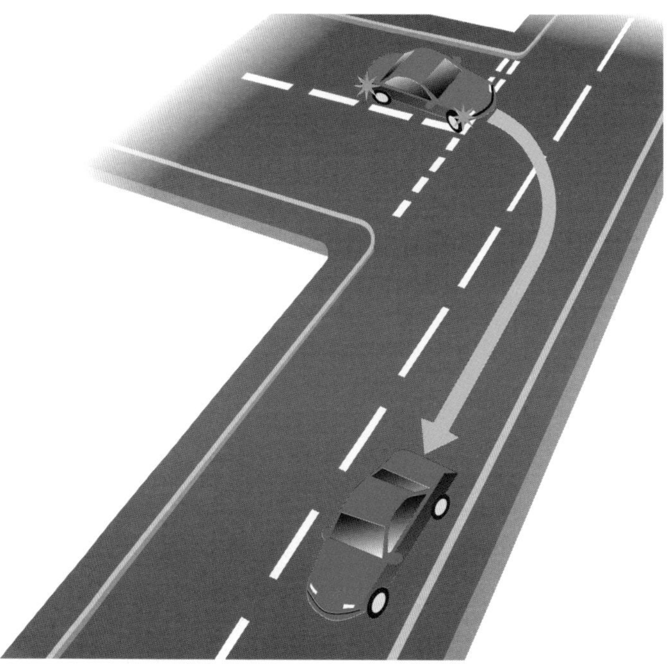

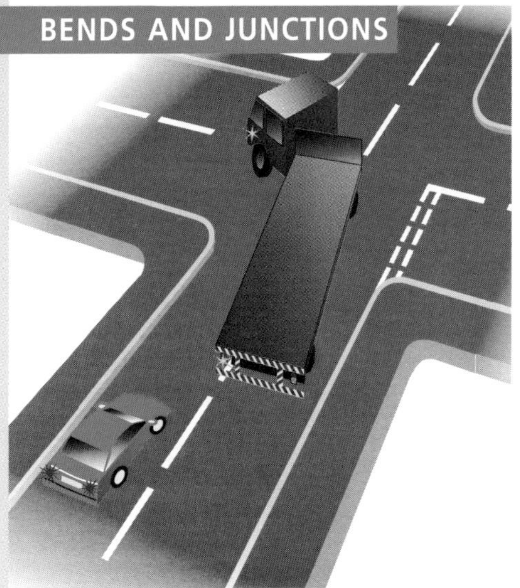

Lanes at junctions

When you approach a junction

- do so in the correct lane for the direction you intend to take; don't switch lanes to gain advantage
- look well ahead and watch for traffic and direction signs
- look out for signals from vehicles about to change lanes
- look out for vehicles suddenly changing lanes without signalling.

Articulated or long vehicles

Stay clear of large vehicles at junctions. These need much more room than smaller vehicles, and may take up a position that seems incorrect to you.

They often swing out to the right before turning left, and to the left before turning right.

Be ready for them to stop if their way is blocked.

Passing minor roads

Look out for road signs indicating minor roads, even if you're not turning off.

Watch out for emerging vehicles. Their view is often obscured at junctions. A vehicle might pull out in front of you.

If this happens, and you're not sure the driver has seen you, slow down. Be prepared to stop.

Be tolerant and don't harass the other driver by sounding your horn aggressively or driving too close.

Remember

Two wrongs don't make a right!

Overtaking

Don't overtake at, or approaching, a junction.

The road surface at junctions

Always watch out for slippery surfaces or loose chippings. Avoid braking while you're turning. Plan ahead. Brake before the junction.

Defensive driving

Adjust your overall speed when passing a series of minor roads so you can stop within the distance you can see to be clear.

Types of junctions

Each type of junction can have many variations.
What you intend to do at the junction determines how you aproach each type.

T-junctions

Where a minor road joins a major road from the left or right.

Normally the road going straight ahead, along the top of the 'T', has priority.

The minor road will either have

- a STOP sign and road markings
- a GIVE WAY sign and road markings
- Give way lines only
- no road sign or markings.

Driving on the major road If you want to go straight ahead

- take note of any road sign and markings
- watch out for vehicles emerging to turn left or right
- avoid overtaking any vehicle on the approach to a T-junction.

Defensive driving

Adjust your overall speed when passing a series of side roads on the left. Watch out for vehicles driving out on to the major road.

Hatch markings On busier roads, the major road is often split before and after the junction, with a turn right filter lane protected by white diagonal hatch markings (or chevrons) surrounded by a broken or an unbroken white line.

Join and leave the major road at these junctions exactly as you would a dual carriageway.

Warning

Areas of hatch markings are painted on the road

- to separate streams of traffic
- to protect traffic waiting to turn right.

Where the boundary line is solid, you must not enter except in an emergency.

Where the boundary line is broken, you should not drive on these markings' unless you can see it's safe to do so.

Junctions on bends

Look well ahead for traffic signs and road markings which indicate priority.

These junctions need extra care, especially when turning right from a major road which bends to the left, because

- your field of vision might be limited
- traffic might be approaching at speed from your left
- you'll need time to manoeuvre safely.

Your position before you turn must not endanger either oncoming traffic or yourself.

Wait until there's a gap in the traffic and act positively.

Only emerge from a minor road at these junctions when it's safe to do so.

Unmarked junctions

Never assume priority over another road if there are no road signs or markings. What's obvious to you might not be obvious to drivers on the other road.

Watch carefully for vehicles

- approaching the junction on the other road
- waiting at the junction
- emerging from the junction to join or cross your path.

Remember

Any vehicle crossing

- might assume priority and expect you to give way
- might not assume priority, but might have misjudged your speed or not seen you.

Such a vehicle creates a hazard.

You should respond in a safe and sensible manner. Anticipate and adjust your speed accordingly to avoid an accident.

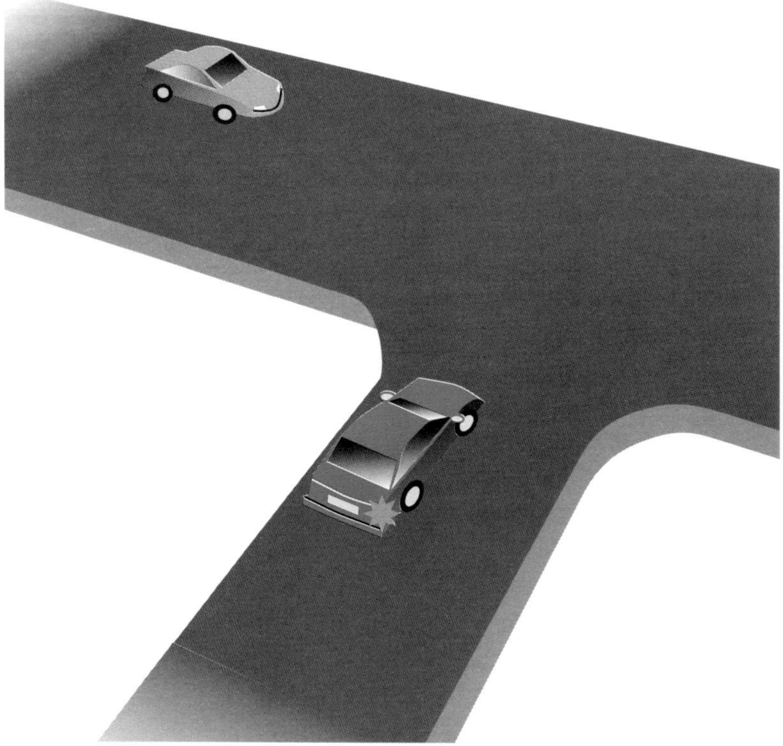

Y-junctions

Y-junctions can be deceptive because they often call for little change in direction.

Normally the road going straight ahead has priority and joining roads have either GIVE WAY or STOP signs. However, there are many exceptions.

Watch out for oncoming vehicles positioned incorrectly. The drivers might have misjudged the junction.

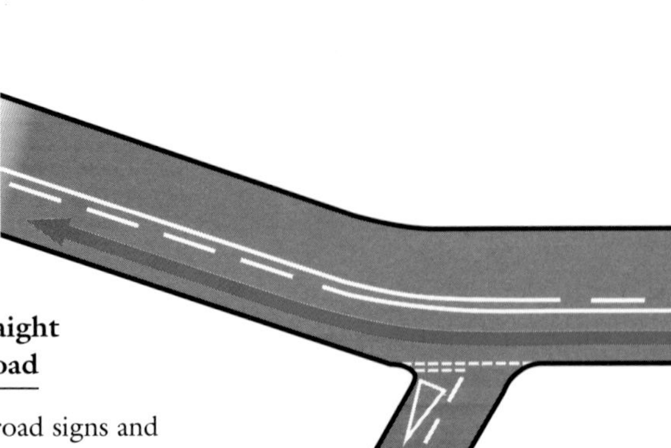

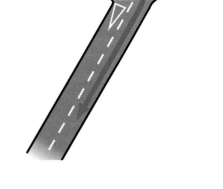

If you want to go straight ahead on the major road

- Look well ahead for road signs and markings.
- Watch out for vehicles emerging to turn left or right.
- You must not overtake approaching any junction.

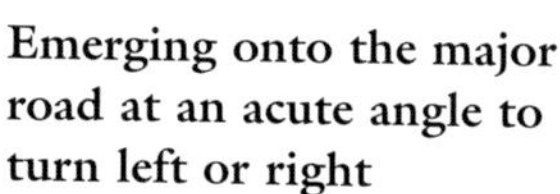

Emerging onto the major road at an acute angle to turn left or right

If the angle of approach to the major road is very sharp and from the right, the view to your left might be restricted.

If you position your vehicle towards the major road at a right angle as you approach the Stop or Give way lines, you will improve your view.

This is especially important if your vehicle has no rear side windows – a van for example.

Staggered junctions

These are junctions where roads join from both the right and the left so that the path from one side road to the other will be staggered.

Driving on the major road

Look well ahead for road signs and markings. Use MSM/PSL.

Adjust your speed as necessary and prepare to stop, especially if your view is limited or if another driver's view of you might be limited.

Watch for vehicles

- emerging from either minor road to turn left or right
- on the major road turning into a minor road on the left or right
- moving across the main road from one minor road into another.

Emerging

When emerging from a minor road to cross the major road and enter the other minor road watch out for traffic approaching in both directions.

Turning left then right

When it's safe to emerge, drive to the centre of the major road opposite the minor road you intend to enter and check the traffic again before entering the minor road.

If you're travelling only a short distance from one minor road to another one almost opposite, take extra care and make sure the gap in traffic is wide enough in both directions.

Look, assess, then decide. Either go if it's safe, or wait.

Crossroads

Crossroads are often accident black spots, so take extra care, especially on roads carrying fast-moving traffic.

Accidents often involve vehicles turning right.

The procedure when turning at crossroads is much the same as at any other junction.

You'll need to assess the crossroads on approach, so look well ahead and check for road signs and markings that might indicate priority.

Driving on the major road

- Watch for road signs and markings.
- Watch for emerging traffic. Be especially careful of vehicles trying to cut across in gaps in the traffic. They may misjudge your speed.
- Adjust your speed approaching crossroads.

Turning right

Getting your position and speed correct is vital. Look out for traffic on the road you're joining as well as on the road you're leaving. Some oncoming vehicles might want to turn right too.

Check your mirrors before starting to turn, especially if you've had to wait.

When two vehicles approaching from opposite directions both want to turn right there are two methods you can use. Either method is acceptable, but will usually be determined by

- the layout of the crossroads
- what course the other driver decides to take
- road markings.

Turning right nearside to nearside

This method is less safe because the view of oncoming vehicles is not clear. Watch out for oncoming traffic hidden by larger vehicles and be ready to stop. Police control or road markings sometimes make this method compulsory.

Turning right offside to offside

The advantage of this method is that both can see oncoming traffic.

In congested traffic conditions, leave a space for approaching traffic to turn right.

Defensive driving

Try and get eye contact with the driver of the approaching vehicle to determine which course is best. Your speed should allow you to stop if the other driver cuts across your path.

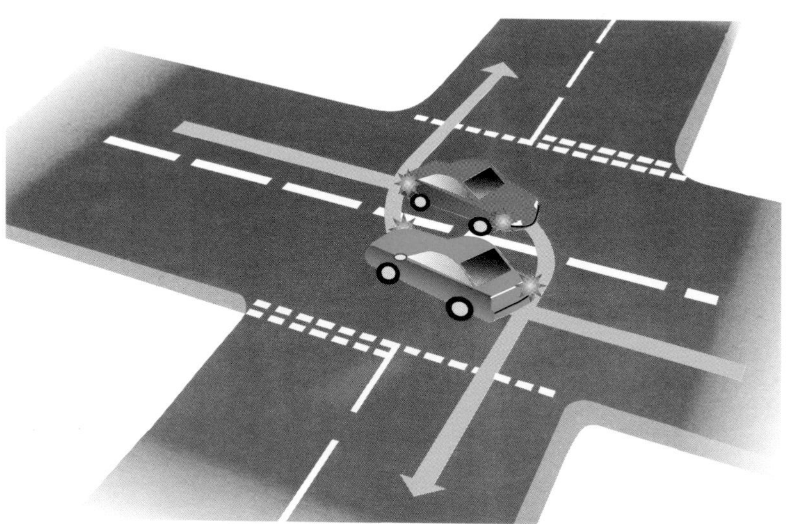

Unmarked crossroads

Treat unmarked crossroads with extreme caution since neither road has priority.

Priority

Never assume you have priority if there are no signs or markings.

Drivers approaching on other roads might also assume they have priority, and an accident could result.

Proceed only when you're sure it's safe to do so.

Remember, you must look, assess and decide, before you act.

Take extra care when your view is restricted (vehicles, walls, hedges, etc.).

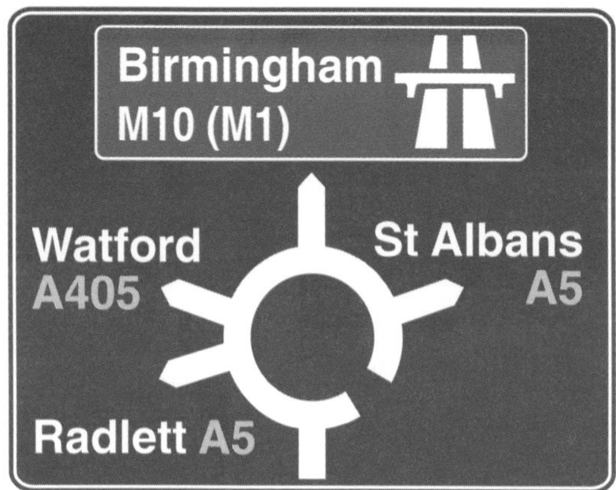

Roundabouts

Roundabouts allow traffic from different roads to merge or cross without necessarily stopping.

Priority

Before you enter a roundabout, you normally give way to any traffic approaching from your immediate right.

In a few cases, traffic on the roundabout has to give way to traffic entering. Look out for GIVE WAY signs and road markings on the roundabout.

Some roundabouts have traffic lights (sometimes part-time) which determine priority.

Always use the MSM/PSL routine an approach.

Traffic mixing

Traffic streams mix at roundabouts.

Be prepared for vehicles to cross your path to leave by the next exit. Always be on the lookout for their signals.

Look out also for long vehicles. These might take a slightly different course approaching the roundabout and when going round it, to allow for the rear of the vehicle cutting in.

Cyclists and horse riders

Cyclists and horse riders also need special consideration.

Remember that both cyclists and horse riders often keep to the outside of the roundabout even when intending to take a road leading off to the right.

Take extra care and allow them plenty of room.

Road surface

As with any junction, roundabouts are places where braking and acceleration occur. The road surface can become polished and slippery when wet. On the roundabout, avoid

- braking
- severe acceleration.

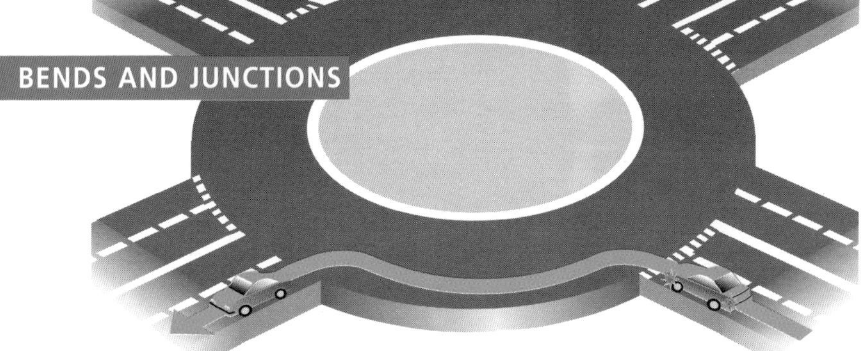

Procedure unless road signs or markings indicate otherwise

Going left

- Indicate left as you approach.
- Approach in the left-hand lane.
- Keep to that lane on the roundabout.
- Maintain a left turn signal through the roundabout.

Going ahead

- Approach in the left-hand lane without signalling. No signal is necessary. If you can't use the left-hand lane, for example, because it's blocked, use the next lane to it.
- Keep to that lane on the roundabout.
- Check your mirrors, especially the nearside exterior mirror, if one is fitted.
- Indicate left as you pass the exit just before the one you intend to take.

Going right or full circle

- Indicate right as you approach.
- Approach in the right-hand lane.
- Keep to that lane and maintain the signal on the roundabout.
- Check your mirrors, especially the nearside exterior mirror, if one is fitted.
- Indicate left as you pass the exit just before the one you intend to take.
- Keep moving if the way is clear.

More than three lanes

Where there are more than three lanes at the approach to the roundabout, use the clearest suitable lane on approach and through the roundabout, unless road signs or markings tell you otherwise.

Defensive driving

Always keep an eye on the vehicle in front as you're about to emerge. Don't assume the driver won't have to stop while you're still looking to the right. Many rear end collisions happen this way. Make sure the vehicle has actually moved away.

Remember

When using the right-hand lane to go ahead or turn right, be aware of traffic in the next lane.

Approaching a large roundabout

Always look well ahead for the advance warning sign.

This will give you a clear picture of the layout of the roundabout together with route directions. The sign will enable you to select the most suitable lane to approach the roundabout.

Watch out also for advance warnings of appropriate traffic lanes at the roundabout. These are often backed-up by road markings which usually include route numbers.

- Get into the correct lane in good time.
- Don't straddle lanes.
- Never change lanes at the last moment.

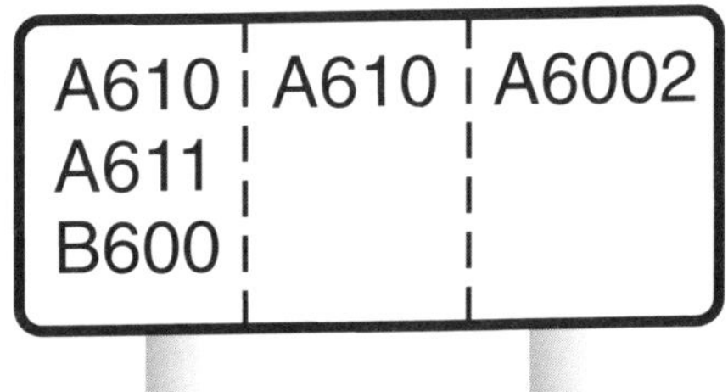

Where possible it's a good idea to look across the roundabout and identify the exit you're aiming to take. This will help you to plan the safest course on the roundabout itself.

Mini roundabouts

- Approach these in the same way as a roundabout, but remember, there's less space and time to signal and manoeuvre. For example, there's often insufficient time to signal left when leaving a mini roundabout.
- Vehicles coming towards you might want to turn right. Give way to them.
- Be sure any vehicle on the roundabout is going to leave it before you join the roundabout.
- Beware of drivers who are using the roundabout for a U-turn.
- Larger vehicles might not be able to avoid driving over the marked centre area.
- In wet conditions this large painted area can be slippery and present a risk of skidding.

Double mini roundabouts

- Don't enter the first roundabout until you're sure you can enter and exit from the second without stopping or interfering with the progress of other traffic.
- Take careful all-round observation before you enter.

Multiple roundabouts

At some complex junctions, a large roundabout can incorporate a series of mini roundabouts at the intersections.

You need to take extra care because traffic can be travelling in all directions around the large roundabout.

Look and assess

Keep a good lookout and assess the situation at each mini roundabout. Look for direction signs well in advance.

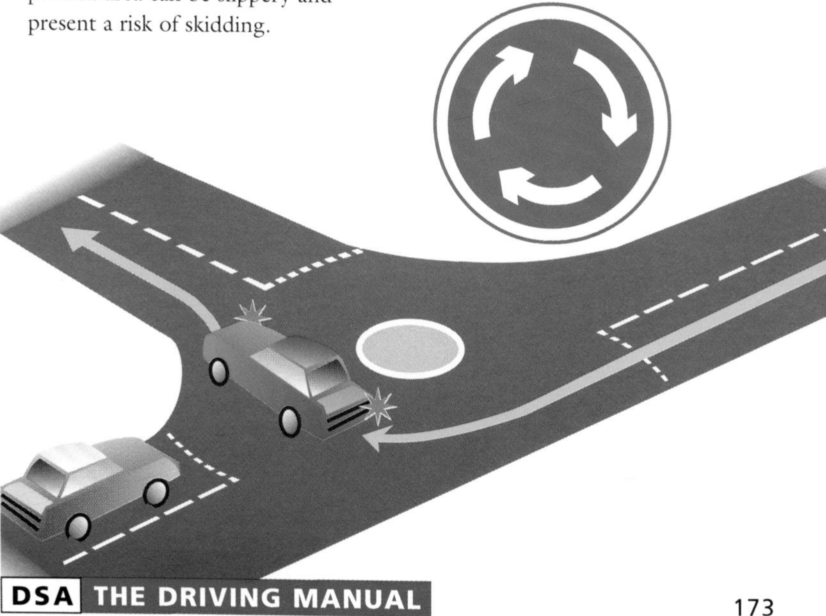

Dual carriageways

Dual carriageways have at least two lanes in each direction, divided by a central reservation where there may be a safety barrier.

Some dual carriageways are very similar to motorways, with acceleration and deceleration lanes to join and leave. However, motorway regulations do not apply and you may come across slow moving vehicles such as cyclists, or farm tractors.

Turning left from a dual carriageway

If there is no deceleration lane use the same procedure as you would for turning left into a side road.

- Use the MSM/PSL routine and get into the left-hand lane in plenty of time.
- Signal left much earlier than you would on ordinary roads because of the higher speeds involved.
- Reduce speed in good time.

If there is a deceleration lane on the left, use the same procedure as you would for leaving a motorway (see Part Eleven).

Turning right from a dual carriageway

The central reserve sometimes has gaps for turning right. Watch out for special approach lanes.

- Use the MSM/PSL routine.
- Signal right and move into the right-hand lane much earlier than you would on normal roads because of the higher speeds often involved.
- Observe any lane markings.
- Reduce speed in good time.

Take particular care when turning. You might have to cross the path of fast oncoming traffic using two or more lanes. If in doubt, wait.

Emerging onto a dual carriageway

To turn left

- If there's no acceleration lane or slip road, emerge as you would to turn left into a major road (see page 156).
- If there is a normal length acceleration lane or slip road, emerge as you would to join a motorway (see Part Eleven).
  - Accelerate to a suitable speed in the acceleration lane.
  - Look for a gap in traffic and move into the left-hand lane.
  - A quick sideways glance might be necessary to check the position of other vehicles (but see page 61).
  - Stay in the left-hand lane until you get used to the speed of the traffic in the other lanes.
  - Don't emerge unless you are sure you won't cause traffic to alter speed or course.

To turn right

- You need to cross the first carriageway before you can join the carriageway you want.
- Look, assess and decide whether it's safe to cross, or if you should wait.
- If the central reserve is wide enough, wait there for a gap in the traffic on the second carriageway.
- If the central reserve is too narrow for the length of your vehicle, you must not begin to cross until the dual carriageway is clear in both directions.
- Don't emerge unless you're sure you won't cause traffic to alter speed or course. This is particularly important if you're driving a longer vehicle, or towing a caravan or trailer.

After you emerge

- Check your mirrors.
- Cancel any indicator signal.
- Drive in the left-hand lane.
- Accelerate as soon as you can to a suitable and safe speed for the new road.
- Don't overtake until you are used to the conditions on the new road.

Always look for signs which might indicate a higher speed limit on dual carriageway. Allow for this when you assess the speed of oncoming traffic.

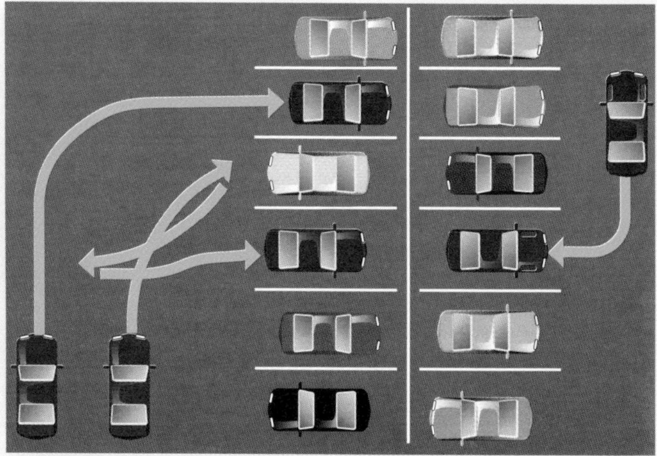

Drivers cannot consider themselves really skilled until they can, safely and confidently, reverse into an opening or side road, turn round in the road, make a U-turn and reverse park.

That includes knowing *when* and *where* to make the manoeuvre just as much as *how*.

This section covers the various methods of reversing, turning round and parking.

The topics covered

- Before manoeuvering
- Reversing
- Turning round
- Parking
- Loading and unloading

Before manoeuvring

Ask yourself

- Is this a safe place?
- Is it a convenient place?
- Is the manoeuvre within the law here?

Safe and legal?

If it's safe and convenient to make a manoeuvre, it's usually within the law.

Your knowledge of *The Highway Code*, road signs, road markings and common sense will help you decide.

You must also ask yourself

Will I be able to control my vehicle here?
You alone can answer that question.

For example, an experienced driver might have no difficulty reversing downhill, but if you've not attempted it before you might feel unsure of yourself.

Only when you can say yes to all four questions can you be sure the place is suitable.

Other road users

Avoid inconveniencing other road users. Another driver or road user should not have to slow down or change course.

Decide if it's safe to continue, or whether it would be better to wait.

Watch for other road users approaching but avoid being too hesitant.

When other vehicles stop for you

If they stop out of courtesy, well and good, but make sure you understand what the other driver means.

Check it's clear in all directions before you act upon any signal.

Reversing

Reversing is not difficult to master, it just needs practice until you become confident.

Start by reversing in a straight line, then go on to reversing round corners and more complicated manoeuvres.

Your vehicle will respond differently in reverse gear. You can't feel the car turning with the steering as you would in forward gears, and you have to wait for the steering to take effect.

The secret is to ensure the vehicle moves slowly enough. This way the steering movements will have the greatest effect.

Avoid turning the steering wheel while the vehicle is stationary (dry steering). It could cause damage to the tyres and increased wear in steering linkages.

- Remember which way the wheels are facing.
- Turn the steering wheel the way you want the rear of the vehicle to turn.

How to sit

Turn slightly in your seat. If you're reversing straight back or to the left, hold the steering wheel near the top – at 12 o'clock – with your right hand, and low on the wheel with your left hand.

If this position is too difficult because of your build, hold the wheel at 12 o'clock with your right hand. Your left arm can rest on the back of your seat or the back of the front passenger seat.

Seat belts

You may remove your seat belt while carrying out a manoeuvre which involves reversing. Don't forget to re-fasten if before driving off.

How to steer

When to begin steering?

In reverse, it's often helpful to begin turning or straightening up sooner than seems necessary.

Remember, reverse *slowly* and you'll have time for

- unhurried control of the vehicle
- checks to the front, side and rear

What to check

All-round observation is just as important when you're reversing as it is when you're going forward.

- Check for other traffic before you reverse.
- Check to the rear particularly for children playing behind the vehicle.
- Check all round – forwards, behind, over both shoulders and in mirrors. Do this before you reverse and especially behind you and to the sides as you reverse.
- If in doubt, get out and check.
- Keep checking all the time you're moving backwards, especially at the point of turn.

Always be ready to stop.

Reversing into a side-road on the left

After selecting a safe side road, use the MSM routine as you approach the corner.

If a signal is necessary, don't indicate too early that you intend pulling up on the left after the corner. You could mislead following traffic or anyone waiting to emerge.

Stop your vehicle reasonably close to the kerb and parallel to it. The sharper the corner, the further out you need to be. Apply the handbrake and select neutral.

Taking observation and starting the manoeuvre

Turn slightly in your seat. You'll find control easier.

Assess the position of your vehicle in relation to the kerb through the rear window. This is the relative position you need to end up with when you finish reversing.

Select reverse gear. Set the engine revs to a steady hum. Bring the clutch pedal to the biting point and check all round.

When you're sure it's safe, start reversing.

As a general rule

Keep the clutch pedal at, or near, the biting point. Keep the vehicle moving slowly enough by making proper use of the accelerator, clutch and brakes. The combination of the controls will depend on the slope of the road.

You should relate the position of the rear nearside wheel, just behind the back seat in most cars, to the edge of the kerb. Try to keep that wheel parallel to the kerb.

Start to turn left as the rear wheels reach the beginning of the corner. As a general guide, you should be able to follow the kerb as it disappears from view in the back window, and reappears in the side window.

The amount of steering needed depends on how sharp the corner is. Remember to keep the vehicle moving slowly.

Continuous observation

Keep a good lookout throughout, but particularly before you start to turn. The front of your vehicle will swing out and present the greatest hazard to any passing traffic.

Remember to check all blind spots before you start to turn. If any other road users are likely to be affected by your actions, pause until it's safe to continue.

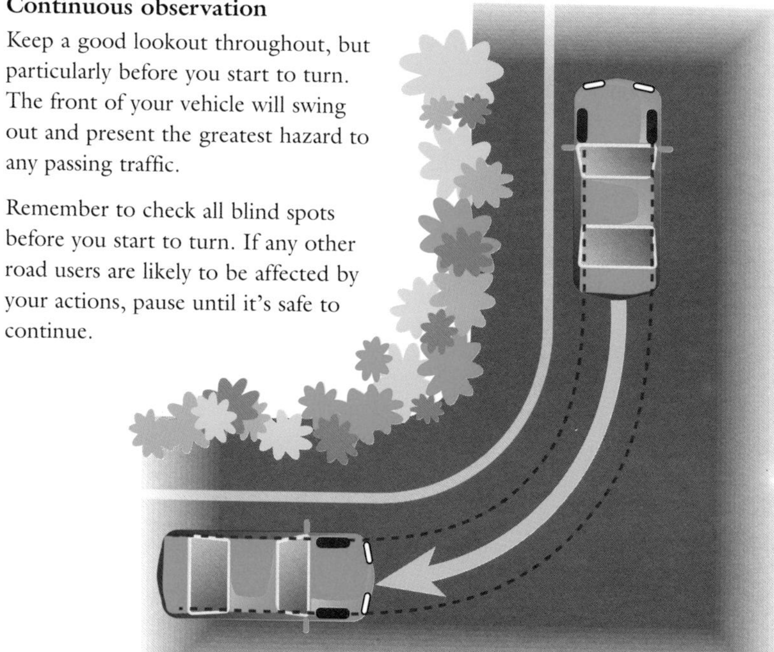

Completing the manoeuvre

When you begin to see into the side road, be ready to straighten up the steering.

Where there's a kerb in the new road, you can use the kerb to help you determine when to take off the left lock.

Try and keep the vehicle about the same distance from the kerb as when you started, and parallel to it.

Remember

Keep on the lookout for other road users, particularly

- pedestrians about to cross behind you
- vehicles approaching from any direction.

Reversing into a side-road on the right

A useful manoeuvre where

- there isn't a side-road on the left
- you can't see through the rear window
- your view to the sides is restricted, for example, in a van or a loaded estate car.

This actually involves two manouevres.

Moving to the other side of the road after passing the junction

For this part of the manoeuvre, you'll need to make

- full use of your mirrors
- proper judgement of position and speed
- a proper assessment of the side road as you pass it.

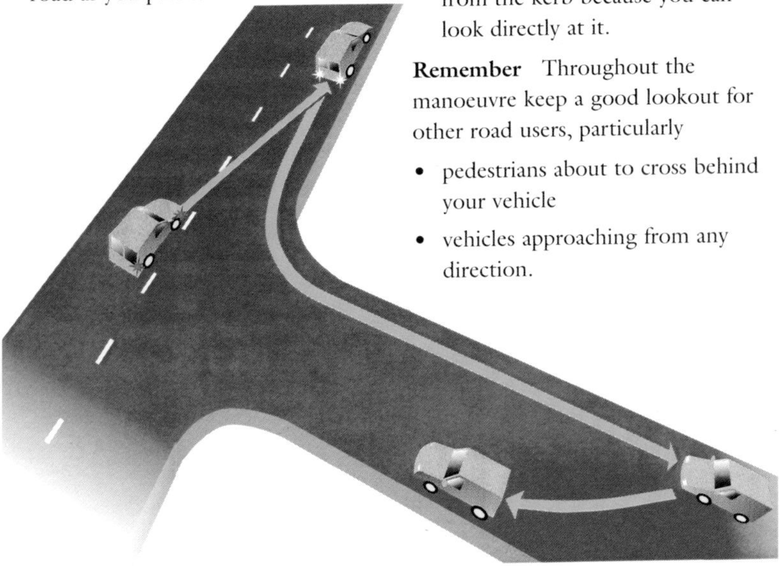

Reversing into the side road itself

You'll need to

- stop your vehicle reasonably close to and parallel with the kerb – the sharper the turn, the further out you'll need to be
- sit so that you can have a good view over your right shoulder and still be able to see forward and to the left.

All round observation is even more important on a right-hand reverse because you're on the wrong side of the road in the path of oncoming traffic.

- When you're sure it's safe, start reversing. Don't rush, but keep the vehicle moving by using the controls as for a left-hand reverse.
- It's easier to judge your distance from the kerb because you can look directly at it.

Remember Throughout the manoeuvre keep a good lookout for other road users, particularly

- pedestrians about to cross behind your vehicle
- vehicles approaching from any direction.

Turning round

There are three methods of turning round.

- Using a side road.
- Turning in the road.
- Making a U-turn.

It's usually safer to use a side road.

On narrow or busy roads

It's normally safer to

- find a side road on the left or right, and use a turning off that road to reverse into
- go into the side road and use forward and reverse gears to turn round (see Turning in the road, page 184).

Remember also

- Never reverse into a main road from a side road.
- Don't reverse without making sure it's safe, even if that means getting help.
- Don't reverse for a long distance. It's an offence to reverse further than necessary for the safety and convenience of yourself and others.
- Always be ready to give way and stop.

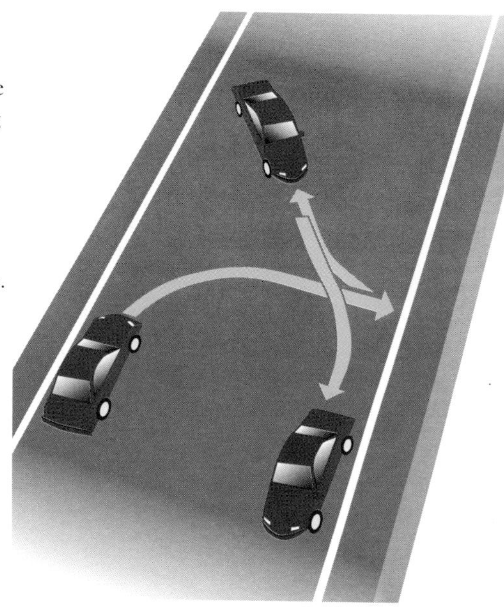

Turning in the road

You'll find this manoeuvre useful for turning when you can't find a side road or an opening.

The secret of this manoeuvre is to keep the vehicle moving *slowly* while steering *briskly*. Tight control of the clutch is essential.

Before you turn

Choose a place where

- you have plenty of room
- there's no obstruction in the road or on the pavement.

Stop on the left. Avoid lamp posts or trees near the kerb.

Select first gear and prepare to move.

Check all round, especially your blind spots. Give way to passing vehicles.

Turning across the road

Slowly move forward in first gear, turning your steering wheel briskly to full right lock. Your aim is to get the vehicle at a right angle across the road.

Just before you reach the opposite kerb, still moving slowly, begin to steer briskly to the left. Your wheels then will be ready to reverse left.

As you near the kerb, declutch and use the footbrake to stop. Use the handbrake to hold the vehicle, which may be necessary because of the camber or slope of the road.

To reverse

Select reverse gear.

Check the way is clear all round. Look through the rear window over your left shoulder to start with. Reverse slowly across the road, turning the steering wheel as far to the left as possible (full left lock).

Look round over your right shoulder as the vehicle nears the rear kerb. At the same time, turn your steering wheel briskly to the right.

Press the clutch pedal, and use the footbrake to stop.

Your wheels should be pointing to the right, ready to drive forward again.

To drive forward again

Apply the handbrake if necessary, and select first gear.

Check that the road is clear and drive forward when it's safe to do so.

You might have to reverse again if the road is narrow or your vehicle difficult to steer.

Straighten up on the left-hand side of the carriageway.

During the manoeuvre, try to avoid overhanging the kerb.

Remember

All-round observation is essential throughout the manoeuvre.

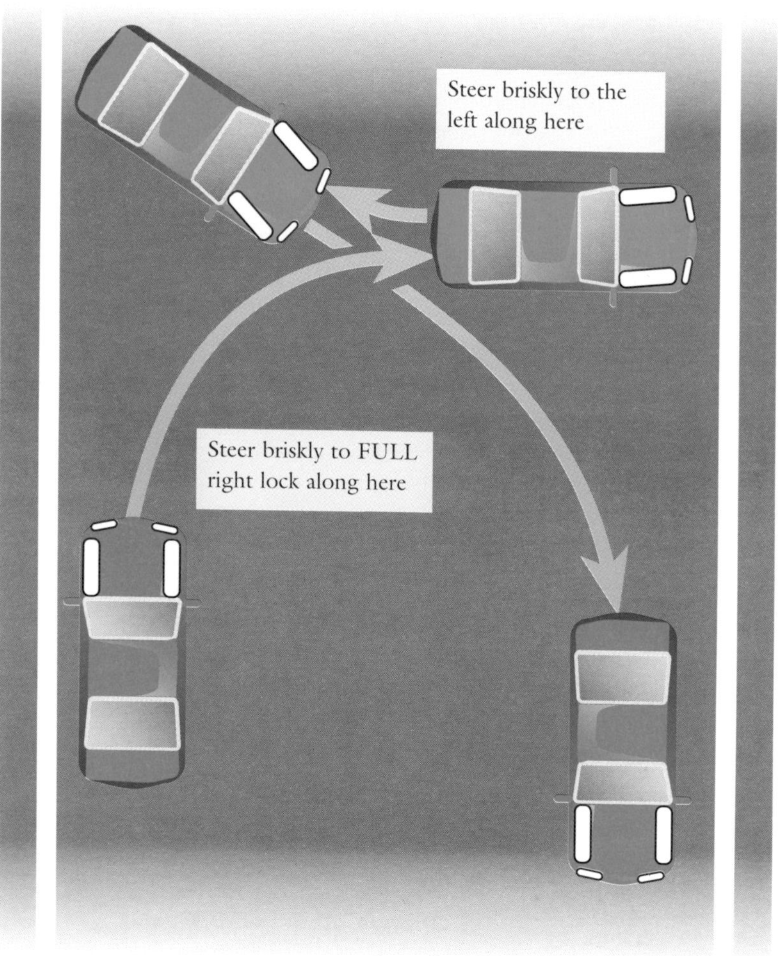
Steer briskly to the
left along here
Steer briskly to FULL
right lock along here

Making a U-turn

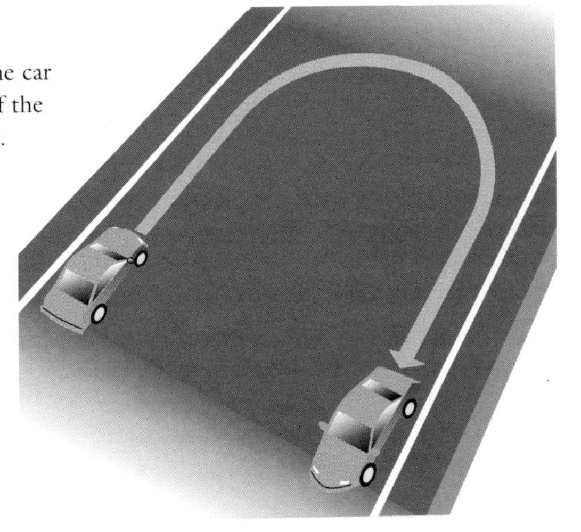

A U-turn means turning the car right round in the width of the road without any reversing.

Never make a U-turn

- on a motorway
- in a one-way street
- wherever a road sign forbids it.

Before making a U-turn

Always ask yourself

- Is it safe?
- Is it convenient?
- Is it legal?
- Is the road wide enough? If in doubt, don't attempt it.

Observation

Good all-round observation is particularly important before a U-turn.

Not a frequent manoeuvre

The U-turn is not a manoeuvre you can use often.

It's potentially dangerous because you may have to cross lines of opposing traffic.

You might find you can do a U-turn in a wide, quiet road.

Watch out for vehicles making U-turns at mini roundabouts.

Be aware that other drivers don't expect this manoeuvre.

Avoid mounting the kerb.

Parking

Whenever possible, park off the road or in a car park.

If you have to park on the road, choose a safe place.

Again, ask yourself

- Is it safe?
- Is it convenient?
- Is it legal?

Road signs and markings

These will help you decide places to avoid, such as at the approach to pedestrian crossings, school entrances, near junctions, etc.

Road signs and markings will also tell you if there are restrictions

- at certain times of the day
- on particular days of the week.

In general, *The Highway Code* lists places where you should not or must not park. Make sure you know these, and use common sense.

Never use your hazard warning lights as an excuse for stopping where you should not.

Other driver's example

Never copy another driver's bad example. It won't excuse you from any penalties.

Parking on the road

Always use the MSM routine and signal, if necessary, before you park.

Try not to touch the kerb when you park. Scraping your tyres can weaken them with possibly serious results.

Don't park so near to other vehicles that it will be difficult for you and them to get out. This is especially important if the vehicle is being driven by a disabled person (orange badge, special parking space, etc.) Allow room to manoeuvre a wheelchair.

As a general rule, park parallel and close to the kerb.

Practice

You'll acquire better parking skills with practice.

Remember

- Take care to plan your parking.
- Always manoeuvre your vehicle slowly.

Reverse parking

This makes use of the vehicle's manoeuvrability in reverse gear to park in a restricted space.

Remember, while you're carrying out this manoeuvre, you could be a hazard to other road users.

Position and observation

Good all-round observation is essential throughout this manoeuvre.

Don't start to manoeuvre if you're likely to endanger other road users.

Other drivers might not be aware of you're intentions, so before you pull up at the place you've chosen to park, remember to carry out the MSM routine.

Positioning your vehicle

Stop your vehicle reasonably close to, and parallel with, the parked vehicle ahead of the gap.

Your vehicle should be about level with, or slightly ahead of, the parked vehicle. This will depend on the size of the gap and the length of your vehicle.

Manoeuvring into the gap

Apply the handbrake, if necessary. Show your brake lights by pressing the footbrake. Select reverse gear to show the reversing light(s). This warns other road users of your intentions.

Check all round.

Bring the clutch up to biting point and, if it's still safe, release the handbrake if you applied it, and ease the clutch pedal up just enough to start to move.

Hold the clutch pedal steady at, or just above, the biting point. Reverse slowly using slight left lock, **but watch the corner of the parked vehicle.**

Don't forget to look round as you begin to reverse into the space. The front of your vehicle could swing out into the path of passing traffic.

Try lining up the offside (right-hand side) of your vehicle with the nearside headlamp of the vehicle behind the space you're entering.*

***Note.** For the sake of safety and consistency, candidates on driving tests are expected to complete the exercise within approximately two vehicle lengths. Only the leading vehicle will be present.

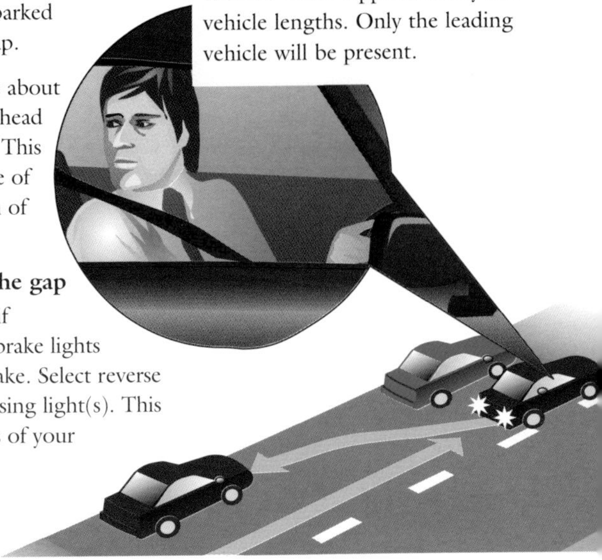

Straightening up in the gap

Straighten up by taking off the left lock. Keep a careful eye on the position of your vehicle. *There's a danger of 'clipping' the vehicle in front at this point.*

When you're sure the front of your vehicle is clear of the parked vehicle, use sufficient right lock to gradually bring the vehicle parallel with and reasonably close to the nearside kerb. Straighten up by taking the right steering off and adjust the position of your vehicle as necessary.

Remember

Keep a good lookout for other road users throughout this manoeuvre, particularly

- pedestrians
- oncoming vehicles
- passing traffic.

Note. You can start practising using only one parked car.

When you have mastered the technique, you should be able to park between two vehicles.

The gap should be at least one-and-a-half times the length of your own vehicle.

Defensive driving

Other road users may not understand your intention. Showing your reversing lights should help.

If another vehicle pulls up close behind, move on and park somewhere else.

Car parks

Arrow markings and signs show you which lanes to take inside the car park.

Follow these. Don't drive against the traffic flow.

Use dipped headlights

Use dipped headlights in multi-storey, underground or indoor car parks.

This helps other drivers and pedestrians to see you.

Parking

Unless there's space at the end of the row, you'll have to fit in between two other vehicles.

Check that there's

- enough space for you to centre your vehicle
- enough room to open the doors safely.

Whether you're reversing in or going forward, move *slowly* so the steering has the maximum effect and gives you time to make corrections.

Park neatly in the marked spaces

Always try to park neatly in the marked spaces. Park squarely within the space, otherwise the car next to you might have to squeeze in, or there might not be enough room for its doors to be opened.

Manoeuvring to park

You might find your exit more difficult if you try to park facing forward in one manoeuvre.

Your wheels will face the wrong way when you reverse to leave.

If you haven't enough room to go forward into a tight space, you might need to nose in, then back out and straighten up to move into the space.

Unless other cars are badly parked, you'll nearly always find it best to reverse into a parking space. You'll have a better view when you drive away, especially with back-seat passengers or at night.

Remember

- Before entering the car park, use your mirrors and signal.
- Look at the layout, markings and signs to guide you. Choose a space.
- Use your mirrors and signal again if necessary.
- Check your position and keep your speed down. Look out for pedestrians.
- Park as neatly as possible with your wheels straight.
- Make sure your vehicle is neatly parked between the white lines in ONE space.

Loading and unloading

Don't use hazard warning lights as an excuse to park or stop where you'll inconvenience others.

Stop only where you're allowed to park.

Remember, yellow lines are there to assist the flow of traffic.

If you park carelessly, your vehicle might be removed or wheel clamped.

Ask yourself: Is it worth it?

Parking on the road

Remember that, unless your vehicle is parked in an authorised parking place, it could cause an obstruction.

Never leave your vehicle where it could prevent emergency vehicles passing, particularly in narrow residential roads where vehicles often park on both sides.

The roads today are busier than they've ever been, and they're getting busier all the time.

As well as heavy traffic, today's driver often has to cope with unpredictable, irrational, offensive and sometimes dangerous driving behaviour.

Such behaviour makes today's road conditions hostile in a very real sense, with a higher risk of accident.

To survive in such conditions, drivers today must learn and practise a defensive strategy.

That strategy is called 'defensive driving', sometimes known as 'planned driving'.

The topics covered

- Defensive driving
- Observation
- Signalling
- Hazards
- Lighting conditions
- Road surface
- Other road users

Defensive driving

Defensive driving is based on effective observation, good anticipation and control. It's about always questioning the actions of other road users and being prepared for the unexpected so as not to be taken by surprise.

Defensive driving involves

- awareness
- planning
- anticipating
- staying in control

and driving with

- responsibility
- care
- consideration and courtesy.

It means putting safety above all else.

This means having real concern not only for your own safety, but also for other road users – including the most vulnerable – those walking or riding.

Expect other people to make mistakes, and be ready to slow down or stop – even if you think you have the right of way.

Never rely on other road users doing the correct thing.

Your safety

Your safety lies mainly in your own hands. The better your control of your vehicle and road space, the safer you'll be.

A good example

Your driving should always set a good example to other road users.

You never know when your good example will make a deep impression on another driver, especially a beginner, and perhaps save lives in the future.

PUT SAFETY FIRST

Reducing hostility

With defensive driving, you'll show more patience and anticipation. This will help to reduce the number of incidents which result in

- open hostility
- abusive language
- threats
- even physical violence.

Avoid

The kind of driving that

- gives offence to other road users
- provokes reaction
- creates dangerous situations.

Competitive driving

Never drive in a spirit of competition.

Competitive driving is, inherently, the opposite of defensive driving. It increases the risks to everyone.

Observation

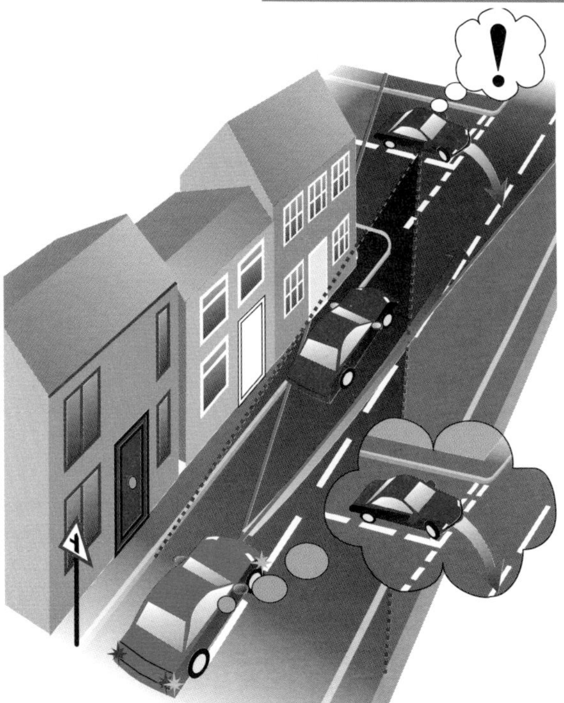

When you check in the mirrors, just looking is not enough. You must act sensibly on what you see.

You must make a mental note of the

- speed
- behaviour
- possible intentions of any other road user.

If you're not observing effectively, you can't assess a traffic situation correctly.

At junctions, there's no point in just looking if your view is obstructed, for example, by parked vehicles.

You must also move carefully into a position where you can see without emerging into the path of oncoming traffic.

- **L**ook
- **A**ssess and
- **D**ecide before you
- **A**ct.

That's what effective observation is all about.

Observing what's ahead

A skillful driver constantly watches and interprets what's happening ahead.

Never

Drive beyond the limits of your vision.

Always drive at such a speed that you can stop safely within the distance you can see to be clear.

A good driver will constantly scan the road ahead and to the side and, by frequent use of the mirrors, be aware of the situation behind.

Screen pillar obstruction

The windscreen pillars can cause obstructions to your view of the road. You should be aware of this effect, particularly when

- approaching junctions and bends
- emerging from junctions.

Approaching a bend Ask yourself

- Can I see the full picture?
- How sharp is it?
- Is my speed right?
- Am I in the right position?
- What might I meet?
- Could I stop if I had to?

Approaching a junction Ask yourself

- Have I seen the full junction?
- Can other drivers see me?
- Am I sure they've seen me?
- Have I an escape route if they haven't?

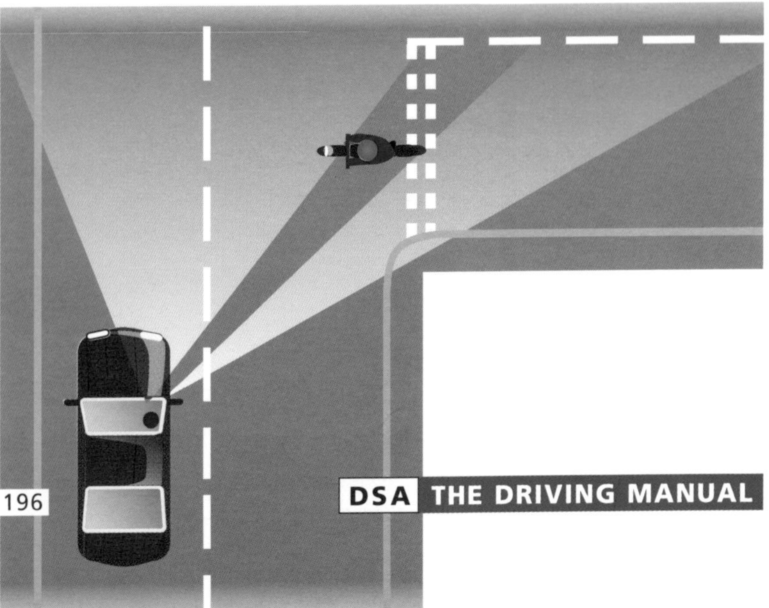

Zone of vision at a junction

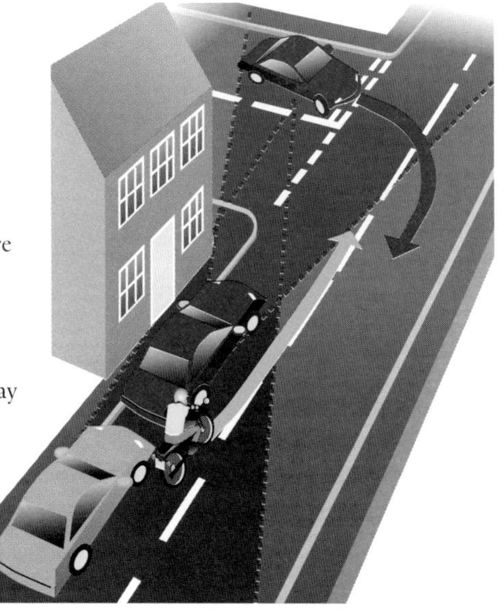

The zone of vision at a junction includes your view into other roads. This usually improves as you get nearer, but can still be limited.

You may need to get close before you can look far enough into other roads to see if it's safe to proceed.

At some junctions, your view may be so restricted that you need to stop and inch forward for a proper view before you emerge.

- Look in every direction before you emerge.
- Keep looking as you join the other road.
- Be ready to stop.
- Use all the information available to you – look *through* the windows of parked vehicles.
- Use the reflections in shop windows to observe oncoming traffic.

Parked vehicles near a junction

The illustration shows how parked vehicles can limit your vision at a junction.

Don't forget

- motorcyclists are often less easy to notice than oncoming motor vehicles

Think once.

Think twice.

Think Bike!

and make sure it's safe to proceed

- cyclists can also be difficult to see, and might be approaching at a higher speed than you expect
- pedestrians frequently cross at a junction and often find it difficult to judge the speed and course of approaching traffic.

Remember

Never rely solely on a quick glance – give yourself time to take in the whole scene.

Observing traffic behind you

You should always know as much as you can about the traffic behind you.

Before you change direction or speed, you must know how your action will affect other road users.

You must also be aware of traffic likely to overtake.

Looking round on the move

Looking round on the move can be dangerous, particularly when driving at high speeds. In the time you take to look round, you lose touch with what's happening in front.

Remember that a vehicle travelling at 70 mph covers about 30 metres (100 feet) per second. Even if it only takes half a second to look round, you will still have travelled 15 metres (50 feet).

Using the mirrors

Using your mirrors regularly and sensibly enables you to keep up-to-date with what's happening behind, *without* losing touch with what's going on in front. They must be clean and properly adjusted to give a clear view.

A quick sideways glance

A quick sideways glance is sometimes helpful. For example, to check your blind spot

- before you change lanes on a motorway or dual carriageway
- where traffic is merging from the left or right.

When should you use your mirrors?

Well **before** you signal your intention or make any manoeuvre. For example, before

- moving off
- changing direction
- turning right or left
- overtaking
- changing lanes
- slowing or stopping
- opening a car door.

Just looking is not enough!

You must act sensibly on what you see, and take note of the speed, behaviour and possible intentions of traffic behind.

Another driver's blind spot

Try to avoid driving in another driver's blind spot.

Approaching green traffic lights

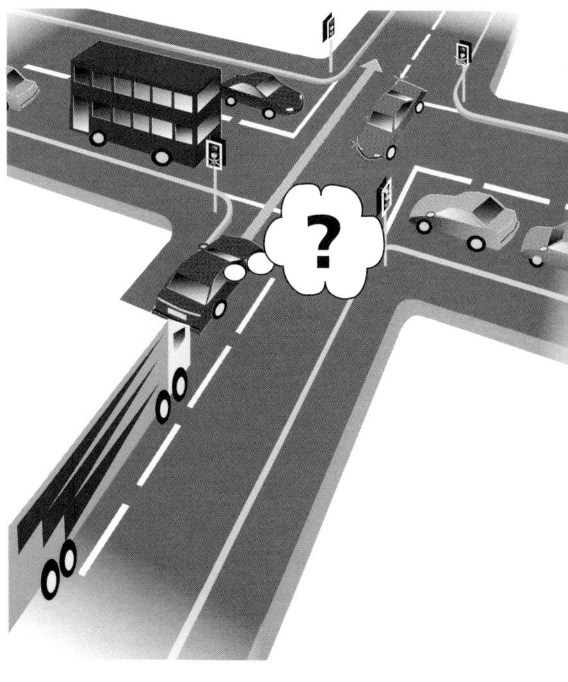

Ask yourself

- How long have they been on green?
- Are there many vehicles already waiting at either side of the junction?

  If there's a queue, the lights are probably about to change.
- Do I have time to stop?
- Can the vehicle behind me stop?

  If it's a large goods vehicle, it might need a greater distance to pull up.

Don't

- try to beat the traffic signals by accelerating
- leave it until the last moment to brake. Remember, harsh braking causes skids.

Traffic signals not working

Where traffic signals are not working, treat the situation as you would an unmarked junction and *proceed with great care.*

Remember

Another driver might anticipate the change of signals by accelerating away while the lights are still showing red-and-amber.

A combination of these actions by drivers often results in a collision that could be avoided.

Signalling

Signal to warn others of your intention and help other road users.

Road users include

- drivers of following and oncoming vehicles
- motorcyclists
- cyclists
- pedestrians
- crossing supervisors
- police directing traffic
- horse riders.

Signal clearly and in good time!

Give only the signals illustrated in *The Highway Code*.

Direction indicator signals

Help other road users to understand your intention by

- signalling in good time so that they have time to see and react to your signal
- positioning yourself correctly and in good time for the manoeuvre you intend to make.

Conflicting signals

A signal with the left indicator means 'I am going to turn left' OR 'I am going to stop on the left'.

Avoid using your left indicator before a left-hand junction if you intend to stop on the left just *after* the junction.

A driver waiting at that junction might think you're turning left and drive out into your path.

- Wait until you've passed the junction, then indicate that you intend to stop.
- Reduce speed by braking gently, so that your brake light warns following drivers.

On the other hand, if you're waiting to emerge, make sure that a vehicle which seems to be indicating its intention to turn left *is* actually turning left into your road.

You might drive into its path.

Remember that roundabouts often have several lanes of traffic with vehicles changing speed and direction. It's important that you give any signals correctly and in good time.

Buses and coaches

- Look well ahead when there are buses and coaches at a bus stop. Watch for a signal that the bus is about to move out.
- If you can do so safely, give way to them. You will often receive a wave or thumbs-up sign in acknowledgement.

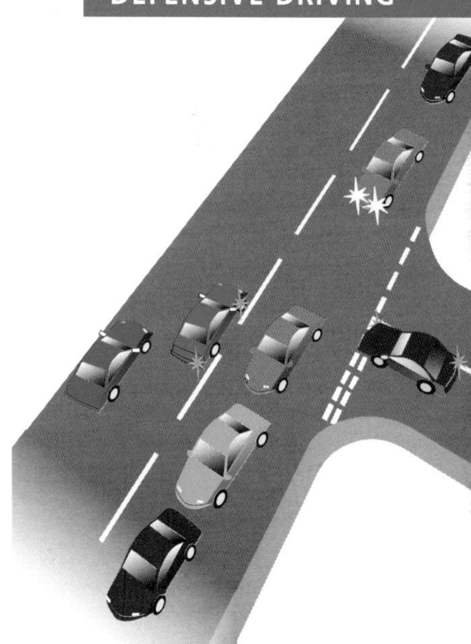

Warning signals

Flashing with headlights

Use only as an alternative to the horn to remind others that you're there.

Assume that other drivers mean the same.

Don't flash at anyone to go ahead or turn!

If someone flashes their headlights at you

Before you act on the signal, make sure

- you understand what they mean
- it's *you* they're signalling to.

Never assume it's a signal to proceed.

Ask yourself

- What's the other driver trying to tell me: 'stop', 'go', 'turn','thank you'?
- If I move, will it be safe?
- Is the signal intended for me or for another road user?
- Am I causing a hold-up by staying where I am?
- Is the other driver really signalling, or were those headlights flashed accidentally?

The consequences rest with you.

On motorways and dual-carriageways

If you think a warning is necessary, flashing headlights is usually better than using your horn.

Be alert for such warnings from other drivers.

If a driver behind starts flashing the headlights and driving dangerously close

- stay calm
- don't be intimidated

Only move back to the left as soon as there's a safe gap and you have checked you can do so without cutting in on vehicles in the left-hand lane.

Remember

Moving off safely and changing course is your responsibility.

There's no official meaning given to the flashing of headlights, apart from letting other road users know you're there – the same as using the horn.

Act sensibly.

The horn

There are few situations when you'll need to use the horn.

Using the horn doesn't

- give you the right of way
- relieve you of your responsibility to drive safely.

Sound it only if

- you think someone may not have seen you
- you want to warn of your presence, for example at blind bends or junctions.

Never use your horn as a rebuke or to attract someones attention.

Don't use your horn

- when stationary, unless it's necessary to warn a moving vehicle
- at night (11.30 pm – 7.00 am) in a built up area, unless you're stationary and a moving vehicle poses a danger.

Remember

- Avoid using a long blast on the horn which can alarm pedestrians.
- If the pedestrian doesn't react to a short signal on the horn, it could mean they're deaf.

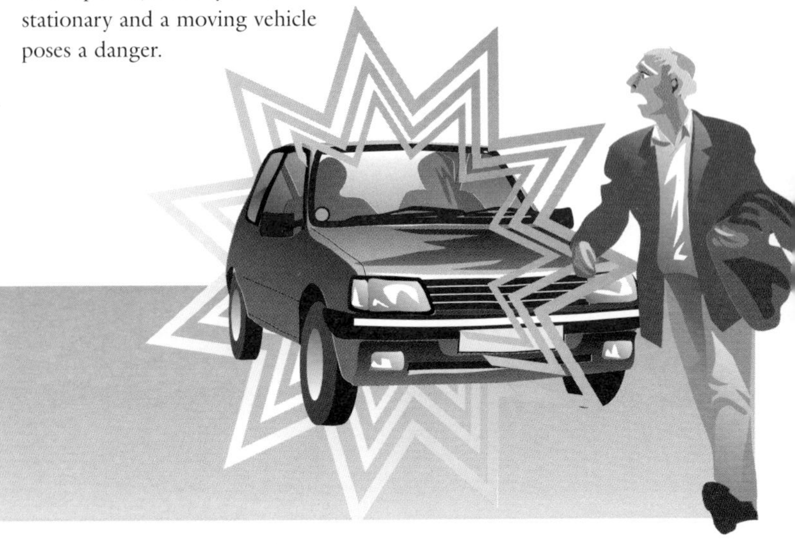

Hazards

A hazard is any situation which could involve adjusting speed or changing course. To identify a hazard, you must look well ahead for

- road signs
- changes in road conditions
- parked vehicles
- junctions
- cyclists
- motorcyclists
- pedestrians
- horse riders
- animals, particularly dogs off the lead.

Remember, as soon as you've recognised a hazard, you must use the mirrors to assess

- how other road users will affect your planning
- how your actions will affect following traffic.

Allowing time and space

Always leave yourself enough time and space to cope with what's ahead.

- Keep your eyes moving.
- Look well ahead, in the far and near distance, especially in town where things change quickly.
- Check regularly on what's following you.
- Watch for clues about what's going to happen next.

For example, a parked car could spell danger if the driver or a passenger is sitting in it, or you see vapour from the exhaust in cold weather.

Remember that

- a door might open suddenly
- the car might pull out without warning.

If you can see underneath a parked vehicle, and you can see feet at the other side, a pedestrian might appear suddenly.

Effective observation and anticipation is your main defence.

Separation distances Always keep a good separation distance between you and the vehicle in front.

Leave a gap of at least one metre or yard for each mph of your speed – use the two second rule.

In bad conditions, leave at least double the distance or a four second time gap.

Tailgating When a vehicle behind is too close to you, ease off very gradually and increase the gap between you and the vehicle in front.

Large vehicles Take extra care when following large vehicles, especially at roundabouts, junctions, entrances, etc.

The driver might well have to take a course that seems incorrect to you. For example, moving out to the right before turning left.

Keep well back from any large vehicles that are in the process of manoeuvring to the left or right.

Don't get caught out by trying to pass on the left.

Remember

The driver might not be able to see you in the mirrors.

Narrow roads with passing places

On single track roads, if you see an oncoming vehicle

- pull into the passing place if it's on the left
- wait opposite to it if the passing place is on the right-hand side of the road.

Look well ahead and be prepared to stop.

If your view ahead is restricted by hedges or bends, reduce speed and take extra care.

If another driver wishes to overtake, use the passing place to allow them to do so.

Recognising hazards

Events can happen at the same time, or in quick succession.

In the illustration, the driver must pull out to pass the stationary van, but

- Is the blue car really going to turn left? The driver might have forgotten to cancel the indicator from a previous turn.
- If the blue car does turn, will the pedestrian decide to cross?
- When will the driver see the red car, which may want to turn left?

If you're travelling too fast, you're not likely to be able to cope with all those events at once.

So, other road users, who might not be doing anything wrong, can turn a straightforward piece of driving into a hazardous situation.

The action you need to take will vary from one hazard to another. Any action which involves a change of speed or course is called a manoeuvre.

A manoeuvre can vary from slowing slightly to turning on a very busy road.

Remember

The defensive driver is always

- travelling at the correct speed for the road and traffic conditions
- in the right gear
- in the correct position
- anticipating and prepared for the next change in the traffic situation.

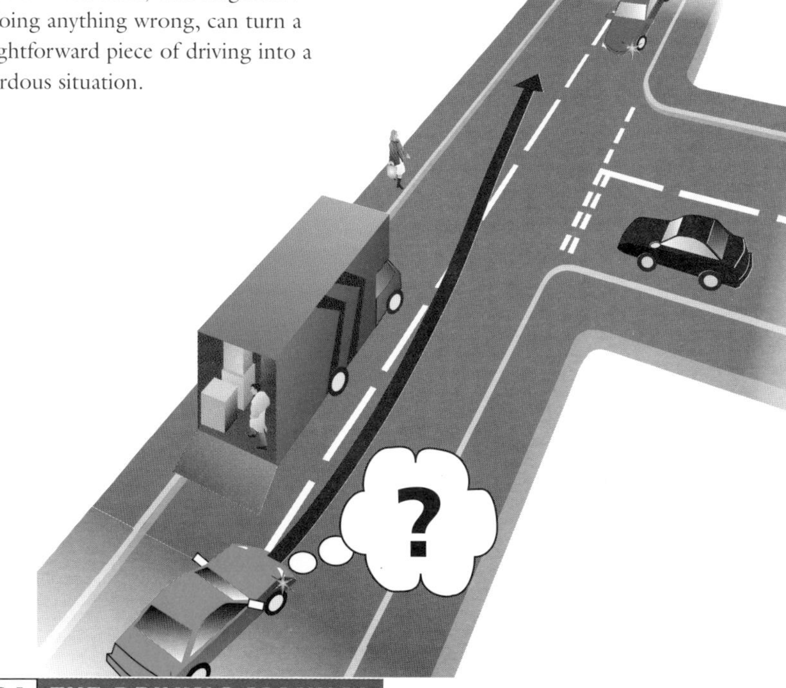

Approaching any hazard

Mirror(s) – Signal – Manoeuvre (MSM)

Follow this routine every time you recognise a hazard.

Manoeuvre Carry out the manoeuvre if it's still safe to do so.

Manoeuvring has three phases, Position–Speed –Look (PSL)

Signal If necessary, signal your intention to change course or slow down.

Signal clearly and in good time.

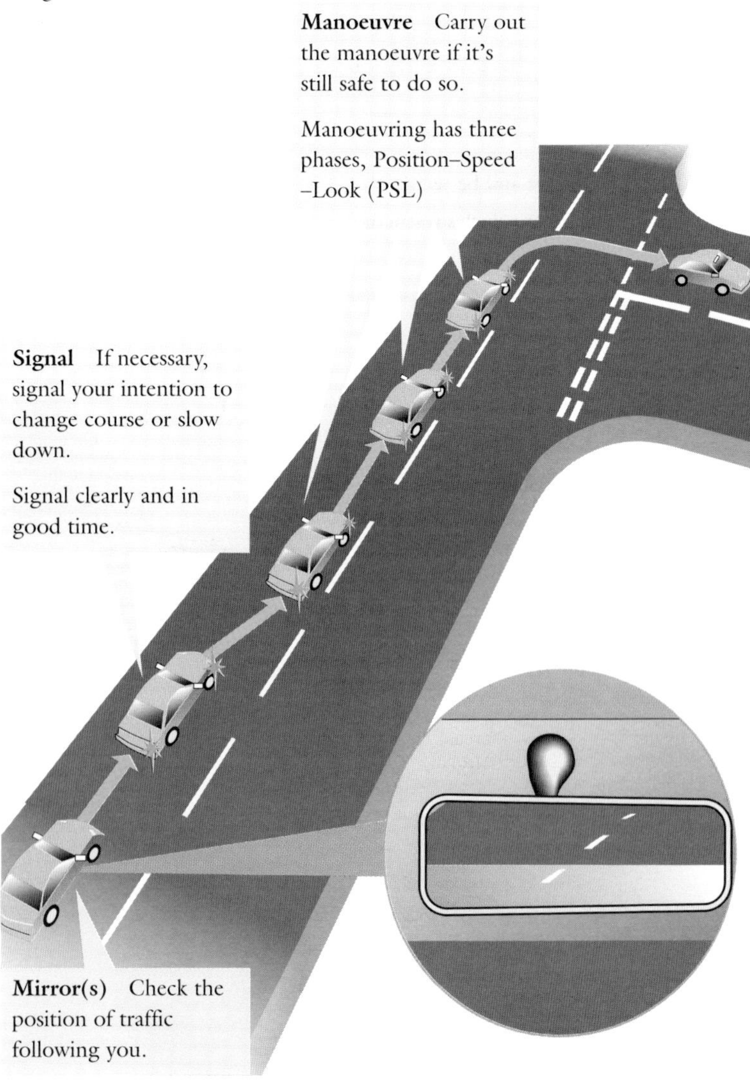

Mirror(s) Check the position of traffic following you.

Position – Speed – Look (PSL)

Positioning Get into correct position in good time to negotiate the hazard. This helps other road users to see what you intend to do.

It helps them anticipate.

Positioning yourself too late can be dangerous.

Ask yourself

- Can I see and be seen?
- Are other vehicles restricting my course of action?
- Have I enough room to get out of any difficulties?

Avoid cutting in front of other drivers or riders.

If lanes are closed or narrow because of roadworks, move into the correct lane in good time.

- Don't wait until the last minute.
- Don't use the situation to overtake and squeeze in later on.
- You'll only increase the frustration of drivers already waiting.

Speed Ask yourself

- Could I stop in time if the vehicle in front suddenly brakes sharply?
- Am I going too fast for the road conditions?
- Am I in the right gear needed to keep control?

Be prepared to slow down as you approach a hazard.

Always be ready to stop.

Look Keep looking ahead to assess all possible dangers.
This is particularly important if the hazard is at a junction.

Look in all directions, even if you're not turning.

If you're joining a road, keep looking as you turn from one road to the other.

Watch out for

- traffic turning across your path
- pedestrians.

Speed limits

40

Don't try to enforce the speed limit by blocking the progress of other vehicles.

It's not your job.

Allow vehicles travelling faster to overtake – even if they're breaking the speed limit.

It's their risk.

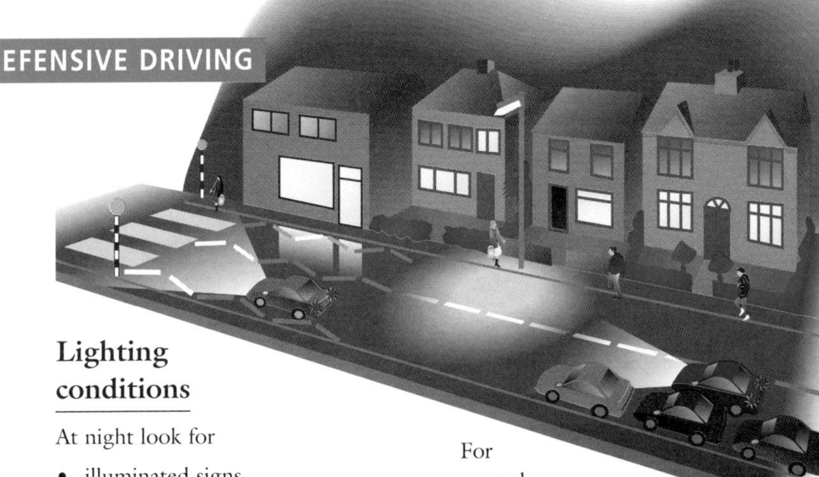

Lighting conditions

At night look for

- illuminated signs
- reflective signs
- reflectors between white lines
- the glow of vehicle headlights on trees and buildings indicating a corner or junction.

Be careful

- It can be difficult to judge distances and speed from headlights.
- Bright lights on some vehicles make it difficult to see less bright lights, such as those of cyclists or low-powered motorcycles.
- Don't let shop and advertising signs distract you. Keep a good lookout for pedestrian crossings, traffic lights, and other road users.

Wet roads

- increase distracting reflected light
- make unlit objects even less visible.

Rain

Rain makes headlights less effective at night.

On dark and poorly lit roads, slow down and watch for unlit objects. For example, builders' skips or parked cars.

Drive more slowly and carefully in rain.

Match your speed to the conditions.

Road surfaces

Stay alert to the road surface ahead because you might have to brake.

Ask yourself

- Is the road wet or slippery?
- Is it a good surface to brake on?

If the surface is wet, allow more time to stop.

A wet road means

- less efficient braking
- a longer distance needed to stop
- a greater risk of skidding.

Drive more slowly on a wet road and take extra care.

Other road users

Cyclists

Make allowances for cyclists. They have every right to be on the road. Allow them plenty of room.

The younger the cyclist, the more you must watch them.

Cyclists might

- glance round, showing they might be about to move out or turn
- make sudden sideways movements into your path
- be carrying light but bulky objects which may affect their control and balance
- weave about, slow down, or stop and get off on a hill
- swerve round potholes or inspection covers
- have problems in bad weather, particularly strong crosswinds
- find difficulties where rails are laid in the road and on other poor road surfaces (see Part Six, pages 120–121).

Motorcyclists

Spare a thought for motorcyclists.

Much of what has been said about cyclists applies also to motorcyclists. They are very vulnerable.

Accidents happen because many drivers fail to notice motorcyclists, particularly at junctions.

Remember

Motorcyclists and cyclists are harder to see than other vehicles and are exposed to

- bad weather
- slippery roads
- uneven surfaces.

Look out for them, especially at junctions.

Think once.

Think twice.

Think Bike!

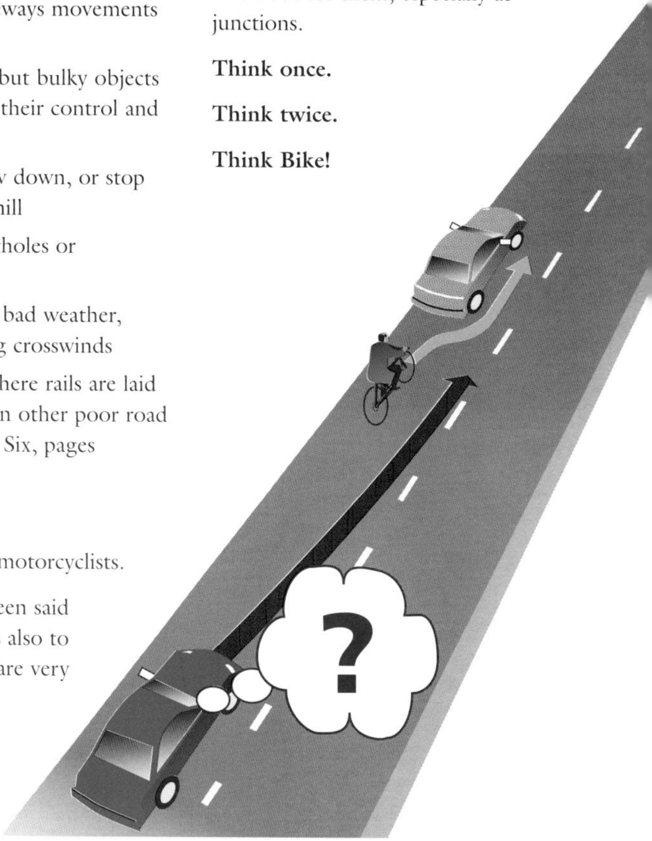

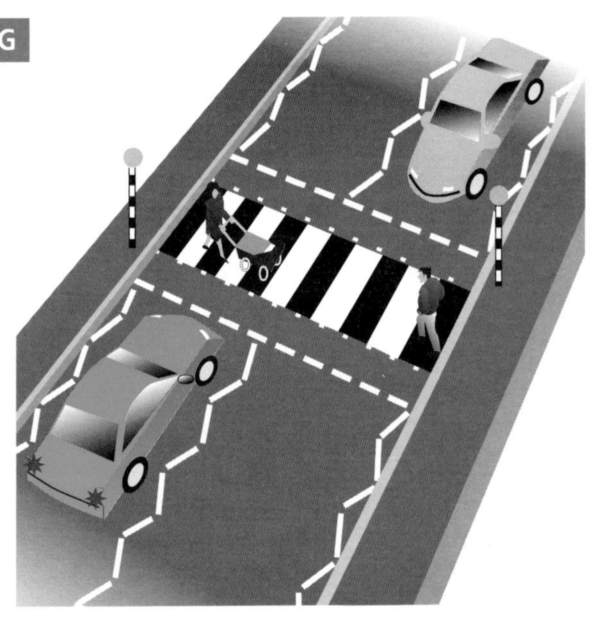

Pedestrians

When turning from one road to another

- always look out for pedestrians
- give way to any who are crossing.

At pedestrian crossings

Never overtake on the approach to pedestrian crossings.

Elderly persons

Several factors make an elderly person more vulnerable.

Poor eyesight or hearing might prevent them from realising the dangers of approaching traffic.

They might not be able to judge the speed of approaching traffic when crossing the road. Even when they do realise the danger, they could be unable to move quickly, or become flustered.

Disabled pedestrians

Take special care with the visually handicapped or disabled.

Remember that a person with hearing difficulty is not easy to identify.

Children

Take extra care where children might be about, particularly in residential areas and near schools and parks.

Always anticipate that a school crossing warden will need to choose a safe opportunity to escort children across a busy road.

Children are impulsive and often unpredictable. Therefore, drive slowly in narrow roads where parked cars obscure your view.

Don't exceed 20 mph.

Look out for parked ice cream vans. Children are more interested in ice cream than they are in traffic.

Animals

Animals are easily frightened by noise and vehicles coming close to them.

You should drive

- slowly and quietly; don't sound the horn
- keep engine speed low; don't rev your engine.

Give animals as much room as possible.

Persons in charge of animals

If someone in charge of animals signals to you to stop, do so and switch off your engine.

Guide dogs

A guide dog for a visually handicapped person usually has a distinctive loop type of harness. Remember, the dog is trained to wait if there's a vehicle nearby.

For a person with hearing difficulty, the guide dog usually has a distinctive orange lead and collar.

Take extra care if a pedestrian fails to look your way as you approach, especially in bad weather.

Horses

Be particularly careful when approaching horses, especially those ridden by children.

Watch the behaviour of the horses. The riders might be having difficulty controlling them.

Take special care when meeting what appears to be a riding-school group. Many of the riders might not be experienced.

Remember

Always think of the other road user, not just of yourself.

Motorways differ from ordinary roads in that they're designed to help traffic travel faster and in greater safety. This puts greater demands on both driver and vehicle.

Motorways are statistically safer than other roads in relation to the *number* of accidents occurring. However, when they do happen, motorway accidents occur at higher speed and involve more vehicles. As a result, injuries are usually more serious – often with greater loss of life.

Traffic travelling faster means that conditions change more rapidly. You need to be alert, rested, and have total concentration.

This section deals with the special skills you need to drive safely on a motorway, and the situations you're likely to meet.

The topics covered

- Driving on motorways
- Getting on to a motorway
- Lane discipline
- Braking
- Overtaking
- Leaving a motorway
- Motorway weather conditions
- Motorway signs and signals
- Stopping on motorways
- Motorways at night
- Contraflow systems
- The novice driver

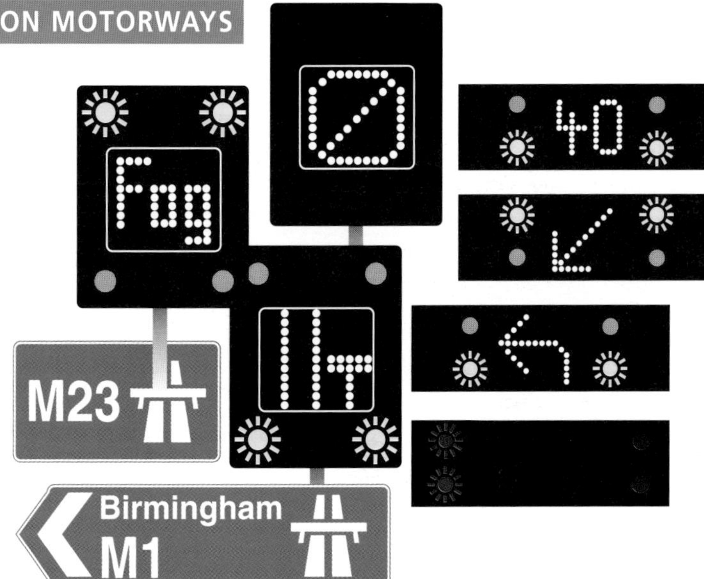

Driving on motorways

- You must hold a Full Driving Licence for the class of vehicle you're driving.
- You should have a thorough knowledge of the sections of *The Highway Code* dealing with motorways.
- You need to know and understand motorway warning signs and signals.
- You need to be fit and alert to drive anywhere, but particularly on motorways. Never use the motorway if you feel tired or unwell.
- Parking is forbidden except at service areas. If you need rest, you'll sometimes have to travel long distances before an exit or a service area. Remember, it's an offence to stop on the hard shoulder, an exit or a slip road, unless in an emergency

Ventilation

Make sure your vehicle is well ventilated.

Use whatever ventilation you can.

If your journey seems monotonous and you feel drowsy, open a window until you reach a service area.

Plan enough rest stops, especially at night.

The vehicle on the motorway

You must

- only drive a vehicle which is allowed on a motorway
- make sure your vehicle is safe and in good working order.

Motorways must not be used by

- pedestrians
- cyclists
- horse riders
- motorcycles under 50cc
- learner drivers
- certain slow-moving vehicles with oversized loads – except with special permission
- invalid carriages less than 254kg unladen weight
- agricultural vehicles and animals.

You must not pick up or set down anyone on any part of a motorway, including a slip road.

Before you use the motorway

High speeds and long distances increase the risk of mechanical failure. You should carry out the following checks on your vehicle.

- Tyres. They must be in good condition and with the right pressure. Consider the sustained high speeds and any additional load. Follow the guidance given in the owner's handbook.
- Instruments. Make sure there are no faults.
- Warning lights. Make sure each is working correctly.
- Mirrors. Make sure they are clean and correctly positioned.
- Windscreen and windows. Make sure they are clean.
- Top up the reservoir for the windscreen washers, and the rear window washer, if your vehicle has one.
- Lights and indicators. Make sure they are all working correctly.

Also make sure that

- your brakes can stop you safely
- your steering is in good order.

For safety, convenience and good vehicle care you should also check the following items.

- Fuel. Make sure you have enough fuel to avoid running out between service areas.
- Oil. High speeds may mean your engine uses oil faster. Running out can be dangerous and costly.
- Water. Higher speeds can mean a warmer engine, especially in traffic tailbacks in hot weather.

Make sure your load is secure

Check that everything carried on your vehicle or trailer is safe and secure.

If anything should fall from your vehicle or from another, stop on the hard shoulder, use the emergency telephone to inform the police.

Never try to retrieve it yourself.

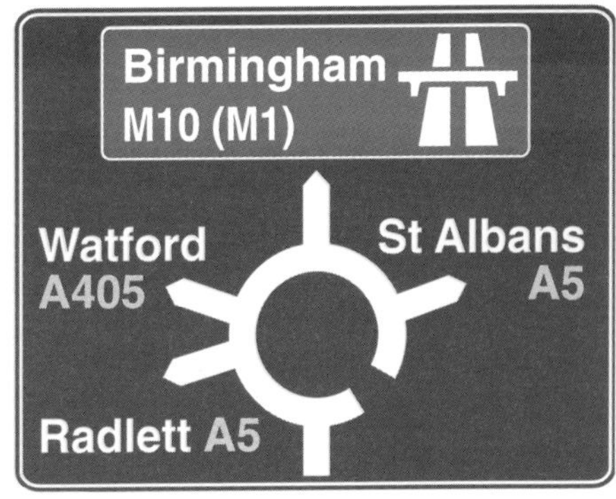

Getting on to a motorway

You can get on to a motorway in three ways.

- A main road becoming a motorway. This is indicated by a specially worded sign.
- Joining at any entry point, by a slip road leading into an acceleration lane.
- At a roundabout.

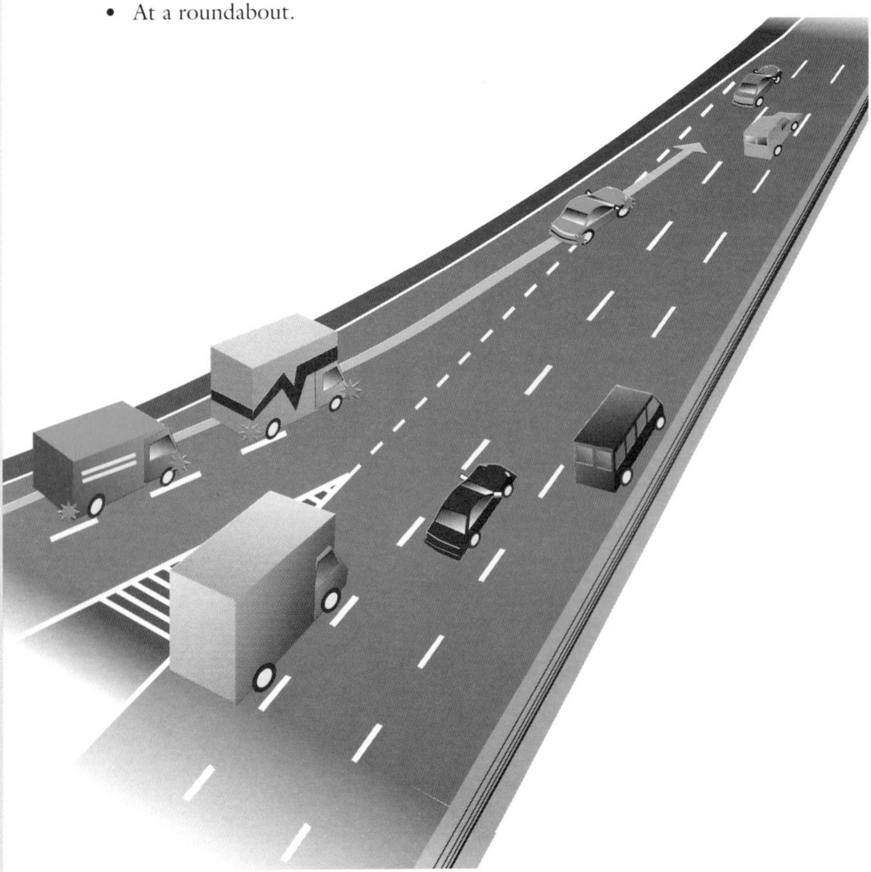

Joining a motorway

At an entry point where the slip road leads to an acceleration lane you can see the motorway and adjust your speed to that of the traffic already on the motorway before joining it.

Giving way

You MUST always give way to traffic already on the motorway.

Join where there's a suitable gap in the left-hand lane.*

Use the MSM/PSL routine.

A quick sideways glance might be necessary to verify the position of other vehicles. Try to avoid stopping at the end of the acceleration lane.

You must not

- force your way into the traffic stream
- drive along the hard shoulder.

Once you've joined the motorway, keep in the left-hand lane* until you've had time to judge and adjust to the faster speed of the moving traffic.

*In a very few cases, the lane merges from the right. Take extra care when joining or meeting traffic at these locations.

Always

- indicate your intention to join the motorway
- make sure you can be seen
- assess the speed of the traffic on the motorway before you try to merge in.

When other vehicles join the motorway

After you pass the exit, there's usually an entrance where other vehicles can join.

- Don't try to race them while they're in the acceleration lane.
- Look well ahead if there are several vehicles joining the motorway – be prepared to adjust your speed.
- If it's safe, move to another lane to make it easier for joining traffic to merge.

Seeing and being seen

Make sure you start out with clean mirrors, windscreen and windows.

Use your washers, wipers and demisters whenever necessary to ensure you can see clearly.

You need to use your mirrors frequently and much earlier. Because of the higher speeds on motorways, they are even more important

Always try to avoid staying where you might be in another vehicle's blind spot.

Effective observation

Keep your eyes moving between the road ahead and your mirrors, so that you always know what's happening all around you.

Continually re-assess the movement of the vehicles

- directly ahead (in the near and far distance)
- alongside you
- behind you.

At high speeds, situations change rapidly. Effective observation helps you prepare for any sudden developments.

For example, an increase in the number of vehicles ahead could mean that traffic is slowing down and 'bunching', or a flashing breakdown light will warn you to slow down until you're sure of what's happening.

If you see serious congestion ahead, you can use your hazard warning lights briefly to alert drivers behind you. This can reduce the risk of rear-end collisions, especially in bad weather.

Being seen on a motorway

Because of the higher speeds, your vehicle must be seen much earlier on a motorway than on an ordinary road.

Poor daylight In poor daylight, you should use your headlights.

In fog, where visibility drops below 100 metres (110 yards), switch on your rear fog-lights. On most vehicles, these will only work if the headlights are already on dip.

Switch them off when visibility improves. They're misleading and can dazzle other drivers in clear weather. They also make the brake lights less conspicuous.

Headlight flashing The level of noise is higher on a motorway, particularly in wet weather, and other road users may not be able to hear your horn.

If you think a warning is necessary, flash your headlights instead.

Watch out for such warnings intended for you.

Keeping your distance

The faster the traffic, the more time and space you need for EVERY driving action.

You must

- give yourself greater margins than on ordinary roads
- make sure there's enough space between you and the vehicle ahead.

How big a gap?

Leave a gap of at least one metre or yard for each mph of your speed. A useful method of judging this is to use the two second rule described overleaf.

Leave at least double the space if the road is wet or slippery.

In extremely poor weather, you'll need up to ten times the stopping distance that you do for dry conditions.

Tailgating

This is a common and very dangerous practice, especially on motorways.

Vehicles often travel with as little as one car length between them at speeds of up to 70 mph.

It's often the cause of serious accidents on motorways.

The two second rule

One way of checking if you're keeping the correct separation distance is to keep at least two seconds behind the vehicle in front.

- Pick an object some distance ahead, for example an emergency telephone post, or a bridge.
- As the vehicle in front passes it, begin to say, 'Only a fool breaks the two second rule'.

If you pass the object before you finish saying it, you're too close. Drop back and try the test again.

This rule is reinforced on some motorways where there are chevrons painted on the carriageway.

Keep at least two chevrons between you and the vehicle in front.

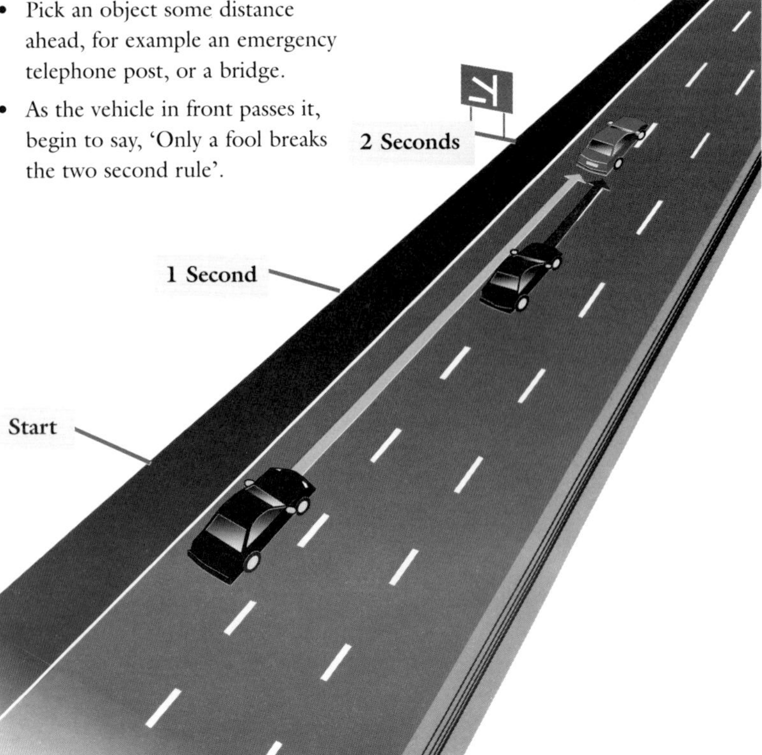

Lane discipline

Lane discipline is vitally important on motorways. You should normally drive in the left-hand lane.

Traffic travels much faster over longer distances, all in the same direction.

There's less reason to slow down, because usually there are no

- ordinary junctions
- sharp bends*
- roundabouts*
- steep hills
- traffic lights.

Slow-moving vehicles are generally forbidden.

*Some motorway links, where motorway regulations also apply, have roundabouts and sharp bends.

MSM routine

Always use the MSM routine well before you intend to change lanes.

At higher speeds, you must start the routine much earlier.

Look and signal early. Remember how quickly vehicles might come up behind.

The sooner you indicate, the sooner other vehicles are warned of your movement. They'll expect a change in the traffic pattern and have time to prepare for it.

Changing lanes on a motorway

- Don't change lanes unless you need to.
- Keep your vehicle steady in the centre of the lane.
- Don't wander into another lane.

Two-lane discipline

On a two-lane motorway, the correct position for normal driving is in the left-hand lane.

The right-hand (offside) lane is for overtaking.

It's not 'the fast lane'.

Large goods vehicles are permitted to use either lane.

Three- or four-lane discipline

Because of the volume of traffic on three-lane motorways, many are being widened to four lanes in each direction.

Keep to the left-hand lane unless there are a great many slower vehicles ahead.

Avoid repeatedly changing lane – it's possible to stay in the second lane, BUT

- don't stay in the second lane longer than you have to
- remember, driver of large goods vehicles are not allowed to use the extreme right-hand lane for overtaking – don't block them

Don't stay in an overtaking lane longer than it takes you to move out, overtake and move in again safely.

Towing

If you're towing a caravan or trailer, you must not use the extreme right-hand lane unless one or more lanes are closed temporarily.

Crawler lanes

A steep hill on a motorway might have a crawler lane to avoid heavy vehicles slowing down the flow of traffic.

Braking

At motorway speeds braking must be

- unhurried
- progressive
- properly spread out.

Stay well clear

You must remember to leave plenty of space between yourself and the vehicle ahead for controlled braking.

Mirrors

Always check in your mirrors before you brake.

Drive defensively

- Anticipate problems; take avoiding action before they develop.
- Slow down in good time.
- Keep your distance from the vehicle ahead.

Never brake suddenly

Defensive driving will reduce the likelihood of having to do so.

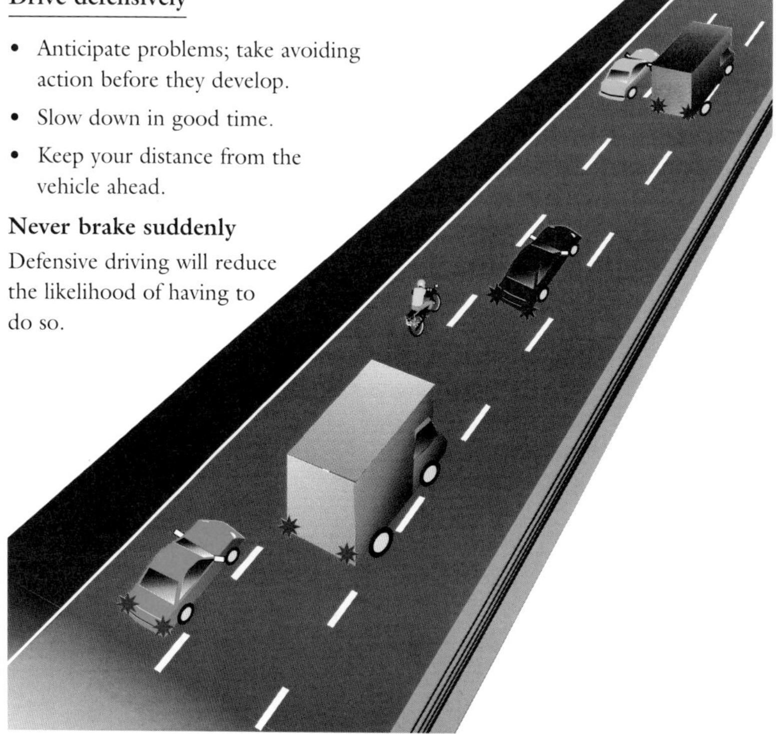

Overtaking

Leave a safe distance between you and the vehicle you intend to overtake.

Use the appropriate parts of the MSM/PSL routine, for example.

Mirror

Check behind to verify the speed, course and position of following traffic.

Position

Make sure you're well back from the vehicle you're going to overtake.

You should be able to move out smoothly to the right without making any sudden movements.

Speed

Make sure you're going fast enough or can accelerate quickly enough to overtake without blocking any vehicle coming up behind.

Look

Look ahead and use your mirrors.

Look to check if there's anything preventing you from overtaking safely. A lane closure, for example, or traffic coming up much faster in the right-hand lane.

Try to anticipate if the vehicle ahead will move out to overtake.

Note. A quick sideways glance into the blind area might sometimes be necessary before you change lanes.

Remember

- Look.
- Assess well ahead.
- Decide – don't rush.
- Act – only when you're sure it's safe.

Mirrors

You must use your mirrors regularly and sensibly.

Remember that vehicles coming up in the right-hand lane are likely to be moving faster than you are.

Watch for vehicles returning to the lane you intend to use.

You must signal well before you start to move out. This gives drivers behind you plenty of time to observe your actions and could influence any manoeuvres they're planning.

Pulling out

Check your mirrors again before pulling out smoothly into the overtaking lane. Overtake as quickly and safely as possible.

Never intimidate the driver ahead by repeatedly flashing your headlights and driving dangerously close behind.

Wait until the vehicle ahead can move safely to the left, then proceed.

Moving back left

Pass the vehicle and signal before moving back into the left as soon as you're sure it's safe to do so.

Don't cut in too soon in front of the vehicle you've just passed.

Look well ahead for any vehicles about to move out into the lane you intend to move into.

Allow plenty of room.

Make sure your indicator signal cancels.

Overtaking on the left

Never overtake on the left, unless

- the traffic is moving in queues

and

- the queue on your right is moving more slowly.

Drive defensively

Let faster traffic pass you.

If they're breaking the speed limit, let them take their reckless driving somewhere else.

Don't add to the danger by trying to enforce the legal speed limit. It's not your job!

Don't move to a lane on the left to overtake.

NEVER USE THE HARD SHOULDER TO OVERTAKE –

unless directed to do so by traffic signs at road works, or by police officers.

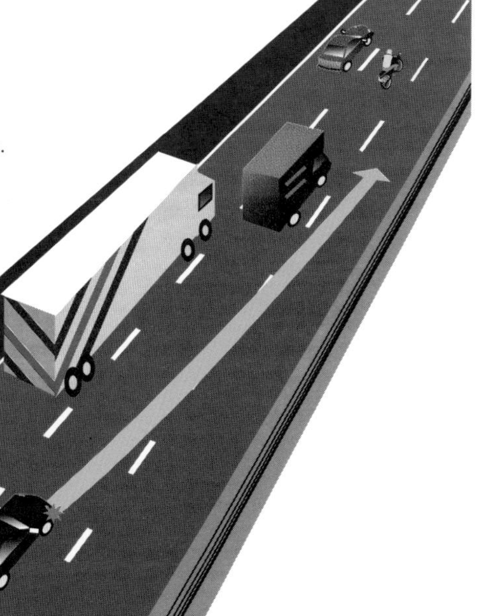

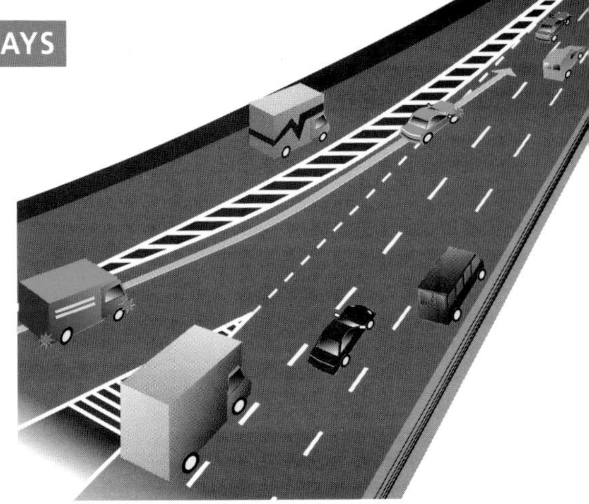

Changes in traffic conditions

Traffic conditions can vary as much on a motorway as on an ordinary road.

There can be rush hour traffic near cities, heavy traffic near road works, and constantly busy sections in other places.

These differences will have a greater effect on two-lane motorways.

Bear this in mind when making any decision about how much space to leave for manoeuvring.

Motorway interchanges

Where motorways merge or separate you might be required to change lanes, sometimes more than once.

Pay attention to the overhead direction signs and move into the correct lane in good time.

Where the hatch markings indicate splitter islands, stay in your lane.

Assess conditions well ahead and watch for other drivers changing lane.

Drive defensively

React to changes well in advance. Don't wait until you're *forced* to react.

Leaving a motorway

Unless you're going to the end of the motorway, you'll leave by moving left from the left-hand lane into the deceleration lane (extra lane) taking you to the slip road. Get into that lane in plenty of time.

Plan well ahead, particularly on three- or four-lane motorways.

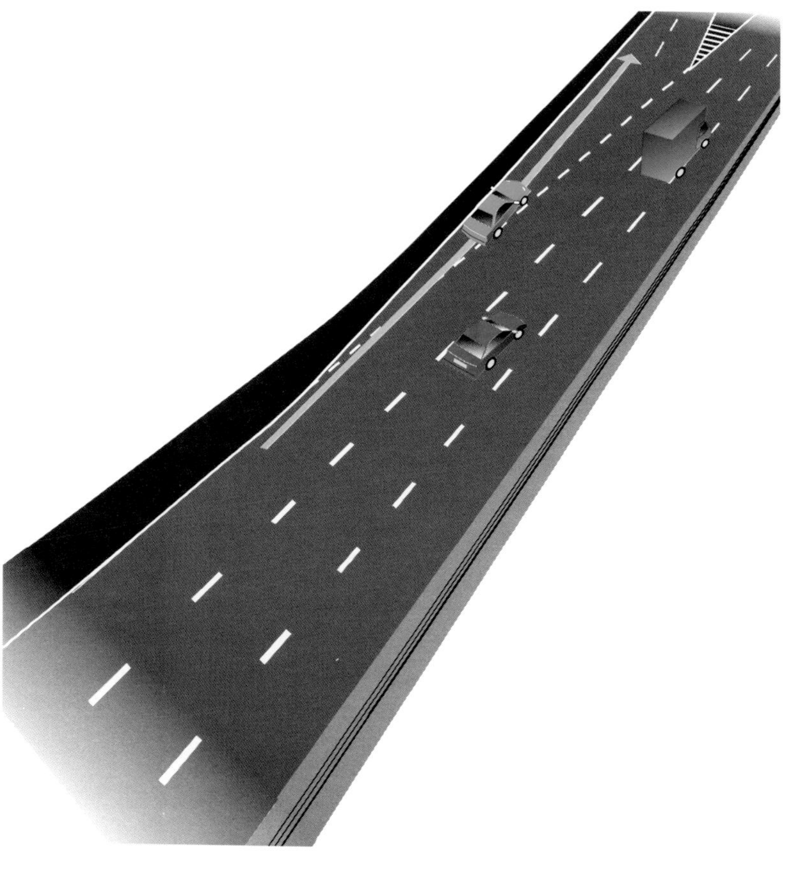

Road signs

Use the road signs and markers to help you time your exit and spread the use of your mirrors and indicators.

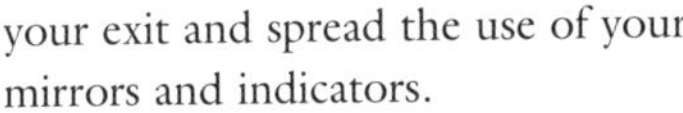

You'll have plenty of time to observe the signs and markers so there's no need to rush.

One mile before the exit

A junction sign with road numbers. Unless there are exits very close together.

A half mile before the exit

A sign with the names of places accessible from that exit.

From 270 metres (300 yards) before the exit

Countdown markers at 270 metres (300 yards), 180 metres (200 yards) and 90 metres (100 yards) before the start of the deceleration lane.

The hard shoulder is NOT an exit road, and you must avoid queuing on it.

Use your mirrors and signal in good time. Remember MSM/PSL.

Get into lane early, unless you're already in the left-hand lane.

On a three- or four-lane motorway, this could mean changing lanes more than once, and you must follow the MSM routine for each change of lane.

Don't cut straight across into the deceleration lane.

Don't move to the left more than one lane at a time.

Use your mirror and signal left in good time to move into the deceleration lane so you can slow down before joining the slip road.

If you miss your exit, carry on to the next exit.

Don't cut across at the last moment, especially from the second lane of a three- or four-lane motorway.

Occasionally, where motorways merge, there may be an exit just prior to the one you intend to take. In these cases, or where there are service areas near to exits, look well ahead for the advance warning signs.

Never

Drive on the white hatch-marked areas which divide the carriageway from the slip road.

End of motorway

There will be 'End of Motorway' signs at all exits. These also mean that the road you're joining will have different rules.

Remember to watch for any signs telling you what these are, particularly

- speed limits
- dual carriageway
- two-way traffic
- clearway
- motorway link road
- part-time traffic lights.

Speed when leaving a motorway

After driving at motorway speeds for some time, your judgement of speed will almost certainly be affected: 40 or 45 mph seems more like 20 mph.

- Adjust your driving to suit the new conditions.
- Check your speedometer. It will give you the accurate speed.

Reduce speed at first

For the sake of safety, reduce your speed until you're accustomed to the change of conditions.

It could take you time to adjust.

Motorway slip roads and link roads often have sharp curves which should be taken at much lower speeds.

Watch ahead for traffic queuing at a roundabout or traffic signals.

Remember the change in traffic conditions; watch for pedestrians, cyclists, etc.

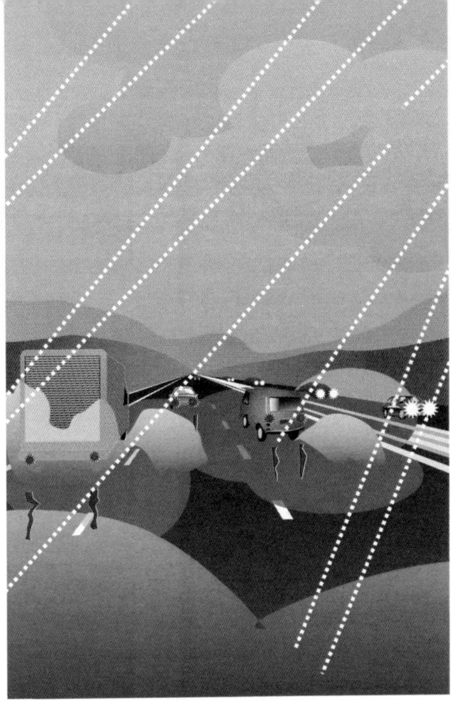

Motorway weather conditions

All that is said in the section on driving in bad weather is even more important on a motorway.

In the wet

Visibility can be made worse because at higher speeds vehicles, especially large ones, throw up more spray. So

- use your headlights to help other drivers see you. Don't use rear fog-lights unless the visibility is less than 100 metres
- always reduce your speed when conditions are poor. Driving is safer at lower speeds
- adjust your speed to suit the conditions and leave larger separation distances.

Ice or frost

If there's any danger of frost or ice, watch out for the way your steering feels.

Any steering lightness is a danger sign. A very gentle touch on your brakes to see their response could help you judge the road surface conditions.

Allow up to ten times the distance for braking.

Crosswinds

Wind is another motorway hazard.

Winds can affect your steering. If they're coming from the left on an exposed stretch of motorway, be especially careful.

A sudden gust as you pass a large vehicle, or come out from the shelter of a bridge or embankment, can send you swerving to the right.

In high wind, be prepared for drivers with high-sided vehicles, or those towing caravans, experiencing difficulties.

Motorcyclists are also often seriously affected by strong crosswinds. Allow for this when overtaking them.

Fog

IF THERE'S FOG ON THE MOTORWAY, YOU MUST BE ABLE TO STOP WELL WITHIN THE DISTANCE YOU CAN SEE TO BE CLEAR.

- USE DIPPED HEADLIGHTS.
- Check your mirrors and SLOW DOWN: fog affects both visibility and judgement of speed and distance.
- Check your speedometer and leave plenty of space between you and the vehicle ahead.

If a motorway warning sign shows 'FOG'

- be prepared
- reduce speed in good time.

Fog can drift quickly and is often patchy.

Multiple pile-ups don't just happen. They are caused by DRIVERS who are

- travelling too fast
- driving too close to the vehicle in front
- assuming there's nothing in the fog ahead
- ignoring the obvious!

Don't

Hang on to the rear lights of the vehicle ahead. You'll be too close to brake if it stops suddenly.

Do

Switch on your rear fog-lamps if visibility drops below 100 metres (110 yards).

Be prepared to leave the motorway.

Be on the alert for accidents ahead.

Watch out for emergency vehicles coming up behind, possibly on the hard shoulder.

Motorway signals and signs

Motorway signs tend to be much larger than ordinary road signs, and can be seen from further away.

This helps you plan well ahead.

Signals

Signal lights will warn of dangers ahead, such as

- accidents
- fog
- danger of icy roads.

Look out for flashing amber lights and signs either on the central reserve or overhead. These warn you of

- lane closures
- speed limits
- roadworks
- other hazards.

Red lights

Some signs have flashing red lights as well.

Red lights warn you that you must not go beyond the red light in that lane.

- Start to slow down in good time.
- Be ready to change lanes.

If the red light flashes on a slip road, you must not enter it.

If a red 'X' shows, do not go beyond the signal in that lane.

Flashing amber lights

These warn of danger and might show a temporary advisory speed limit.

- Slow down to the speed limit.
- Be ready to slow down still more to pass the obstacle or danger.
- Look out for police signs.
- Don't speed up until you see the sign ending the temporary restriction (or no more flashing amber lights).

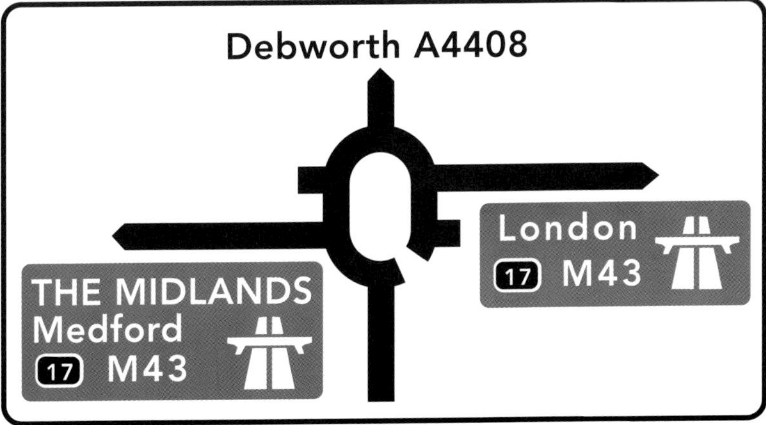

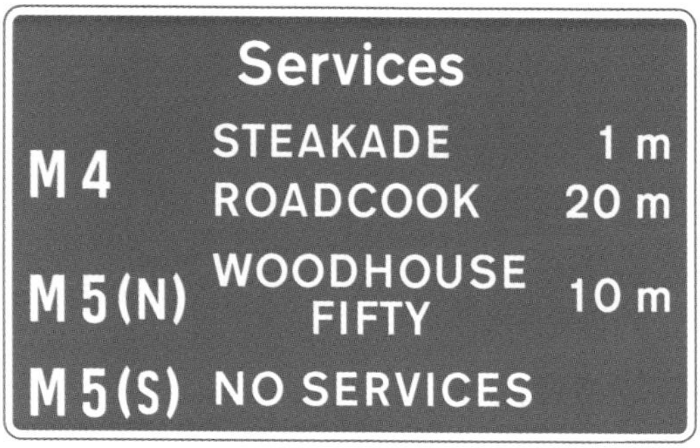

Speed Limits

- Road works might have circular signs indicating mandatory maximum speed limits.

  You MUST obey these signs. If you don't, you risk prosecution.
- Black and white rectangular signs recommend maximum speed limits which you should observe.

Services
M 4 STEAKADE 1 m
ROADCOOK 20 m
M 5(N) WOODHOUSE FIFTY 10 m
M 5(S) NO SERVICES

Signs

Direction signs from ordinary roads to the motorway have white lettering and figures on a blue panel, often bordered in white.

These signs may

- stand alone
- be included in other larger signs of various colours.

Types of sign

- Advance direction signs.
- Countdown markers.
- Signs giving information about service areas.
- Signs on motorways which have a brown background indicate tourist attractions which can be reached by leaving at the next exit.

All these signs are very much larger than those on ordinary roads.

You need to be able to see them from a distance – a good reminder that you must leave more room for error on motorways.

Each junction has an identifying number which corresponds with current road maps, to help you plan your route and know where you need to leave the motorway.

Stopping on motorways

You must only stop on motorways if

- the red lights tell you to
- it's an emergency
- it will prevent an accident
- police or road signs or signals indicate you must.

If you have to stop on the carriageway or hard shoulder, switch on your hazard warning lights to warn following traffic.

Remember to switch them off before you move away.

Never leave them on when you're moving, except briefly to warn drivers behind of a traffic tailback ahead.

Accidents

It only takes a few seconds inattention for a multiple accident to occur.

If you come across an accident, concentrate on your driving. 'Rubber-necking' often causes further accidents.

The hard shoulder

Use the hard shoulder only in an emergency.

Breakdowns

If you break down, pull off onto the hard shoulder.

If you can, try to stop near an emergency telephone. They're about a mile apart.

Steer your vehicle onto the hard shoulder as safely as possible, and as far to the left as you can, away from traffic.

If the breakdown affects your control of the car

- try to keep in a straight line by holding the steering wheel firmly
- avoid braking severely
- steer gently on to the hard shoulder as you lose speed.

When you stop

- Switch on your hazard warning lights.
- Make sure your sidelights are on in poor visibility or at night.
- Don't open the offside doors.
- Warn your passengers of the dangers of passing vehicles.
- Keep animals inside.
- With your passengers, leave the vehicle by the nearside door, away from the traffic.
- Ask your passengers to wait near the vehicle, but on the embankment away from the hard shoulder.
- Place an advance warning triangle at least 150 metres (160 yards) back from your vehicle. Don't forget it when you resume your journey.

Never

Attempt even simple repairs on the motorway.

Emergency telephones

Police-controlled emergency telephones are on most stretches of motorway at one mile intervals.

Look for a telephone symbol and arrow on marker posts 100 metres (110 yards) apart along the hard shoulder.

The arrow directs you to the nearest phone on your side. Never cross an exit or entry slip road to reach a phone.

Reaching a phone

Lock all doors, except the front passenger door.

With central locking, leave all doors unlocked, unless you're alone and the telephone is a long distance away.

Walk to the telephone. Keep on the inside of the hard shoulder.

Never

Cross the carriageway to use a phone, or for any other purpose.

Using the emergency phone

Face oncoming traffic when you use an emergency phone.

If you're a woman travelling alone, make this clear to the operator.

Waiting for the emergency services

Wait on the bank near your vehicle, so you can see the emergency services arriving.

Don't wait in your vehicle unless another vehicle pulls up near you, and you feel at risk. If anyone approaches

- get into the vehicle
- lock ALL the doors
- lower the window slightly
- speak through a small gap

Then

- ask for identity
- tell them that the police have been told and the emergency services are coming.

A person claiming to be from the emergency services should have

- an identity card
- your details: your name and information about the breakdown.

Leave your vehicle again as soon as you feel the danger has passed.

To rejoin the carriageway

From the hard shoulder, use a stretch of the hard shoulder to gain speed and wait for a safe gap in traffic before moving into the left-hand lane.

Don't try to move out from behind another vehicle or force your way into the stream of traffic.

Remember

Many motorway deaths are caused by vehicles driving into people on the hard shoulder.

When you're on the hard shoulder, you're five times more likely to be injured by motorway traffic than suffer personal attack.

Disabled drivers

You should display a HELP pennant which will alert police patrols.

Don't try to reach an emergency telephone, if you can't stop near one.

Special 'emergency only' car phones have been developed to assist rescue.

Parking

Service areas are the only parking places provided.

To reach the services, follow the same procedure as for a motorway exit.

Once off the motorway, slow down and be aware that a low speed will feel very different after motorway driving. Watch out for sharp turns into car parking areas.

Other drivers could fail to reduce their speed sufficiently. Keep children and animals well under control.

When you leave your vehicle, remember to lock it. Don't leave valuables (cameras, etc.) on view. Be a careful pedestrian.

To rejoin the motorway, follow the same procedure as when joining the motorway at any entrance.

Motorways at night

Part Thirteen deals in general with driving at night and much of it applies to motorway driving.

Take special note of 'Your eyes at night' on page 265.

Remember, if you've just left a well-lit service area, give your eyes time to adjust to the darkness.

Use your headlights

Always use your headlights, even on lighted motorways.

Use dipped beam if you're likely to dazzle drivers ahead or oncoming drivers, particularly on a left-hand curve.

If you're dazzled

You may have to slow down, but don't brake too hard. Remember, there might be a vehicle behind.

Judging speed

It's harder to judge speed and distance both on a motorway and at night.

If you change lanes to overtake, or to leave the motorway, use your indicators earlier and give yourself even more time.

Reflective studs on motorways

- Red: between hard shoulder and carriageway.
- White: lane separation.
- Amber: between edge of carriageway and central reserve.
- Green: slip road exit and entrances.
- Bright green/yellow: contraflow systems and road works.

Contraflow systems

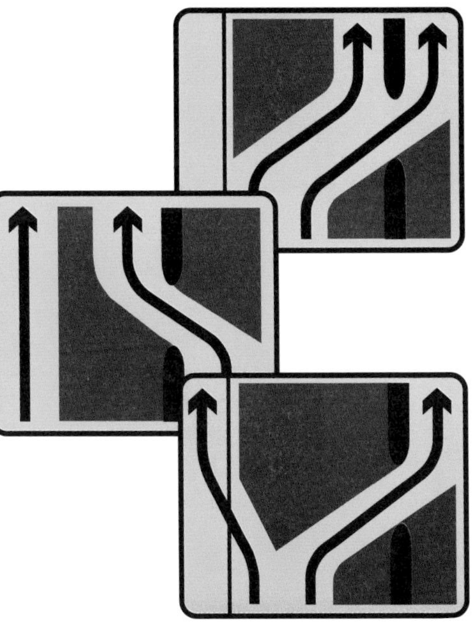

Temporary systems where traffic travelling in opposite directions shares the same carriageway are known as contraflow systems.

These allow traffic to keep moving during repairs or alterations on the other carriageway.

Red and white marker posts separate traffic travelling in opposite directions.

Fluorescent or reflective bright green/yellow studs often replace normal ones.

Accidents can often happen at contraflows when drivers fail to observe simple rules of safety. So

- reduce speed in good time when warned by the advance warning signs or flashing signals
- get into the lane indicated for use by your vehicle in good time
- obey all speed limits
- keep the correct separation distance from the vehicle ahead
- avoid sharp braking and sudden steering movements
- don't change lanes when signs tell you to stay in your lane
- don't let you concentration wander
- don't speed up until you're clear of the roadworks.

Watch out for

- Lane change signs.
- Vehicles broken down ahead. There's often no hard shoulder
- Vehicles braking ahead – KEEP YOUR DISTANCE.

Note. While contraflow systems may be found on many motorways, they may also be used on other roads carrying fast-moving traffic.

Roadworks

Roadworks often affect only one carriageway.

Follow the same safety rules and comply with any lower speed limits in force.

The novice driver

Driving on motorways places greater demands on the driver's skill, observation, anticipation, planning and concentration.

It's important that you get proper guidance before you attempt to drive on your own on a motorway.

If you've recently passed your test, not driven for a while, or your driving hasn't included busy fast-moving traffic, your decision-making skills might not be up to the standard needed.

Remember

The next move you make on a motorway always has to be the right one.

Bear in mind that the vehicles on either side and behind you could weigh over 30 tonnes and be travelling at 50/60 mph or even faster.

So

- ask advice from a professional instructor who can give you valid, safe instruction
- use every chance to observe and learn as a passenger
- select fairly quiet sections of motorway to practise on
- get used to driving at 60–70 mph and keeping up with the flow of the traffic
- don't drive on a motorway until you're fully prepared.

Different weather conditions can lead to a variety of different hazards both from season to season and from region to region.

You might find the task of dealing with a potential weather hazard as easy as putting a sun visor down or as difficult as dealing with wheel-spin in deep snow.

Extreme weather conditions, either very hot or very cold, will show up any deficiencies in both driver and vehicle.

The best thing to do in extremely bad weather is to stay off the road. Take heed of warnings not to go out.

This leaves the emergency services free to deal with real emergencies instead of rounding up stranded motorists.

If you must drive, training and preparation are very important – as with other aspects of driving.

This section deals with the main problems of driving in extremes of weather and the techniques of dealing with them safely.

The topics covered

- Your vehicle
- Weather and vision
- Driving on wet roads
- Driving in cross winds
- Driving in fog
- Driving in snow and ice
- Driving in sunshine and hot weather
- Skidding

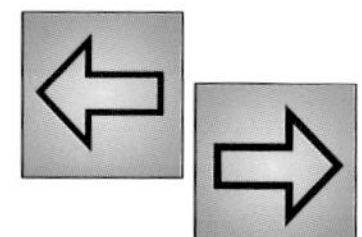

Your vehicle

Whatever the weather, make sure your vehicle and equipment are in good condition and regularly checked and serviced.

Tyres

Check tyre condition and pressure frequently. Make sure they have a good tread and are properly inflated Don't forget to check the inside faces.

Also check your tyres for uneven wear of the tread, either across or around the tyre, which could be due to a mechanical defect. Have your vehicle checked, any fault put right and a new tyre fitted if necessary.

Be prepared: don't wait to examine your tyres until the bad weather shows up the deficiency. It might be too late, and your life could depend on a few millimetres of rubber which should have been there.

Good tyres are especially important in snow, on icy roads and in heavy rain.

Brakes

Keep your brakes in top condition. Stopping takes much longer on wet, slippery roads, even with perfect brakes.

Fuel, oil and water

Check your fuel, oil and water frequently in extreme weather conditions, both hot and cold. The adverse weather can affect how quickly these levels change which can lead to breakdowns.

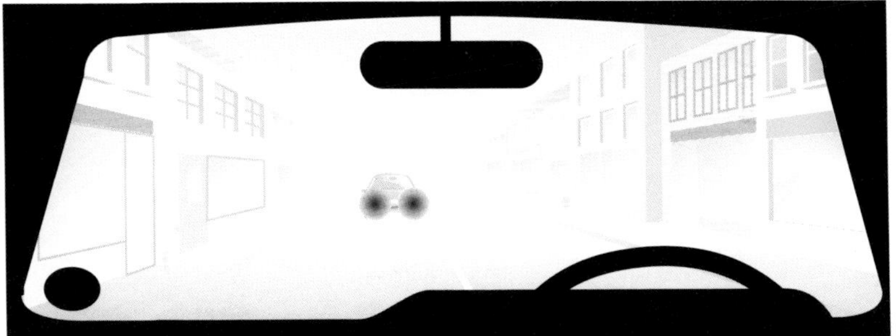

Weather and vision

The biggest single danger to any driver is being unable to see properly. You won't be able to make the right decisions if you can't see the road clearly.

Always keep your windscreen, mirrors and windows clean and clear.

Wipers and washers

Make sure your wiper blades are efficient.

Make sure washers are working and keep the reservoir filled. Use an additive. It helps

- in winter to prevent freezing
- in summer to clear dead insects and smears off the windscreen and maintain full vision.

Misting up

Misting up of the mirror and glass inside the car affects your ability to see. Even on a summer's day a sudden shower can mist up glass inside.

- Keep a dry cloth handy and clean all inside glass.
- Wipe the windows dry before you set out.
- Use your demisters. If your car has a heated windscreen, use it early. Also, use your heated rear window to maintain your rear vision.
- Open your windows to clear mist, if necessary.

Read your vehicle owner's handbook and follow the maker's suggestions for best results in heating and ventilation.

Many anti-mist and anti-frost accessories are available, including

- liquid for keeping glass clear
- de-icers
- prepared cloths
- electrically heated glass.

Warm, dry air

Warm, dry air works best, is by far the cheapest and is usually in plentiful supply once the engine has warmed up.

However, when you start from cold, you won't be able to create warm air, so use a dry cloth or a chamois leather. Ask passengers to help keep side windows clear – essential when manoeuvring.

Icy weather

If the weather is particularly icy, your windows and screen can be frozen over.

Give yourself plenty of time to clear the screen. Before setting out, wait until your demister and heater are working well enough to keep the whole of the screen and rear window clear.

Take care not to damage wiper blades which may have frozen onto the windscreen or rear screen. Never use boiling water to clear the windscreen. You could break the screen.

Rain and vision

You must use dipped headlights in poor visibility (such as rain, drizzle, mist, or very poor light) so that other drivers can see you.

Rain can drastically reduce your view through the windscreen and windows and in the outside driving mirrors.

The cleaner the glass the sooner the wipers can clear the outside of the screen.

Always keep the washer bottle topped up.

Keep your speed down in very wet weather. Some windscreen wipers are not efficient enough to deal with very heavy rain.

In dirty weather conditions, take time to clean your windscreen, windows, indicators and lights as often as necessary.

Warning

In all weather conditions, don't drive unless you can see properly all round.

Driving on wet roads

Wet roads reduce tyre grip. Give yourself plenty of time and room for slowing down and stopping. Keep well back from other vehicles.

Your allowance for braking distance on a wet road should be at least double that on a dry road.

After a spell of dry weather, rain on the road can make the surface even more slippery. Take extra care, especially when cornering.

Be prepared for different road surfaces which might affect your tyre grip.

Remember, the less tread on your tyres the greater the increase in braking distance.

Aquaplaning

When driving at speed, a great danger in very wet weather is the build-up of water between the tyre and the road surface. As a result your vehicle actually slides forwards on a thin film of water as your tyres lose contact with the road surface. Even good tyres cannot grip in this situation.

This is called aquaplaning.

A clear indication that this is happening can be the steering suddenly feeling very light.

When this happens slow down by easing off the accelerator. Never brake or try to change direction.

When you're aquaplaning, you've no control at all over steering or braking.

The higher your speed on a wet road, the more likely you are to aquaplane. You must keep your speed down and watch for water pooling on the road surface.

Even at lower speeds, if the front and rear tyres on one side of the vehicle hit a patch of deeper water, the vehicle may swerve due to the additional resistance on that side.

Spray

Another reason for keeping your speed down in the wet is the amount of water thrown up by passing vehicles.

Overtaking or being overtaken by heavy vehicles on a motorway can be an unnerving experience.

Sometimes, even wipers working at full speed can't keep the windscreen clear, and this results in the driver being temporarily blinded to conditions ahead.

Breakdowns

If water sprays up under the bonnet it can stop the engine or affect electronic controls.

Your brakes

Water can also affect the effectiveness of your brakes. You should allow for this and test your brakes when it's safe to do so.

Dealing with floods

When you have to pass through a flood, take your time.

Stop and assess how deep the water is. Don't just drive into it.

Sometimes roads likely to flood have depth gauges. Check the depth on these, and keep checking as you drive through.

Deep water If the water seems too deep for your vehicle, turn back and go around the flood by another road.

It might take a little longer, but that's better than finding yourself stranded in a flood.

If the water is too deep it could

- flood the exhaust causing the engine to stop
- find its way into the air intake on some vehicles, causing serious engine damage

Shallow water If the water is not too deep, drive on slowly, but be sure to keep to the shallowest part. Remember, because of the camber of the road, the water is probably deepest near the kerb and shallowest at the crown.

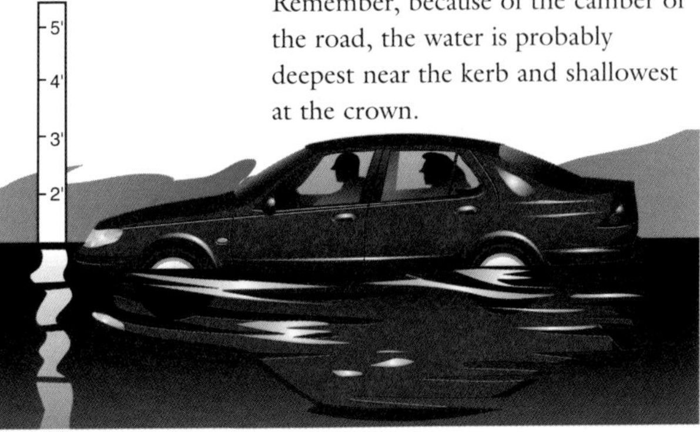

Consider pedestrians Pedestrians can easily get drenched by passing vehicles. Look well ahead and show consideration by slowing down or giving them more room when it's safe to do so.

Driving through floodwater Drive in first gear as slowly as possible but keep the engine speed high and steady by slipping the clutch.

- If the engine speed is too low, you might stall.
- If you go too fast, you could create a wave. Water will flood the engine and it could cut out.
- Try to strike a balance.

Engines and water Some types of diesel engine will tolerate a certain amount of water, but many modern fuel systems are electronically controlled and are therefore affected by water.

All petrol engines can be seriously affected by even small amounts of water being splashed on to the electrical components, such as engine management systems, the coil, distributor, leads and so on.

When you're through When you've driven safely through, test your brakes.

Check your mirrors first, then drive slowly while pressing your left foot lightly on the brake pedal.

Make sure your brakes work properly before you drive at normal speed.

Crossing a ford

The depth of water at fords varies with the weather and is usually greater in winter.

There may be a depth gauge.

If the water is not too deep for your vehicle, cross using the same technique as you would for a flood.

Remember to test your brakes after you cross. There might be a notice reminding you to do so.

Don't

Don't try to displace the water by 'charging' at the flood or ford.

- You could lose control.
- Your vehicle will probably stall.
- You could end up blocking the road.

Driving in crosswinds

Some vehicles can become unstable in strong crosswinds, because of their large surface area and comparatively low weights.

This can happen particularly on exposed stretches of road such as motorways, viaducts and bridges.

The effect can vary from a pull on the steering wheel, to a distinct wander, possibly into the path of another vehicle.

In very bad cases, the whole vehicle can be lifted bodily off the road with very serious results.

Cyclists and motorcyclists

In gusty conditions, watch for cyclists or motorcyclists being blown sideways and veering into your path. Allow extra room when overtaking.

High-sided vehicles

Drivers of high-sided vehicles, or towing caravans, trailers, horse-boxes, etc., particularly empty ones, should

- pay special attention to forecasts of strong winds
- avoid well-known trouble spots and high bridges.

Drivers of these vehicles should be constantly alert for the effects of wind near bridges and embankments, even on normal journeys in reasonable conditions.

Other drivers should bear this in mind when about to overtake, or when being overtaken by these particular vehicles.

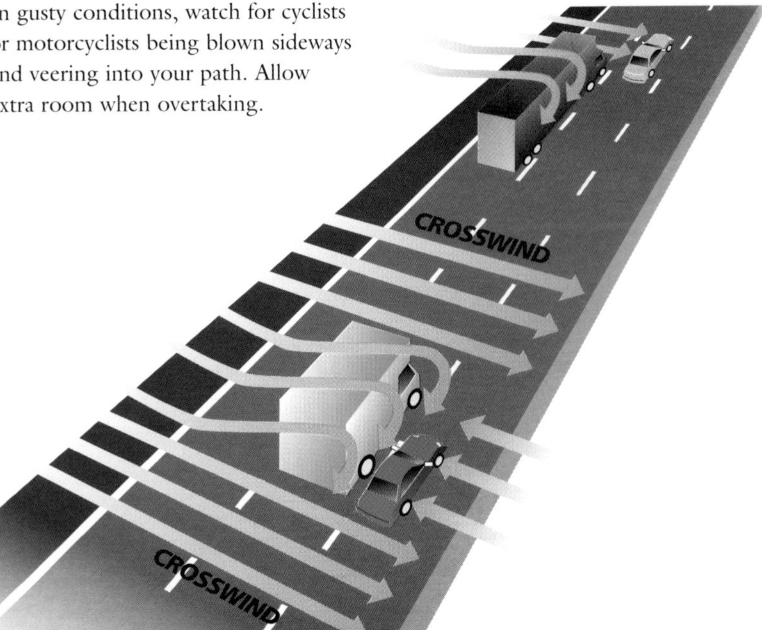

Driving in fog

Fog is one of the most dangerous weather conditions.

An accident involving one vehicle can quickly involve many others, especially if they're driving too close to one another.

Motorway pile-ups in fog have sometimes involved dozens of vehicles.

All too often, there's a loss of life or serious injury, which could so easily be prevented.

Observe the obvious

It doesn't need a sign to tell you it's foggy if you can only see a short distance ahead!

REMEMBER

If the fog is very thick and you can see the rear lights of the vehicle ahead

YOU'RE PROBABLY TOO CLOSE TO STOP IN AN EMERGENCY.

Avoid driving in fog

Take alternative transport or postpone your journey, if at all possible.

If you must drive, give yourself time to prepare, check all lights, clean your windscreen, and so on. Allow more time for the journey.

Fog patches

The density of fog varies. Sometimes the fog is patchy. One moment it can be fairly clear, the next extremely dense. Avoid the temptation to speed up between the patches.

Poor visibility is frustrating and a strain on the eyes. The driver's ability to anticipate is dangerously restricted.

You MUST

- SLOW DOWN – check the speedometer from time to time
- be able to stop well within the distance you can see to be clear
- use your windscreen wipers to keep the outside of the screen clear
- use your demister to keep the inside of the screen clear. use your heated windscreen, if your vehicle has one.

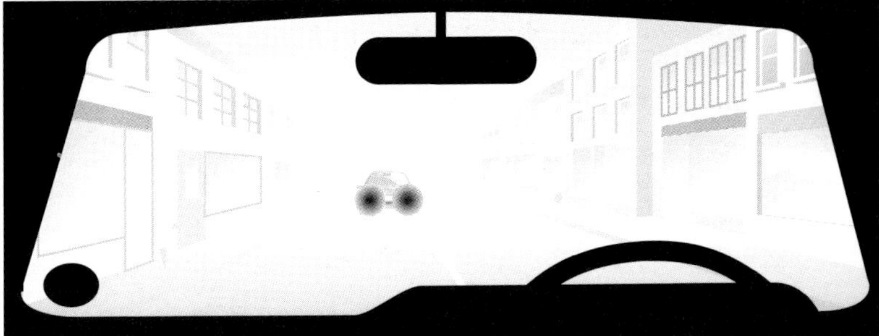

Lights in fog

Correctly adjusted fog lights can be a valuable aid when driving in fog.

In daylight You must use your dipped headlights in daylight when visibility is seriously reduced.

- They'll be seen from a much greater distance than sidelights.
- They won't dazzle other drivers or pedestrians in the day-time.
- Use fog lights if your vehicle is fitted with them.

At dusk Use dipped beams at dusk and other times when visibility is poor.

At night In darkness, you might need to depend entirely on fog lights, or alternate between fog lights and dipped beams, through stretches of thick and thin fog.

High-intensity rear fog lights If your vehicle has high-intensity rear fog lights, use them only in fog when your vehicle might not be seen, that's when visibility drops below 100 metres (110 yards). Using them at other times, such as in the rain, can cause dazzle for following drivers.

Remember

Don't forget to switch them off when visibility improves.

Change your lighting with the conditions.

For example, when you're queuing in traffic and the driver behind has already seen you, it can be helpful to switch off your front or rear fog lights temporarily to avoid dazzle.

It's much more difficult to judge distances and speed in fog when outlines become confusing. The driver can easily become disoriented – especially on an unfamiliar road.

Following another vehicle in fog

SLOW DOWN and leave plenty of room for stopping.

There may be something ahead which you cannot possibly see until you're close to it.

If the vehicle ahead has to stop suddenly, you must have ample time to react and brake.

You may not see or recognise that the vehicle ahead is braking, or has stopped, as soon as you would in clear weather.

You need to be able to brake safely, so remember the road surface is often slippery in fog.

Overtaking

Overtaking in fog can be particularly dangerous. You could well find that visibility ahead is much worse than you thought, and you won't be able to see oncoming traffic soon enough.

Don't

- follow the vehicle in front too closely
- try to keep up with the vehicle ahead or play 'follow my leader' – it's a dangerous game in fog. You'll get a false impression that the fog isn't too bad if you hang on to the lights of the vehicle ahead because it will displace some of the fog
- use main beam when you're following a vehicle in fog as
  - the beam will cast a shadow of the vehicle ahead on the fog in front of it and the driver won't be able to see as well
  - you'll dazzle the other driver.

Do

- give yourself plenty of time and space to deal with whatever is ahead. Decide what's a safe speed for the conditions and stick to it. Don't let other drivers push you into driving faster
- watch out for emergency vehicles. There could well be an accident ahead.

Remember

Fog itself doesn't claim lives, but the standard of driving in fog results in death and destruction which could be avoided.

Junctions in fog

Dealing with junctions in fog needs particular care, especially when turning right.

Do

- open your window(s) and switch off your radio/tape/CD so you can hear any approaching traffic
- start indicating as early as you can
- make the greatest possible use of your lights. If you keep your foot on the brake pedal while you're stopped, your brake light will give drivers behind an extra warning
- use the horn if you feel it will help, and listen for other vehicles.

Don't

- Turn until you're absolutely sure it's safe

Road markings in fog

Dipped headlights will pick out reflective studs, but it's not so easy to recognise other road markings in fog.

Local knowledge helps, particularly knowledge of the edge of a carriageway or similar markings.

Try to keep a central position between lane lines or studs.

- Red reflective studs appear on the left-hand edge of some carriageways.
- White reflective studs are lane markings.
- Amber reflective studs are placed between the right-hand lane and the centre reservation of some dual carriageways.
- Green reflective studs indicate slip roads and lay-bys.

Don't mix up lane lines and centre lines.

Driving too close to the centre could mean you're dangerously near someone coming the other way doing the same thing.

Driving on the centre line as a means of finding your way is extremely dangerous.

Parking in fog

Never park on a road in the fog if you can avoid it. Find an off-street parking place.

If you break down, get your vehicle off the road if you possibly can.

Inform the police, and make arrangements to remove it as soon as possible if it creates an obstruction.

Never leave it without warning lights of some kind or on the wrong side of the road.

Driving in snow and ice

When falling snow reduces visibility, use your dipped headlights, as you would in heavy rain or fog. Falling or freshly fallen snow need not cause too much difficulty providing you remember to

- increase the gap between you and the vehicle in front
- test your brakes, very gently from time to time. Snow can pack behind the front wheels or around brake linkages under the car and so affect steering and braking
- be prepared to clear the windscreen by hand. Your wipers, even with the aid of the heater, may not be able to sweep the snow clear. Snow might collect and pack around your lamps and indicators
- always clear your rear window before setting off and keep it clear.

In areas which are subject to prolonged periods of snow, it may be an advantage to fit

- snow chains (attachments which fit over existing wheels and tyres)
- 'M & S' (mud and snow) tyres with a tread pattern designed for these conditions.

Remember

Snow will cover up road markings – take care when you cannot see which road has priority.

Braking on snow and ice

ALL BUT THE MOST GENTLE BRAKING WILL LOCK YOUR WHEELS ON PACKED SNOW AND ICE.

If your front wheels lock, you can't steer. If you can't steer, you can't keep out of trouble.

Get into a lower gear earlier than normal. Allow your speed to fall and use the brake pedal gently and early to keep your speed well under control.

Braking distances Braking distances on ice can easily be ten times normal distances.

Downhill braking Downhill braking calls for careful speed control well before reaching the actual hill, as well as while you're on it.

By selecting a low gear, the engine compression will help to hold the vehicle back and reduce the overall speed.

Anti-lock brakes Anti-lock brakes will not help your tyres stay in contact with the road surface in ice or snow.

Ice

Overnight freezing usually results in an icy surface, especially on less-used roads.

It's even more dangerous when the roads are just beginning to freeze or thaw.

The combination of water and ice adds up to an extremely slippery surface.

Rain freezing on roads as it falls (black ice) is an invisible danger. As with aquaplaning, your steering will feel especially light.

When driving on ice

- you need to keep your speed down
- treat every control – brakes, accelerator, steering, clutch and gears – very delicately
- look for signs of frost on verges, etc.

If it's very cold, treat all wet looking surfaces as though they are frozen, because they probably are. If the road looks wet but there is no sound from the tyres, expect ice.

Cornering on ice and snow

Time your driving and adjust your speed so that you don't have to touch your brakes at all on a bend.

Approach a corner at a steady speed, using as high a gear as you reasonably can.

- Be gentle with the accelerator.
- Don't touch the clutch unless you absolutely have to.
- Steer smoothly – sudden movements must be avoided.
- Take just as much care coming out of a turn.

Braking on an icy or snow-covered bend is extremely dangerous.

The centrifugal force will continue to pull you outwards and the wheels will not grip very well. This could cause your vehicle to spin.

Starting off on snow

If you experience wheel-spin when you're starting off in deep snow, don't race the engine because the wheels will dig in further.

Try to move the car slightly backwards and then forwards out of the rut. Use the highest gear you can.

In these conditions, it's worthwhile carrying a spade and some old sacks. These can be useful to help get you going when you've become stuck in snow

Snow chains are available which can be fitted over existing wheels and tyres to help avoid getting stuck and to reduce the danger of skidding.

Climbing hills on snow and ice

Speed must be kept down on icy and slippery roads. But this can bring with it other problems.

For example, going uphill you might lose momentum. Trying to regain speed and keep going could cause severe wheel-spin and loss of control.

If you have to stop, it could well be difficult to start again.

Leave a good gap between you and the vehicle in front. If it stops, you'll at least have a chance to keep going while it restarts, or even pass it altogether.

To reduce the chances of wheel-spin, use the highest gear you reasonably can.

Don't rush a hill thinking you'll change down on the way up. Before reaching the hill, get into a gear which will take you all the way up.

Changing gear is not easy on an icy slope. It takes very delicate footwork to avoid wheel-spin, and loss of speed

Other vehicles on snow and ice

If you find a vehicle heading toward you that is obviously out of control try to make maximum use of engine braking if there's time.

If you must use the brake pedal, be as gentle as possible.

Avoid braking and steering at the same time to get out of the way. Both are dangerous in icy conditions.

Constantly assess what's ahead. Be prepared, and look for escape routes.

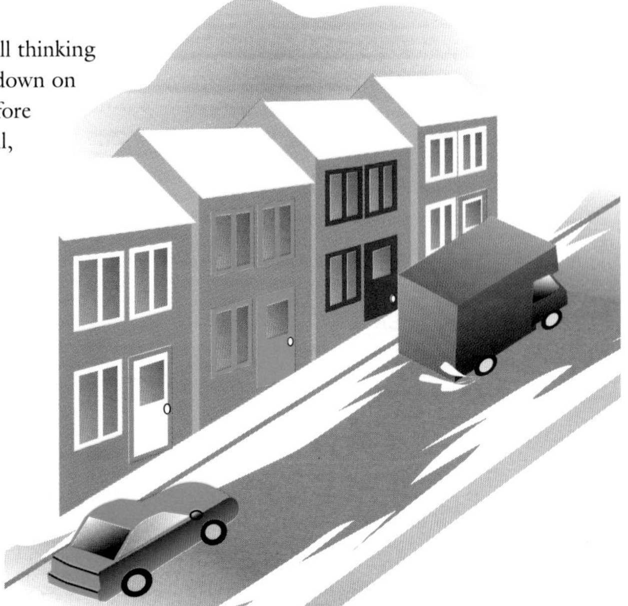

Driving in sunshine and hot weather

Before you begin a long journey, make sure you're prepared for the weather.

Tyres

Tyre pressures should be checked and adjusted when they're cold.

Don't check the pressure when you've been driving for a while because tyres will be warm and the reading inaccurate.

Coolant

Before you start your journey, check the level of coolant in the system.

Clear windscreen

There are generally more flies and insects about in hot weather, and your windscreen needs to be kept clean.

Keep the windscreen as clear as possible of water and grease marks. This helps to cut down glare.

Check the level in the washer reservoir and top up if necessary.

Glare

Constant sun in your eyes can be exhausting on a long journey and may well affect your concentration.

Even if you don't feel the need, the correct sun-glasses can reduce the glare and keep your eyes efficient for longer.

This is especially important if you're driving abroad, where conditions are hotter and the sunlight brighter than you may be used to.

Low-angle sun

Glare can be worse in the winter when the sun is low in the sky. Wear sun-glasses and/or use your visor to cut out as much glare as possible. Avoid looking directly into the sun.

If the roads are wet, reflected glare seriously reduces your ability to see. Reduce speed and take extra care.

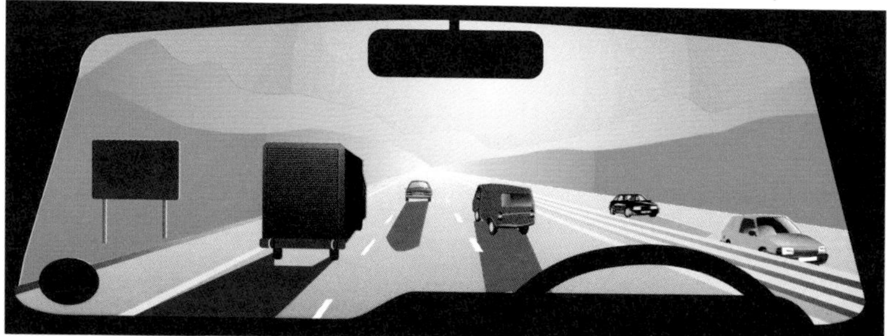

Coping with heat

Make sure you use adequate ventilation inside the car. Air-conditioning helps, if you have it. Take plenty of breaks and refreshment on a long trip.

If you feel sleepy, stop where it's safe and rest.

Never stop on the hard shoulder of a motorway because you feel tired. Use the service areas or get off the motorway.

Once again, oil and water can make the hot surface of the road slippery and dangerous, particularly if there's a sudden rain shower after a long dry spell.

Take extra care: watch your speed and keep your distance.

Soft tarmac

During long periods of hot weather, many tarmac road surfaces become extremely soft. Take care braking and cornering.

Loose chippings

Many highway authorities replace the granite chipping road surfaces during the summer. Always observe the special warning speed limits and keep well back from the vehicle in front.

Flying stone chips can not only cause expensive damage to your vehicle, but also cause serious injury to pedestrians and other road users.

Remember

Listen to travel information and avoid known traffic hold-ups.

Overheated engines in long traffic queues are the most frequent causes of breakdowns in these conditions.

Skidding

Three important factors cause a skid. In order of importance, they are

- the driver
- the vehicle
- the road conditions.

Skids don't just happen. They're caused by a driver asking too much of the vehicle for the amount of grip the tyres have on the road at that time.

A skid happens when you change speed or direction so suddenly that your tyres cannot keep their grip on the road.

There's an increased risk of skidding as you

- slow down
- speed up
- turn a corner or round a bend
- drive uphill or downhill.

The risk increases on a slippery road surface.

Skids caused by braking

Harsh and uncontrolled braking is one of the chief causes of skidding. Brakes have their greatest stopping power when they're nearly, but not quite, locked.

The weight of the car is thrown forward and the heavier the braking the more weight goes to the front and the less there is on the rear wheels.

The less the weight on the rear wheels the more likely they are to lock. It's the rear wheels locking first that causes the skid, because the vehicle tends to swing, if not spin.

Skidding on dry roads

Skids happen on dry roads with good tyres, as well as in wet conditions. They'll happen if you suddenly brake harshly when you've not left enough stopping space.

All weight is thrown forward and its impossible to keep the vehicle straight. It begins to swing and only has to touch something to be in danger of turning over.

Anti-lock brakes

Anti-lock systems help you to continue steering while braking, but on wet or slippery roads this will be less effective. The brakes are only as good as the tyre grip on the road.

Skids caused by steering

When a vehicle is cornering at speed, more weight is thrown onto the front wheel on the outside of the curve. This not only affects the steering, but also lessens the weight on the back wheels which can cause them to lose grip and slide.

Skids caused by acceleration

Sudden or harsh acceleration, particularly in the lower gears, can cause the driving wheels to spin on the road surface. Unless you ease off the accelerator very quickly, the vehicle could go into a skid due to the wheel-spin.

Skids caused by both braking and steering at the same time

If you combine wrong braking with wrong steering, you're asking for trouble.

You're bound to skid if your tyres are only just gripping while you're cornering and you start braking.

You could also skid if you're braking when you start cornering.

Don't expect your tyres to do the impossible.

The answer is simple: adjust your speed to the conditions and give yourself plenty of space. If the road is wet or icy, the amount of grip your tyres have is much less.

Excessive braking

Over-acceleration

Over-steering

Avoiding skids

There's no better protection against skids than driving in a way that will avoid them. Drivers cause skids, they don't just happen.

Take the following advice.

- On very slippery surfaces your stopping distance can be as much as TEN TIMES longer than on a dry road.
- Look out for signs of slippery roads. Any wet road, even in summer, is likely to be slippery. Be wary of rain, ice, packed snow and frost in shady places, wet mud, loose surfaces and wet leaves
- If you suspect the road is slippery, keep your speed down.

  Your brakes will not get you out of trouble when your tyre grip is poor. Brakes are far more likely to get you into trouble.

  Use engine braking. Change down in good time, but be very careful with the accelerator and clutch, particularly in very slippery conditions. They can cause skids too!
- Keep your vehicle in good condition.

  Brakes that snatch or pull unevenly are dangerous on slippery roads.

  An accelerator pedal linkage which is jerky can lead to wheel-spin.

Dealing with skids

If you find you're in a skid there are a number of things you should do.

- Release the brake pedal fully. Drivers often instinctively do the opposite, keeping their right foot hard down on the brake pedal throughout the skid. This makes matters worse, so keep *off* the brakes.
- Turn the steering wheel in the same direction as the skid and ease off the accelerator at the same time, particularly if the skid is little more than a slight slide. This should bring the wheels into line again.
- If the skid is more than a slight slide, ease right off the accelerator and turn more definitely into the skid. That is
  - if the rear of the vehicle is going left, you should steer left to bring front wheels into line with the back
  - if the rear of the vehicle is going right, steer to the right.

Be careful not to over-correct with too much steering. Too much movement of the front wheels will lead to another skid in the opposite direction.

If the front wheels are sliding instead of, or as well as, the back wheels, release the accelerator and don't try to steer until the wheels regain some of their grip.

Too much power on a front-wheel drive vehicle can produce the same problem. Again, ease off the accelerator.

Remember

- Prevention is far better than cure.
- Adopt safe driving techniques which avoid the build-up to a skid.
- Adjust to the conditions and give yourself time to react safely.

Rear of car skids to the right

Driver steers to the right

Driving at night is another aspect of driving which demands special techniques and precautions.

The problems of driving at night vary widely with the type of road and the amount of traffic; this section deals with the most important aspects.

The topics covered

- Driving at night
- Built up areas
- Your vehicle lights
- Overtaking or following at night
- Parked vehicles
- Meeting other vehicles

Driving at night

You'll find you're very much more limited by conditions at night. You can't see as far as you can in daylight, so less information is available.

Problems vary widely with the type of road and amount of traffic.

Speed at night

You need to be more alert and aware that you can't safely drive as fast at night as you can in the daylight. This includes driving at dusk or dawn, even in good weather.

Never drive so fast that you cannot stop well within the distance you can see to be clear. That is, within the range of your lights.

If you can't stop safely within the range of your lights, you're going too fast.

Note. Fluorescent material shows up well in daylight or at dusk, but is of little use in the dark. Only reflective material shows up well in headlights.

At dusk

You may find it best to put your lights on before lighting-up time.

Don't be afraid to be the first driver to switch on.

It's better to see and be seen.

At dawn

The opposite applies.

Don't switch off your lights until you're sure it's safe. Make sure you can see and be seen.

Dark-coloured cars – navy blue, brown, dark grey, etc., should

- switch on earlier
- switch off later.

When you drive with your lights on, other drivers can not only see you earlier, they can also tell which way you're heading.

This is often difficult in the half-light without lights.

Your eyes at night

You should have your eyesight checked regularly.

Ask yourself, 'Can I really see as well as I would like?'

If you can't see so well at night, it might be your eyes that are to blame, night driving showing up the need for a check.

How far can you see?

Test yourself in a suitable place.

Pick an object within the range of your lights and see if you can stop by the time you reach it.

You'll be surprised how difficult this is with dipped lights on an unlit road, and shows you should take a good look before you dip your lights.

Notice too how lighter coloured objects are easier to see at night.

Adjusting to darkness

Give your eyes a minute or two to adjust to the darkness, particularly when you're coming out of a brightly lit area or building.

You can always fill in the time cleaning your lights, mirrors, windscreen, etc.

Remember this when you leave a motorway service area after a rest or refuelling stop.

A clean screen cuts down dazzle.

Don't

At night don't

- wear tinted glasses, sun-glasses or night-driving glasses
- spray the windscreen or windows with tints.

Built-up areas

Always use dipped headlights in built-up areas at night. It helps others to see you!

In areas where street lights cause patches of shadow, watch out for pedestrians especially those in dark clothes, who can be difficult to see.

Remember

- Be on the alert for pedestrians.
- Approach pedestrian crossings at such a speed that you can stop safely if necessary.
- Watch for cyclists and joggers.

Noise at night

Keep all noise to a minimum.

- Don't rev your engine.
- Close your car doors quietly.

Remember that neighbours and children may be asleep.

- Take extra care setting/disarming the anti-theft alarm on your vehicle.

Using the horn at night The law says you must not use your horn between 11.30 pm and 7 am in a built-up area. (Except when stationary, to avoid danger from a moving vehicle.)

If you need to warn other road users of your presence, flash your headlights.

Your vehicle lights

At night, your vehicle lights are your most important source of information for both you and for other road users.

They also tell other drivers your movements. Use them with care and consideration.

Always

- keep your headlights clean
- use your headlights at night, dipped or full beam, as appropriate
  - on all roads where there's not street lighting
  - on roads carrying fast-moving traffic
  - on motorways, even if they're well lit
- use dipped headlights at any time when the light is poor, even during the day.

You should

- check all your lights before and during a long journey
- fix any lighting fault immediately, for your own safety, and the safety of others. Carry spare bulbs.
- remember that extra weight at the rear of your vehicle could cause your headlights to dazzle other road users. Some models have headlamp adjusters to deal with this.

Auxiliary driving lights

When you're using dipped beams, auxiliary driving lights can help pick out pedestrians and cyclists. If your vehicle doesn't have them, it's possible to have a set fitted.

Make sure these lights are correctly adjusted and don't dazzle oncoming drivers.

Junctions at night

Brake lights can dazzle.

Don't keep your foot on the brake pedal if you're waiting at a junction or queuing in traffic, except in fog – use the handbrake.

However, switch off your indicator light only if it's dazzling the driver behind and, if you do switch off, make sure you switch on again before you move off.

Overtaking or following at night

You'll need to take extra care before attempting to overtake at night. It's more difficult because you can see less.

Don't overtake if there's a chance you are approaching

- a road junction
- a bend
- the brow of a bridge or hill, except on a dual carriageway
- a pedestrian crossing
- road markings indicating double white lines ahead

or if there's likely to be

- a vehicle overtaking or turning right
- any other potential hazard.

Stay clear and dip

Make sure you don't get too close to the vehicle ahead, and always dip your lights so you don't dazzle the driver.

Your light beam should fall short of the rear of the vehicle in front.

Remember your separation distance.

On a dual carriageway or motorway where it's possible to overtake, don't use full beam in the face of oncoming drivers.

If you're being overtaken

Dip your lights as soon as the vehicle passes you.

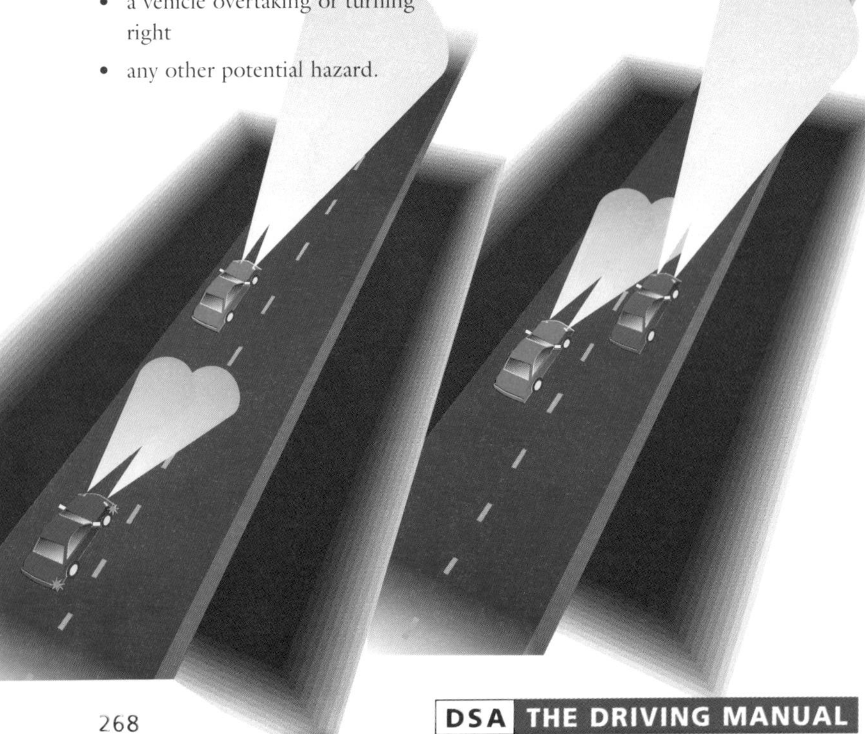

Parked vehicles

Cars and light goods vehicles (1525 kg or less unladen), invalid carriages and motorcycles can park without lights on roads with a speed limit of 30 mph or less, so long as they're not within 10 metres (11 yards) of a junction.

They must also be parked parallel to, and close to, the side of the road or in a designated parking place and facing in the direction of the traffic flow.

Parking in fog

If you can't get your vehicle off the road, always leave the lights on.

Never

- leave your vehicle on any other road without lights unless a sign indicates that lights are not required; better to get it off the road altogether
- leave your vehicle standing on the right-hand side of the road, except in a one-way street.

Always

Switch your headlights off when you stop, even for a short while.

It's an offence to leave them on when the vehicle is parked. The fixed glare can be very dazzling especially if, for any reason, the vehicle is on the offside of the road facing oncoming traffic.

Meeting other vehicles

Another vehicle's lights can tell you which direction they're heading and can give you an idea of their speed. Oncoming lights should raise a number of questions in your mind, such as

- How far away is the vehicle and how fast is it moving?
- Should I slow down while we pass each other?
- How soon should I dip?
- How far ahead can I see before I dip?
- Before I dip, is there anything on my side of the road
  - that I might endanger?
  - that might endanger me?

  For example, a stationary vehicle, a cyclist, a pedestrian, or an unlit builder's skip.

Headlights on full beam

When your headlights are on full beam,

- dip early enough to avoid dazzling oncoming drivers, but not too early
- check the left-hand verge before you dip.

When you're dazzled

If the headlights of oncoming vehicles dazzle you, slow down and, if necessary, stop.

Don't look directly at oncoming headlights.

Don't retaliate.

On a left-hand bend

Dip earlier.

Your headlights will cut straight across the eyes of anyone coming toward you.

On a right-hand bend this might not happen, or it won't happen so soon.

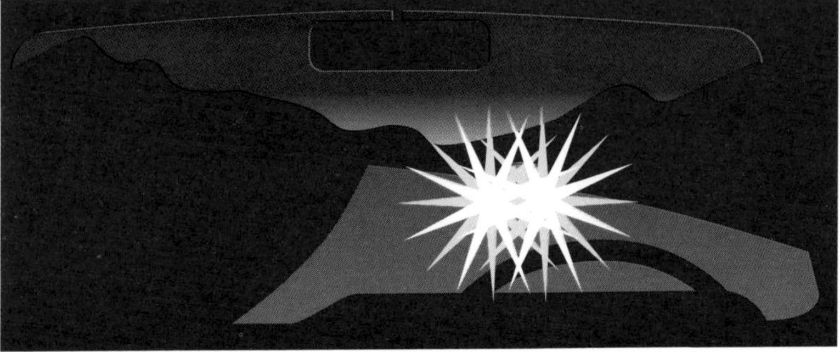

PART FOURTEEN BASIC MAINTENANCE

Your vehicle needs routine attention and maintenance to keep it safe and in good mechanical condition. Some of this can be done with the help of the owner's handbook.

Routine checks of the oil, fuel, water, tyres and tyre pressures, particularly before a long journey, can help save trouble and expense, and prolong the life of your car.

You'll find that regular service checks on brakes and engine by a qualified mechanic can also save time and money.

Neglecting the maintenance of vital controls, such as brakes and steering, is dangerous.

The topics covered

- Fuel
- The engine
- Steering and suspension
- Brakes
- Tyres
- Electrical systems
- Basic fault finding

Fuel

Keep an eye on the fuel gauge on your instrument panel.

Don't let the fuel in your tank run too low. When the fuel level runs very low you risk drawing sediment through into the engine. This can cause running problems and even damage the engine. Fill up before you reach that stage.

Some vehicles have a warning light which shows when the fuel is getting low. The light flashes at first, and then stays on as the fuel runs out.

Fuel cans Some drivers carry 4 or 8 litre (1 or 2 gallon) cans as an extra reserve. If you do this, make sure the can is of an approved type for carrying fuel. It's illegal and dangerous to carry petrol in a container not intended for that purpose.

Motorway driving Make sure you've plenty of fuel for motorway driving.

Driving at higher speeds tends to use more fuel.

Petrol engines

Choose the right grade of petrol for your engine.

Using the wrong type could damage the valves and cylinder head, because of the differences in the temperatures at which the fuel burns.

Leaded or unleaded? Because it releases no lead into the atmosphere, unleaded petrol is more environmentally friendly.

If your vehicle can use unleaded fuel, you should use it. Check in the owner's handbook.

Your vehicle might need a small adjustment first. Consult your dealer or garage if you are in any doubt.

New vehicles *must* be capable of running on unleaded petrol.

Some earlier models cannot be converted to use unleaded petrol.

Vehicles fitted with catalytic converters

Leaded fuel must not be used in vehicles fitted with a catalytic converter. Even one tankful can permanently damage the system.

Diesel engines

Diesel fuel is also environmentally friendly, provided the engine is tuned correctly. Take care to avoid spilling diesel fuel when refuelling, since it will cause an extremely slippery surface.

Warning

Take care never to put petrol into a diesel vehicle, or diesel fuel into a petrol engined vehicle. Look carefully at the pump you're going to use!

The engine

Oil

Oil is necessary to lubricate your engine. You need to keep the oil at the level recommended by the vehicle manufacturer.

Check regularly and top up the oil when necessary, especially before a long journey.

Preferably, check the oil level every time you fill up with fuel.

How to check the oil level The dipstick will tell you the amount of oil in the engine. See owner's handbook.

You'll need a clean, dry cloth to wipe the dipstick.

- Ensure the vehicle is on a level area. Make sure it's not on a sloping surface.
- Look for the dipstick on the engine block of your vehicle.

Take particular care if your vehicle is fitted with automatic transmission when there may be an additional dipstick for transmission oil level checks. (Consult the handbook.)

Oil changes Observe manufacturer's recommendations. If a large number of short journeys are involved, change the oil at more frequent intervals, especially in dusty conditions. Remember to have the filter changed at the same time.

Warning Oil is toxic and can cause skin problems. Wash oil off your hands immediately.

Keep containers storing oil out of reach of children.

Oil use The amount of oil an engine will use depends on

- the type of engine
- the amount of wear
- how you drive.

Don't

- run the engine when the oil level is below the minimum mark
- add so much oil that the level rises above the maximum mark. You'll create excess pressure that could damage the engine seals and gaskets, and cause oil leaks.

Warning light If the oil pressure warning light on your instrument panel shows when you're driving, stop as soon as you can and check the oil level.

Lubricating oils – engine The oil in your engine has to perform several tasks at high pressures and temperatures up to 300°C. The oil

- helps resist wear on the moving surfaces
- helps combat the corrosive acids formed as the hydrocarbons in the fuels are burnt in the engine
- helps keep the engine cool
- has to withstand gradual contamination from both fuel and dirt.

Make sure you always use the lubricants recommended in the handbook.

Lubricating oils – gear box Most vehicles have a separate lubricating oil supply for the gearbox.

This oil is especially formulated for use in the gearbox and you should always follow the instructions in the vehicle handbook.

It's not necessary to drain the gearbox in most cases, but the level should be checked at service intervals.

Lubricating oils – final drive/ rear axle Front-wheel drive vehicles often have a separate supply for the final drive and gear box, but most have a common filler/level plug and specified gear oil should be used to top up.

With rear-wheel drive vehicles, there's a filler/level hole at the rear of the differential (on the rear axle) which can be more easily reached when the vehicle is raised, but remember to keep the vehicle level.

It's important that the correct hypoid type EP (Extreme Pressure) oil specified in the vehicle handbook is used.

You may have to squeeze the top-up oil in via a plastic bottle and tube.

Coolant

Water is used to keep most engines comparatively cool.

Vehicles today use a mixture of water and anti-freeze to make up the coolant. This is kept in the radiator all the year round.

The anti-freeze contains corrosion inhibitor which reduces rust and prolongs the life of the system. In cold weather, maintain the recommended strength of anti-freeze. Have it checked annually.

You should frequently check the coolant level, particularly before a long trip, topping up with water as necessary. The need to top up often might indicate a leak or other fault in the cooling system. Have it checked by your garage/dealer.

It's a good idea to always carry a supply of water with you.

Air filter

Replace the air filter at the intervals recommended by the manufacturer, or sooner if the vehicle is used in exceptionally dusty conditions.

Overhead camshaft engines

On this design of engine it's vital to replace the camshaft drive belt at the recommended intervals. Serious damage can be caused to the engine if the belt breaks.

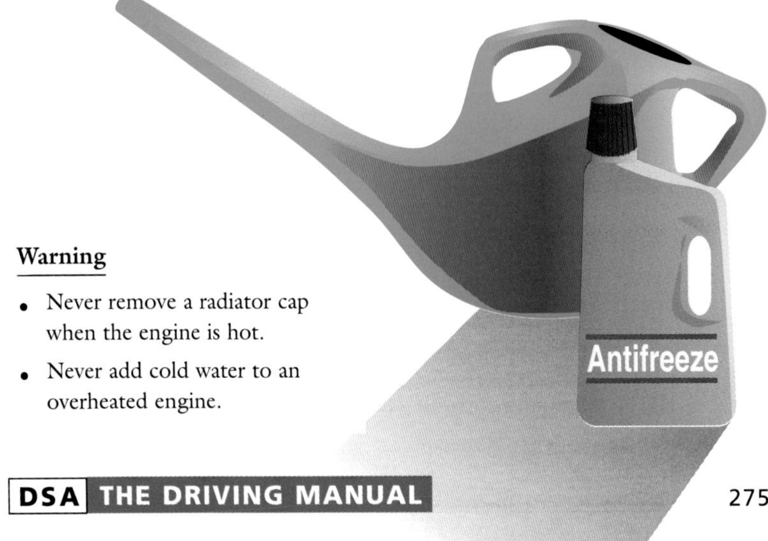

Warning

- Never remove a radiator cap when the engine is hot.
- Never add cold water to an overheated engine.

Steering and suspension

Steering

If you suspect any wear in the steering mechanism, you should seek qualified advice without delay.

Watch for excessive movement or play at the steering wheel, for example.

Power Assisted Steering (PAS) pump reservoir Check the level of fluid regularly when the engine is switched off. The level should be between the min and max marks.

Never run the engine without oil in the pump reservoir. You could severely damage the pump or cause it to seize up completely.

Suspension

Check the condition of shock absorbers and examine the dampers for signs of leaks.

The vehicle should not continue to bounce unduly when tested. If in doubt, seek qualified assistance.

Remember, worn shock absorbers make a vehicle difficult to control and can increase your stopping distance.

Brakes

Brakes are one of the most important elements in driving safety.

Footbrake

Note any variations in braking efficiency. If the brakes feel too spongy or slack, get them checked by a mechanic.

Brakes are too important to be ignored.

Testing your brakes

Test the brakes every day as you set out. Choose a safe spot on the road.

If you hear any strange noises, or if the vehicle pulls to one side, consult your garage immediately.

Check the brake fluid level regularly.

Make sure the brake fluid reservoir is kept topped up. Consult the handbook.

Handbrake

Adjust the handbrake setting if

- the amount of travel is above the limit specified in the handbook
- the vehicle can roll on a gradient when the handbrake is fully set.

Regular servicing

Regular servicing will help to make sure your brakes are safe. Follow the manufacturer's recommendation on service intervals.

Unless you're an enthusiastic and skilled amateur mechanic, leave brake checking, adjustment and replacement of pads and shoes to your garage.

If you're in any doubt about your vehicle's ability to brake safely, don't use it. Have it checked immediately.

Warning lights

Some vehicles have warning lights that indicate brake condition. If a warning light shows make sure your brakes are still operating, then drive carefully to the nearest garage.

If in doubt, don't drive the vehicle.

Anti-lock brake systems

If your vehicle has anti-lock brakes, there will also be a warning light for that system. If the light indicates a fault, have the brakes checked immediately.

Only if it's safe, drive carefully to the nearest garage.

On a motorway

If you have any reason to suspect that your brakes are defective when you're driving on a motorway leave at the next exit, and drive carefully to a garage.

Tyres

Your tyres are your only contact with the road. The area of contact is as small as the sole of a large shoe for each tyre. Tyres won't grip properly and safely unless they're in good condition. Make sure you check wear and tear and replace them when necessary. They can easily become damaged.

The condition of your tyres

- Check that the walls of the tyres are free from cuts and bulges. Don't forget the inner walls, (i.e., those facing each other under the car).
- Check that all your tyres have a good depth of tread right across and all around them. The legal requirement for cars, vans and trailers/caravans is not less than 1.6mm thread depth across the central three-quarters of the breadth of the tyre and around the entire outer circumference. Replace worn tyres as soon as you can.
- Have the wheel alignment and wheel balance, suspension and braking system checked. If there's a fault get it put right as soon as you can, otherwise the wear on the tyres will be excessive or uneven.

Don't let grease and oil stay on your tyres. Remove anything (stones, glass, etc.) caught in the treads. These can work their way in and cause damage.

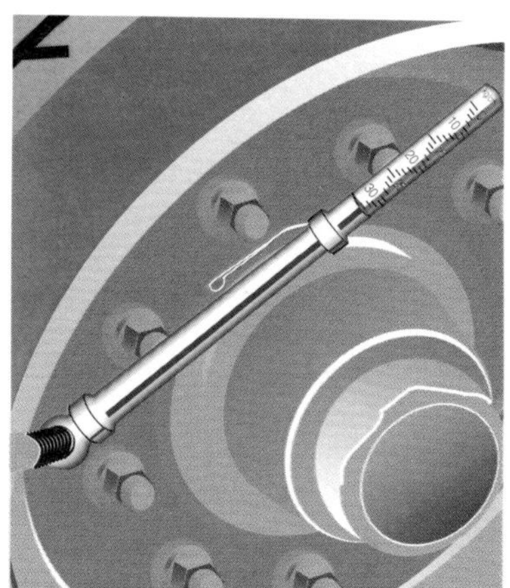

Tyre pressure

You can't guess pressures just by looking at a tyre, except when it's obviously flat.

Check your tyres regularly – at least once a week. Use a reliable gauge and follow the manufacturer's guide for the correct tyre pressure.

Check your tyres and adjust the pressure when they're cold.

Don't forget the spare tyre.

Remember to refit the valve caps.

The handbook will also tell you if you need different pressures for different conditions.

Generally, the pressure should be higher for a heavily loaded vehicle or if you're intending to drive at high speed for a long distance, e.g., motorway journeys.

Remember, it's an offence to use a car with a tyre not properly inflated.

Burst tyres

The main problem with a tyre burst is that the vehicle swerves and weaves. This is made worse if you brake heavily.

- Avoid heavy braking.
- Use as little braking as possible.
- Grip the steering wheel firmly to check the swerving, but again beware of over-correction. Aim to let your vehicle roll to a safe stopping place.

Replacing tyres

You'll need to distinguish between the two main types of tyre in general use: cross-ply and radial-ply.

In cross-ply tyres the cords making up the structure of the tyre run diagonally across it, with alternative layers at opposite angles, forming a trellis structure.

In radial-ply tyres the cords run at right angles across the tyre, resulting in thinner and more flexible walls.

The tread of a radial-ply tyre gives extra grip in the wet because of the way it's structured.

New cars generally have the same type of tyre for each wheel. If you have to change one or a pair, stick to the same type.

> **Note.** Although most cars are now fitted with radial tyres, cross-ply tyres are still available. Make sure you only fit the appropriate type.

Mixing tyre types It's not safe to put radial-ply tyres at the front with cross-ply at the rear. There are no exceptions to his rule. It applies whether the vehicle has front- or rear-wheel drive. It's an offence to mix cross- and radial-ply tyres on the same axle.

Mixing radial- and cross-ply tyres makes rotating tyres, where it's recommended for your vehicle, difficult if not impossible.

If you want to change the type, change ALL the tyres, including the spare.

Keep to the same type all round – all cross-ply or all radial. If you can't avoid mixing types, then make sure the radial-ply tyres go on the back. The car will handle differently from the way it would with the same type of tyres all round.

Ask expert advice Get the advice of a tyre expert if you're changing type, particularly if you're changing to something other than cross-ply or radial-ply, e.g., bias-belted. Good garages and specialist tyre services know the regulations; ask them.

Tubeless tyres When you're replacing a tubeless tyre, fit a new valve to the wheel.

Punctures should only be repaired if the damaged tyre can be vulcanised (a specialist hot-weld process) to meet legal requirements.

You should run in new tyres at reasonable speeds for the first 100 miles (160 kilometres).

How to save wear and tear on tyres

- Check tyre pressures.
- Avoid driving over pot-holes and broken road surfaces. If you can't avoid them, slow down.
- Don't drive over kerbs or scrape the wheels along them when manoeuvring. You'll damage the wall of the tyre. this could cause a blow-out later.
- Hitting the kerb can also affect the tracking of the front wheels. If there are any signs of uneven front tyre wear, have the steering checked.
- Think and plan ahead. Avoid high speeds, fast cornering and heavy braking, all of which increase tyre wear.

Electrical systems

Battery

Some modern batteries are maintenance free and sealed for life. The terminals should be secure, clean and greased.

When the battery is fitted with a filler cap or caps, check the level of the fluid. The plates in each cell should be covered. Top up with distilled water if necessary, but avoid overfilling.

Lights

Check the operation of the front and rear lights, brake lights and indicators, including hazard lights, each time you use the vehicle.

Make use of reflections in windows and garage doors, or ask someone to help you.

It's a good idea to carry a selection of spare bulbs. See your vehicle owner's handbook for bulb replacement procedure.

Headlights must be properly adjusted to

- avoid dazzling other road users
- enable the driver to see the road ahead adequately.

All lights must

- be clean and in good working order
- show a steady light.

Indicators

- must be clearly visible and in good working order
- must flash at 1–2 times per second.

Windscreen washers and wipers

Check the windscreen washer mechanism and the washer reservoirs. Make sure there's enough liquid.

The washer can be very important in wet, muddy conditions. If you carry a supply of water, you can use a sponge to wash away any heavy dirt wherever you happen to be.

Check the wipers. Replace worn or damaged blades.

If your vehicle is fitted with headlight washers, the same attentions should be paid to these.

The horn

Check the horn is working properly and sounding clearly. Take care not to alarm or annoy others when doing so.

Basic fault finding

For detailed advice consult either the owner's handbook, a workshop maintenance manual or a qualified mechanic.

The tables on pages 284 and 285 give only a brief guide to simple fault finding and remedies.

If you have any doubts about the road-worthiness of the vehicle, obtain specialised assistance without delay. Don't ignore the warning signs.

Some minor faults can be easily identified and corrected comparatively simply, but with the more complex engine management and electronic systems in modern motor vehicles, anything beyond a simple repair is better left to qualified mechanics, especially when the vehicle's warranty might be affected.

Remember

Prevention is better (and cheaper) than cure. Stick to the maintenance schedules. If you notice any fault, consult your garage.

Check all levels and systems as recommended.

Changing filters and spark plugs at recommended intervals will help keep your vehicle reliable and prolong its life.

Don't drive on ignoring noises or symptoms which are unusual.

Don't drive on if you're concerned that the problem might be serious.

Describe the problem as clearly as you can when seeking qualified advice.

Always follow the manufacturer's instructions.

Always have repairs carried out by a qualified and reputable mechanic.

In addition to carrying a first aid kit and fire extinguisher in your vehicle, the following items are useful to keep for emergency use

- a warning triangle
- spare bulbs and fuses
- a torch
- vinyl tape
- wire
- jump leads
- a tow rope
- pliers
- a plastic container of water.

Additionally, on winter journeys, especially in snow

- a thermos flask with a hot drink
- biscuits
- a rug/blanket
- a spade
- old sacks
- matches

and, of course, de-icer and lock defroster.

Recognising basic faults

Symptom	Probable cause	Remedy
BRAKES		
Vehicle pulls to one side when braking	Incorrect adjustment	Seek qualified assistance
Warning light shows	Undue wear in pads/shoes	Seek qualified assistance
	System fault	Seek qualified assistance
	Low brake fluid level	Check level
	Brake lamp failed	Replace bulb
Brakes inefficient on good road surfaces	Possible component failure	Seek qualified assistance
	Brakes require adjusting	Seek qualified assistance
Handbrake will not hold vehicle	Cable adjustment or replacement needed	Seek qualified assistance
LIGHTS		
Lamp does not light	Bulb failure Fuse failure	Check and replace Check and replace
Indicator flashing irregularly	Possible bulb failure Relay failure	Check and replace Check and replace
Main/dip beam not lit	Part failure of unit	Check and replace
TYRES/STEERING		
Steering 'heavy' or erratic	Puncture	Change wheel and repair/repace tyre
	Power assisted steering fault	Seek qualified assistance
Vibration in steering at specific speeds	Front wheel out of balance (check for loss of balance weight or bulge in tyre)	Seek qualified assistance or change tyre

Recognising basic faults

Symptom	Probable cause	Remedy
ENGINE		
Misfiring or won't run	Fuel or electrical fault	Examine connections Seek assistance
	Defective spark plugs	Examine and replace if necessary
Fails to start	Out of fuel Damp in electrical circuits	Check gauge Use anti-damp spray
Starter doesn't operate	Battery discharged (flat)	Change battery Jump start Push start
Starter or solenoid clicks	Starter motor jammed	Rock vehicle backwards/forwards in gear with ignition OFF Turn 'square' end on starter with a spanner
Squealing noise from engine area	Fan belt/alternator belt slipping	Adjust/replace
Overheating	Fan belt snapped or hose leaking	Replace belt/hose Tape hose for temporary repair
	Fuse blown on electric cooling fan	Replace fuse

You can reduce the chances of breakdown with preventive maintenance and regular vehicle checks. However, no matter how careful you are, your vehicle can still break down – a puncture or burst tyre is always possible.

Knowing how to deal with such a situation efficiently and safely is essential knowledge for every driver.

The topics covered

- Breakdowns
- Breakdowns on dual carriageways
- Breakdowns on motorways
- National organisations
- Punctures and blow-outs

Breakdowns

Many breakdowns are the result of

- neglect
- failing to make routine checks
- inadequate preventive maintenance
- abuse of the vehicle.

Preventive maintenance will reduce the likelihood of a breakdown. However, even a well maintained vehicle can break down occasionally.

You need to know how to deal with a breakdown with a minimum of risk to other road users.

When you break down As a general rule, brake as gently as possible and pull over as far to the left as possible to keep your vehicle away from approaching traffic.

If possible, get your car well off the road.

- Use your hazard warning lights to warn others.
- Use your warning triangle, particularly if you've broken down near a bend, or over the brow of a hill.

Keep children and animals well under control, and away from the road.

Contact the police if your vehicle is causing an obstruction, and a breakdown service if you're unable to rectify the fault yourself.

Breakdowns on dual carriageways

Some dual carriageways are similar to motorways; they have

- a hard shoulder to pull on to
- emergency telephones at regular intervals.

Most dual carriageways do *not* have a wide hard shoulder. If you break down on one of these

- get your car safely away from the road, if you can – onto the grass verge or lay-by if there is one. Take care if there's long grass which could ignite from the heat of a catalytic converter
- use your hazard warning lights and advance warning triangle to warn others
- go to the nearest telephone and arrange assistance
- keep animals safely in the car.

Breakdowns on motorways

If you cannot reach the next exit or service area

- pull over as safely as possible onto the hard shoulder as far from the carriageway as possible. Don't brake suddenly
- switch on your hazard lights to warn other drivers you've broken down
- don't open the offside doors
- warn your passengers of the danger of passing vehicles
- with your passengers, leave the vehicle by the nearside doors, away from traffic
- ask your passengers to wait near the vehicle, but on the embankment away from the hard shoulder
- position your warning triangle back on the hard shoulder to warn other drivers.

Telephone marker posts There are marker posts 100 metres (110 yards) apart with arrows to show the direction of the nearest emergency telephone.

Emergency telephones Never cross a slip road to reach an emergency telephone.

The telephone connects you to police control, who will put you through to a breakdown service. Always face the traffic when you speak on the telephone.

You'll be asked for

- the number on the telephone, which gives your precise location
- details of your vehicle and your membership details, if you belong to one of the motoring organisations
- details of the fault.

You'll also be told about how long you'll have to wait.

Return to your vehicle and wait for the breakdown service. It's safer to wait outside your vehicle on the embankment. Leave the front passenger door unlocked so you can get back inside.

To re-join the motorway after a breakdown

Use the hard shoulder as an acceleration lane to build up speed before joining the other traffic when it's safe to do so. Remember to switch off your hazard warning flashers and retrieve your warning triangle.

Don't

- attempt to change a wheel or carry out any repairs on the motorway, hard shoulder or slip roads
- cross to the other side of the motorway to use an emergency telephone, it's illegal and it's dangerous.

Advance warning triangles Advance warning triangles fold flat and don't take up much space in the car. You should carry one and use it to warn other road users if your car is obstructing the highway or is in dangerous position as a result of a breakdown or an accident.

Where to position the triangle You should place the triangle on the road, in the same lane, well back from the car.

- On a straight level road: put the triangle 50 metres (55 yards) from your vehicle.
- On a dual carriageway or motorway: put it at least 150 metres (165 yards) away.
- On a winding or hilly road, put the triangle where drivers will see it before they have to deal with any bend or hump in the road.
- On a very narrow road put the triangle on the nearside verge or footpath.

Always use your hazard warning lights as well as a warning triangle, especially at night.

Don't

- use the triangle as an excuse to leave your car in a dangerous position

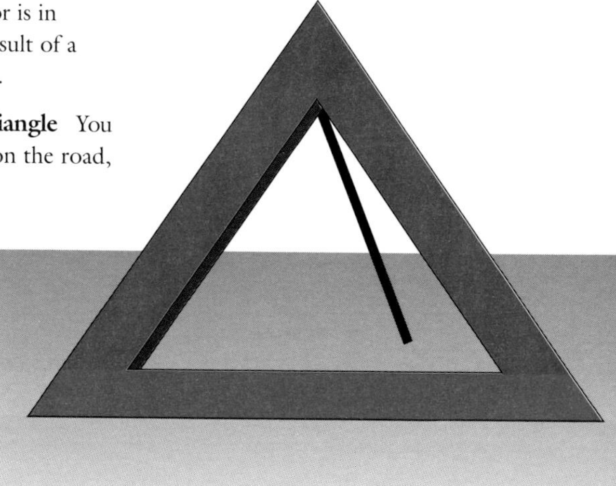

National organisations

By joining a national organisation or taking out breakdown insurance, you'll save a great deal of time and money if you break down.

Most services include an option to take your vehicle and passengers either to your destination or to your home.

The annual fee is usually less than the cost of a single motorway breakdown call-out.

Drivers travelling alone

You might feel vulnerable if you're travelling alone and you break down, especially on an isolated stretch of road, dual carriageway or a motorway.

You should spend as little time as possible away from your vehicle.

When you telephone for assistance, make it clear to the operator that you're travelling alone. Priority will often be given in these cases.

Disabled drivers

Display a HELP pennant. This will alert police patrols. Don't try to reach an emergency telephone if you can't stop near one.

Once you've managed to report to the police or breakdown service

- lock all doors except the front passenger door
- if possible, remain near the vehicle so that you can get back in easily if a vehicle approaches and you feel concerned
- tell anyone who approaches you that the police have been informed and that assistance is already on its way to you.

Don't

- ask for help from passing strangers
- accept help from strangers
- leave your vehicle for any longer than you really have to.

Remember
The likelihood of being injured on the hard shoulder by motorway traffic is five times greater than the risk of assault.

Defensive driving

If you come across an accident, concentrate on what is happening ahead or you could cause another one!

Punctures and blow-outs

If your car suddenly becomes unstable or you begin to feel steering problems you might have a puncture or a blow-out (burst tyre).

Try not to panic.

- Don't brake suddenly.
- Try to keep a straight course by holding the steering wheel firmly.
- Stop gradually at the side of the road.
- Get the vehicle away from the traffic, (on to the hard shoulder if you're on the motorway).

If you have to move the vehicle, do so very slowly to avoid further damage to the tyre or wheel rim. If the tyre has burst, it can't be used again.

Get the vehicle to a place of safety before attempting to change the wheel.

If you can't get off the road altogether, use your warning triangle, particularly if you're near a bend, to warn other drivers.

If necessary, wait for assistance.

Don't

- try to change the wheel on the carriageway, especially on a dual-carriageway or motorway
- work unaided particularly on the side nearest fast moving traffic.

  (Recovery crews wear high visibility clothing, and their vehicles usually have flashing amber warning beacons.)

Remember

- Secure the vehicle when changing any wheel by applying the handbrake and using chocks if available.
- Always try to work on a level surface.
- Re-tighten wheel nuts/studs after changing a wheel.

Warning

If you have any doubts about your ability to carry out the procedure for changing a wheel exactly according to the owner's handbook, you should seek professional assistance.

Carry a legal, serviceable spare in your vehicle at all times.

Do not attempt to change a wheel in an exposed or dangerous position. Call for assistance.

As we have seen in earlier sections, you can reduce the chances of being involved in an accident by driving defensively. Accidents, unfortunately, are always possible, even with the greatest care.

You might also come upon the scene of an accident. It could happen that you're the first to arrive and the safety of others, both the existing casualities and other road users, might be in your hands.

Knowledge and preparation can save lives.

The topics covered

- At the scene of an accident
- First aid on the road
- Fire

At the scene of an accident

If you're involved in an accident you must stop.

If you're the first or among the first to arrive at the scene of an accident, remember

- further collisions can, and do, happen
- fire is a major hazard
- both the accident victims and helpers are in danger.

What to do

Warn other traffic by

- displaying an advance warning triangle
- switching on hazard warning lights or other lights
- using any other means to warn other drivers.

Put out cigarettes or other fire hazards. Switch off your engine and warn others to do the same. Call the emergency services if necessary.

Give full details of the locations and casualties. On a motorway, this could mean going to the next emergency telephone.

Don't move casualties trapped in vehicles unless they're in danger. Give first aid as described in this section.

Move uninjured people away from the vehicles involved to a place of safety.

On a motorway, this should be away from the carriageway, hard shoulder or central reservation.

When the ambulance arrives, give the crew as many *facts* as you can (not assumptions, diagnoses, etc.)

Dangerous goods

If the accident involves a vehicle containing dangerous goods

- give the police or fire brigade as much information as possible about the labels and other markings
- keep well away from the vehicle unless you have to approach to save life
- beware of dangerous liquids, dust or vapours, no matter how small a concentration, or however minor the effects on you may seem.

Full details of hazard warning plates are given in *The Highway Code.*

Defensive driving

Always give way to emergency vehicles. Watch out for their blue flashing lights and listen for their warning sirens.

Attending to injuries

If there are injuries, ask someone to call the ambulance and police.

- Give whatever help you can. People who seem to be unhurt may be suffering from shock, and may in fact be unaware of their injuries.
- Ask yourself if you're hurt too? If in doubt, get a check-up at the hospital.

You must call the police

- if anyone's hurt
- if you've damaged someone else's property but can't find them to tell them.

Report the accident to the police, in person, as soon as possible, or in any case within 24 hours.

Witnesses

Note any witnesses and try to make sure they don't go before you get their names and addresses.

Make a note of the numbers of any vehicles whose occupants might have witnessed the accident.

You'll need to exchange details and obtain

- the other driver's name, address and phone number
- the make and registration number(s) of the other vehicle(s) involved
- insurance details.

Find out the vehicle *owner's* details too, if different.

Information Gather as much information as you can.

- Damage and/or injuries caused.
- Weather conditions.
- Road conditions.
- Details of other vehicles. Record all information: the colour, condition, whether the lights were on, were they showing any indicator signals?.
- What was said by you and other people.
- Identification numbers of police involved.

Take photographs If you have a camera it can be useful to take photographs at the scene.

Draw a map Showing the situation before and after the accident, giving the distances

- between vehicles
- from road signs or junctions
- away from the kerb.

Note skid marks, where any witnesses were situated, street names and car speeds and directions.

Statements

If the police ask you for a statement, you don't have to make one straight away.

It could be better to wait a while, even if you don't appear to be suffering from shock.

Write your statement later. Take care with the wording, and keep a copy.

First aid on the road

Every car should carry a first aid kit and every driver should have a basic knowledge of first aid.

If you haven't any first aid training the following points could be helpful.

Accident victims

It's essential that the following are given urgent priority (within three minutes) if the casualty is unconscious and permanent injury is to be avoided.

- The airway must be cleared and kept open.
- Breathing must be established and maintained.
- Blood circulation must be maintained and severe bleeding stopped.

If breathing has stopped

Unless you suspect head or neck injury

- remove anything that obstructs the mouth, (false teeth, chewing gum, etc.)
- keep the head tilted backwards as far as possible. Breathing should begin and colour improve.

If there's no improvement

- place a clean piece of material, such as a handkerchief, over the injured person's mouth
- pinch the casualty's nostrils together
- blow into the mouth until the chest rises. Take your mouth away and wait for the chest to fall
- repeat regularly once every four seconds until the casualty can breathe without help
- with small babies and children let your mouth surround their mouth and nose and blow *very gently*
- *don't give up*. Never assume anyone is dead. Keep giving mouth to mouth resuscitation until the ambulance arrives.

Unconscious and breathing

Move a casualty only if there's further danger. Movement could add to a spinal/neck injury.

If breathing is difficult or stops, treat as recommended above.

It's vital to obtain professional assistance as soon as possible. Ensure someone dials 999.

Don't attempt to remove an injured motorcyclist's safety helmet unless it's essential – otherwise serious injury could result.

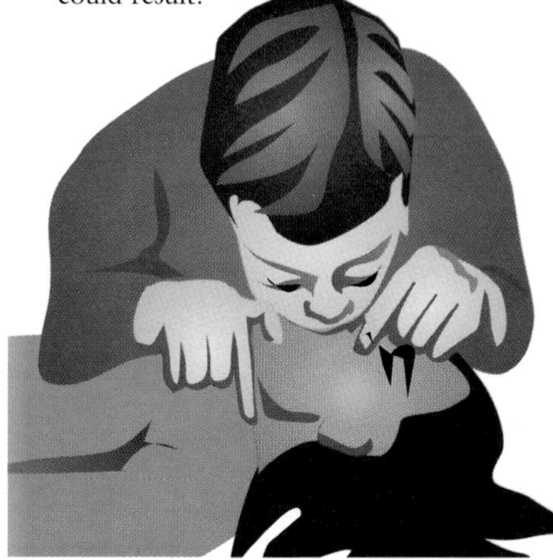

Bleeding

Put firm pressure on the wound, without pressing on anything which might be caught in the wound. Use clean material if you can.

Secure a pad with a bandage or length of cloth.

If it's a limb that's bleeding but not broken, raise it to lessen the bleeding.

Reassurance

Even apparently uninjured persons could be in shock; prompt treatment will help minimise it.

- Avoid unnecessary movement and reassure the casualty confidently.
- Keep the casualty comfortable and warm.
- Try to make sure they're not left alone.
- Give casualties nothing to eat and drink.
- If the casualty has to be moved for safety reasons place him or her in the recovery position.
- Calm an hysterical person by talking to him or her in firm, quiet tones.

Carry a first aid kit

You might never need it, but it could save a life.

Learn first aid

You can learn first aid from

- the St John Ambulance Association and Brigade
- the St Andrew's Ambulance Association
- the British Red Cross Society.

Fire

Always carry a suitable fire extinguisher in your vehicle.

If you suspect a fire in the engine compartment

- pull up as safely and as quickly as possible
- get all passengers out safely
- summon assistance or get someone to dial 999
- DO NOT open the bonnet wide
- direct any available fire extinguisher through the small gap available when the release catch is operated.

Many incidents could be reduced in their severity by prompt action.

Remember

Fire can spread through a vehicle with alarming speed.

If you notice a strong smell of petrol, don't ignore it – investigate!

PART SEVENTEEN THE DRIVER AND THE ENVIRONMENT

Transport is an essential part of modern life, but we cannot ignore its environmental consequences – local, regional and global.

There's increasing public concern for the protection of our environment with the result that many motor vehicle manufacturers are devoting more time, effort and resources to development of environmentally-friendly vehicles.

Considerable research and effort is taking place to develop lighter, smaller and more efficient vehicles for town use. Much of that effort has concentrated on developing electrically powered vehicles with the ability to operate for longer periods before recharging.

Other methods of reducing pollution have resulted in much wider use of engines able to run on unleaded petrol and the introduction of catalytic converters.

This section explains the effects of pollution and what you, the driver, can do to help.

The topics covered

- The effects of pollution
- Exhaust emissions
- What you can do to help
- Traffic management

The effects of pollution

Motor vehicles account for most of the movement of people and goods.

The increased number of vehicles on the roads has damaged the environment; it has resulted in

- changes to the landscape
- building deterioration
- bridge weakening
- changes to communities
- the using-up of natural resources
- disruption of wildlife
- air pollution.

Fuel combustion produces carbon dioxide, a major greenhouse gas, and transport accounts for about one-fifth of the carbon dioxide we produce in this country.

MOT tests now include a strict exhaust emission test to ensure that cars are properly tuned.

This means they need to operate more efficiently and cause less air pollution.

Exhaust emissions

New petrol-engined cars have to be able to run on unleaded petrol.

Ever-stricter controls on exhaust emissions require catalytic converters to be fitted to the exhaust system of all new petrol-engined vehicles.

Some older normal carburettor fuel systems won't be able to reduce exhaust gases to specified levels. If the engine is running at the levels it was originally designed for, then it will remain acceptable.

Catalytic converters

Greater efforts are being made to reduce levels of pollution caused by motor vehicles.

Catalytic converters reduce the exhaust gases containing carbon monoxide, nitrogen oxide and hydrocarbons by up to 90%.

The converter is a honeycombed filter with a total surface area about equal to a football pitch.This surface is coated with precious metals such as platinum, palladium and rhodium. These speed up a chemical reaction in the exhaust gases as the engine heats up.

The oxygen content of the exhaust is monitored and a sensor triggers controls to adjust the air-fuel mixture.

The converter only deals with toxic and polluting gases. Carbon dioxide is still produced.

Leaded petrol cannot be used in vehicles fitted with a catalytic converter. Even one tankful can permanently damage the system.

Diesel engines

Diesel engines are even more environmentally friendly than a petrol engine.

However, heavier diesel engines will be required to meet stricter exhaust emission requirements.

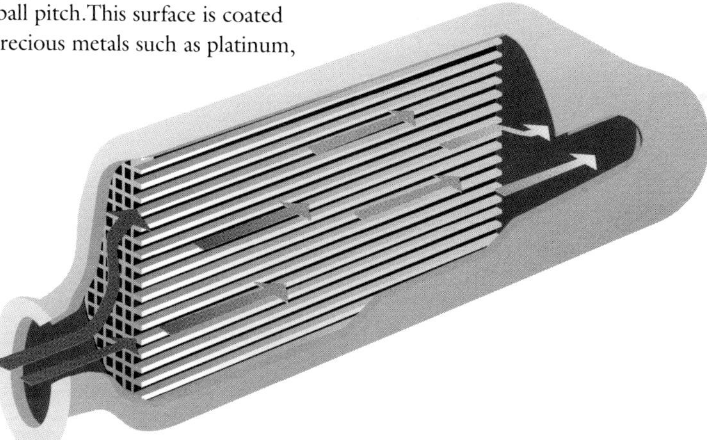

What YOU can do to help

- Walk or cycle whenever it's safe to do so.
- Use public transport when you can.
- Make sure your vehicle is properly tuned and serviced.

  A vehicle in good condition uses less fuel and produces cleaner exhaust.
- Make sure your tyres are properly inflated. Under-inflated tyres waste fuel.
- If your engine is cold when you start, push in the choke as soon as the engine will run smoothly without it.
- When buying a new vehicle, choose a fuel-efficient model. Use the Department of Transport's guide to the fuel consumption of new vehicles.
- Look well ahead to avoid harsh braking, one of the biggest fuel wasters.
- Drive sensibly. Good driving habits save fuel. Plan ahead, watch the traffic flow.
- Use the appropriate gear and avoid over-revving in low gear.
- Don't accelerate harshly.
- Use unleaded fuel, or, if possible, convert the engine to use it. Consult your dealer or garage.
- Check your fuel consumption to make sure you're getting the most from your car
- Slow down. Driving at 70 mph uses up to 30% more fuel than driving at 50 mph
- Send waste oil, old batteries and used tyres to a garage or local authority site for recycling or safe disposal. Otherwise they can cause serious pollution

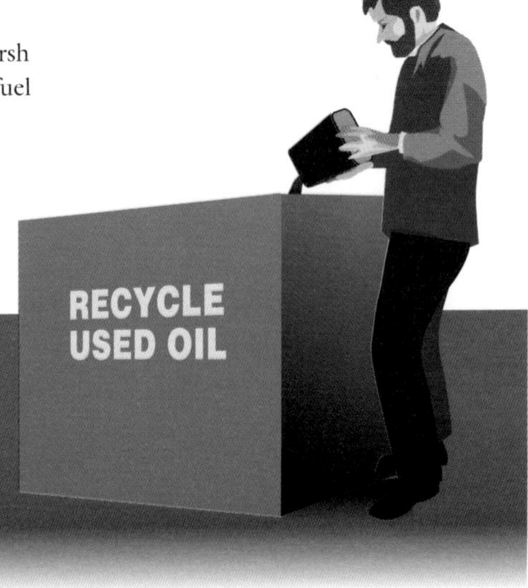

Don't

- use your car for very short journeys, especially when the engine is cold. (Walk, cycle or use public transport.)
- carry unnecessary weight in your car; it uses extra fuel. So does your roof rack, even when it's empty, so if it's removable, take it off when you're not using it
- pour used oil down the drain or into the ground. It's illegal, and could lead to prosecution

Off-road activities

Whatever type of vehicle you drive, whenever you take part in off-road activities, remember

- avoid damaging walls, fences, paths, grassland, etc.
- take care not to harm livestock or wildlife
- respect the countryside in general
- drive in a responsible manner at all times.

Traffic management

Continuous research has resulted in new methods of helping the environment by easing traffic flow.

All drivers need to be aware of the restrictions that apply and consider using alternative transport systems.

The strict parking rules in major cities and towns help the traffic flow. Use public transport whenever you can.

The 'Red Routes' in London have cut journey times and stopped traffic using short cuts through residential streets.

Traffic calming measures, including road humps and chicanes help to keep vehicle speeds low in sensitive areas (20 mph). Children are much more likely to survive an accident with a motor vehicle travelling at 20 mph than at 40 mph.

Cyclists and pedestrians are safer too in these conditions.

Light Rapid Transit (LRT) systems, trams or 'Metros' are being introduced in cities and large towns to provide more efficient public transport which is also environmentally friendly as it uses electric power (see page 120).

For further information

Contact:

Public Enquiry Unit
Department of Transport
2 Marsham Street
LONDON SW1P 3EB
Tel: 0171 271 5388

Environmental Transport Association
10 Church St.
WEYBRIDGE KT13 8RS
Tel: 01932 828882

The Automobile Association
Fanum House
BASINGSTOKE RG21 2EA
Tel: 01256 320123

The Royal Automobile Club
Technical Control
RAC House
P.O.Box 200
WALSALL WS5 4QZ
Tel: 0990 313131

PART EIGHTEEN

Caravanning and camping have become very popular because not only do they offer complete flexibility, they are also a more economical way of touring than staying in hotels.

They can be extremely enjoyable providing you follow the basic principles of safe towing.

Most of the skills and precautions involved in towing a caravan are no different from those needed for towing a trailer.

This section deals with the regulations, skills and precautions needed for safe towing.

The topics covered

- Towing regulations
- Weight distribution
- Experience
- Safety checks
- Driving technique

Towing regulations

Car drivers who passed their test before 1 January 1997 are generally allowed to drive a vehicle and trailer combination up to 8.25 tonnes.* (7.5 tonnes under 21 years old.)

New drivers regulations

Drivers who pass their car test on or after 1 January 1997 and wish to tow trailers may drive

- a 3.5 tonne vehicle with a trailer up to 750kg
- a category B vehicle† with a trailer exceeding 750kgs provided
  - the combination doesn't exceed 3.5 tonnes

  and

  - the laden weight of the trailer doesn't exceed the unladen weight of the towing vehicle

and providing the towing vehicle has no more than 8 passenger seats.

In practice most small trailers, caravans and horseboxes should be well within the category B entitlement.

If you wish to drive

- a 3.5 tonne vehicle with a trailer of more than 750kg
- a combination which exceeds 3.5 tonnes
- a trailer whose maximum authorised mass exceeds the unladen weight of the towing vehicle

then you will have to take a B+E test.

B+E test The minimum test vehicle is a Category B vehicle with a trailer of at least
1 tonne. Full details of this test are available in the sister publication *The Driving Test* (published by The Stationery Office)

Larger vehicles New drivers who wish to tow trailers behind

- minibuses

or

- larger vehicles

can obtain full details of the current regulations on factsheet INF 30 available from The Driver and Vehicle Licensing Agency.

Note.
* All trailer weights refer to the maximum authorised mass (MAM) also known as the maximum authorised weight or gross vehicle weight.

† A category B vehicle is

- a four wheel vehicle capable of at least 100 kph (62.5 mph)
- no heavier than 3.5 tonnes
- not capable of carrying more than eight passenger seats.

The combination

As a general guide, the laden weight of the caravan or trailer should never exceed the kerbside weight of the towing vehicle. Ideally, the actual weight of the loaded caravan or trailer (laden weight) should be no more than 85% of the empty weight of the towing vehicle (kerbside weight), especially for drivers new to towing.

Take care not to exceed the limits set out in the vehicle owner's handbook.

Remember that the overall length of the combination is generally double that of the normal family car.

You will need to

- fit exterior towing mirrors so that you have a clear view along both sides of the caravan or trailer
- allow more time and brake earlier when slowing down or stopping
- give yourself three times the normal distance and time to overtake safely
- take account of the extra length, particularly when turning or emerging at junctions.

Stabiliser A good stabiliser fitted to the towbar can make the combination safer to handle, but it will not relieve you of the responsibility of loading the combination correctly.

Neither will it cure instability caused by a poor towing vehicle/trailer combination.

The stabiliser will give you added security in cross-winds, when large goods vehicles overtake you on the motorway.

Weight distribution

The overall stability of both the caravan and the towing vehicle depends on correct weight distribution.

For example, heavy items should be loaded as low as possible in the caravan or trailer so that they are mainly over the axle(s).

Bulkier, lighter items, such as bedding or clothing, should be distributed to give a suitable 'noseweight' at the towing coupling.

If in doubt, adjust the noseweight by using a gauge available from caravan accessory stockists.

Riding in the caravan

You must not allow anyone to ride in the caravan when it's being towed.

Entering the caravan If you stop for a break, always lower the jockey wheel and corner steadies of the caravan before entering or letting anyone in.

Don't forget to raise them fully before you move off.

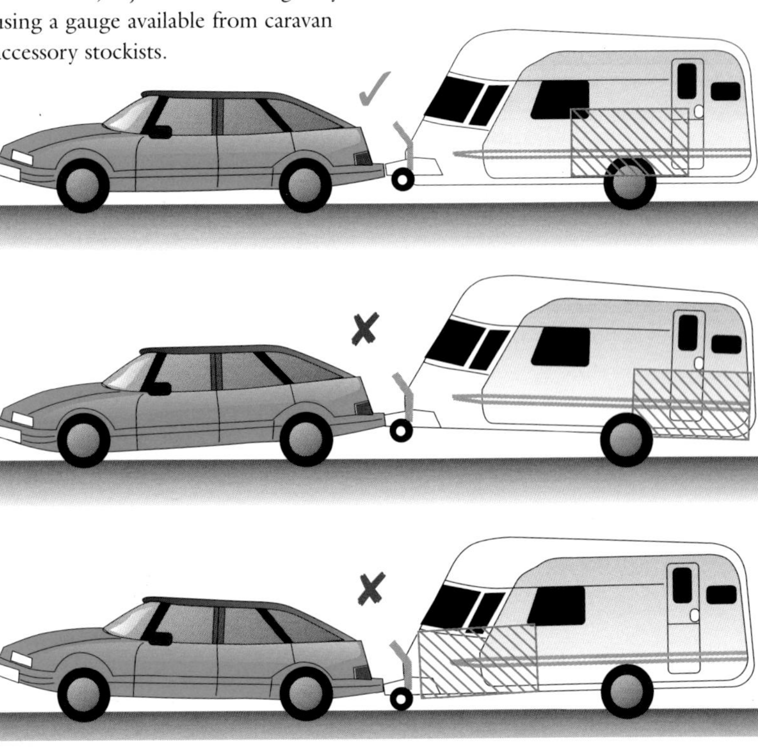

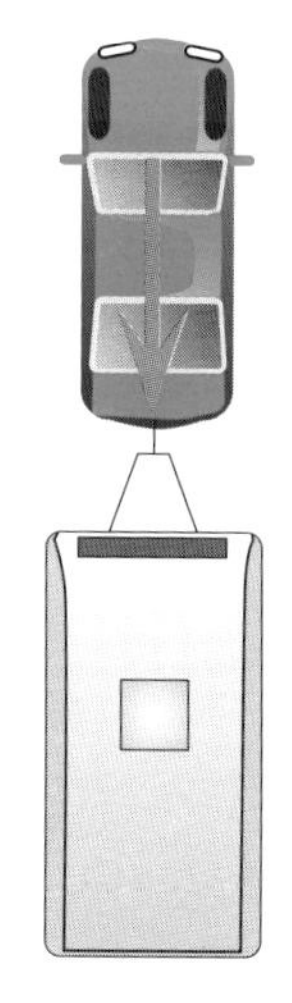

Experience

Experience of towing is desirable but not essential. Drivers without experience need to take great care, particularly when manoeuvring.

Don't be afraid to practise reversing in a quiet car park until you have mastered the technique.

If you're new to towing a caravan seek advice from one of the large caravanning organisations.

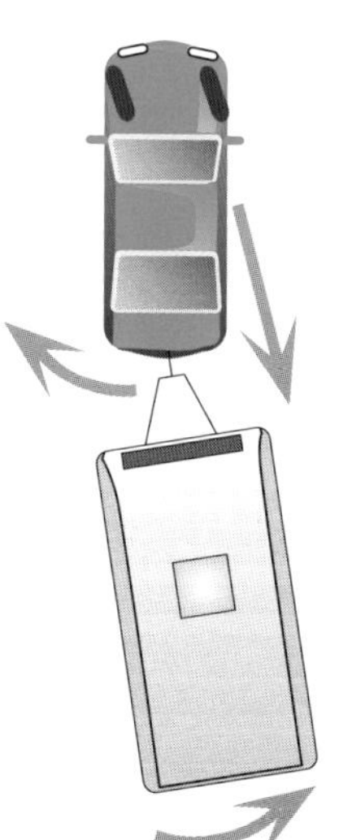

You should also consider attending their excellent courses which cover such safety aspects as loading, manoeuvring, and driving techniques.

You can find detailed guidance on all aspects of towing in the booklet *The Caravan Towing Guide* which you can obtain from

The National Caravanning Council
Catherine House
Victoria Road
ALDERSHOT
Hants GU11 1SS
Tel: 01252 318251

Safety checks

Before starting a journey, check that the caravan or trailer

- is loaded correctly with the right pressure on the towbar
- is correctly hitched up with the breakaway cable, if fitted, properly connected and the hitch fully locked on
- lights and indicators are connected and working correctly
- jockey wheel and assembly is fully retracted and in the stowed position
- braking system is working correctly
- windows, roof light and door are closed
- tyre pressures are correct.

In addition

- check the caravan or trailer tyres for signs of cracking even if the tread pattern is above the legal limit.
  Remember that tyre regulations also cover the tyres on your caravan or trailer.
  A caravan that has to be left standing for long periods should be raised on supports that take the weight off the tyres. This will help prolong tyre life
- check that your caravan or trailer is fitted with tyres of the specified rating (see manufacturer's handbook)
- check that you've secured and turned off all fuel supplies, such as liquid gas cylinders.

Driving technique

Always be aware of the increased weight, length and width of the combined vehicles by planning well ahead.

You'll soon adjust to the different techniques involved in towing so long as you remember not to hurry any manoeuvres and to plan well ahead.

Speed limits

You must not exceed the speed limits when you're towing, which are, unless road signs tell you otherwise

- 30 mph (48 kph) in built up areas
- 50 mph (80 kph) on single carriageways
- 60 mph (96 kph) on dual carriageways or motorways.

Reduce speed

- in high or cross-winds
- when going downhill
- in poor visibility.

Motorway driving

Caravans or trailers must not be towed in the outside lane of a motorway, unless other lanes are closed.

Snaking Never attempt to correct swerving or 'snaking' by increasing speed, steering sharply (zig-zag), or braking hard.

The safe technique

- ease off the accelerator slowly
- allow a certain amount of 'twitch' in the steering
- reduce speed until the snaking has stopped.

High-sided vehicles

You need to take extra care when passing or being passed by high-sided vehicles.

Allow as much space as possible to avoid the affects of turbulence or buffeting.

Remember

On narrow roads, be prepared to pull up at suitable passing places to let faster traffic overtake.

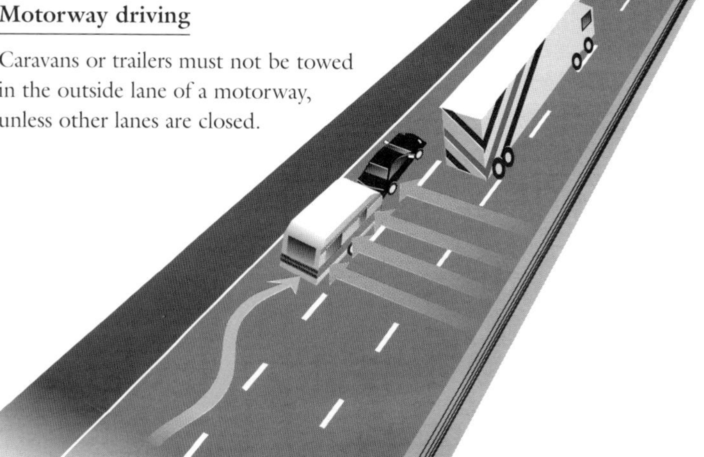

Theft of vehicles, especially cars, has risen to unacceptable levels. In some urban areas, it has become an epidemic.

The thieves vary from the opportunists to the professional thieves who often work in gangs and target specific models for which they already have a buyer, sometimes in another country.

Even more common are thefts *from* private cars. Once more the thieves vary from the opportunists, who snatch valuables from unlocked cars, to the professionals, who comb whole areas and steal car radios from poorly secured vehicles.

Having your vehicle stolen or broken into is at best an inconvenience and at worst very distressing.

While determined thieves would probably be able to steal or get into any vehicle, they are usually too busy with the poorly secured ones. If your vehicle is secured, and preferably alarmed and immobilised, they may well leave it alone.

This section deals very briefly with the precautions you can take to secure your vehicle.

The topics covered

- Security measures
- Parking

Security measures

Taking a vehicle without the owner's consent, or with the intention of driving it recklessly, is a criminal offence. Such actions sometimes end in death, usually of innocent passers-by.

If you don't want your vehicle stolen

- fit an anti-theft device (alarm and/or immobiliser)
- lock it in a secure garage overnight
- use a visible security device (to lock steering wheel, handbrake, etc.)
- have the vehicle registration number etched on all windows.

Vehicle watch

Join one of the Vehicle Watch schemes in your area.

Parking

Avoid leaving your vehicle unattended in poorly lit areas, which are known to be a high risk.

Whenever possible

- use attended and secure car parks
- at night park in an area that will be well lit
- if you have a garage, use it.

When you leave your vehicle

- lock it
- remove the key
- engage the steering lock
- set the alarm or anti-theft device, if you have one
- close all windows completely (But don't leave pets in a vehicle with the windows completely closed.)
- either remove all valuables or lock them out of sight
- never leave the vehicle documents inside.

Radios

Car radios are one of the prime targets for thieves.

Install a security coded radio. This can deter thieves since the radio is likely to be of little use once removed from the vehicle.

Some manufacturers provide security coding for radios supplied in new vehicles.

Another alternative is to install a removable radio. One of these looks exactly like any other radio, but it slides out of its housing. You can lock it away in the boot or take it with you.

Soft-top vehicles

Never leave a cabriolet or soft-top vehicle where it will obviously be vulnerable.

Remember

Lock it or lose it!

Taking your car abroad or hiring one in the country you're visiting gives you freedom and mobility.

You can

- plan your holiday around your interests or business commitments
- travel at your own pace
- stop when and where you like
- visit places of interest on the way
- discover the more remote places
- carry extra equipment such as camping, sports gear, canoes, surfboards, etc.

This section summarises what you need to do to prepare for driving in Europe.

The topics covered

European driving

Many East European countries have recently opened up their borders and now there's even more of Europe to explore.

Travelling to Europe

An extensive motorway network runs through most of the continent and there are regular ferry links from many of the UK ports.

You have more opportunity to choose alternative routes and arrive in Europe closer to your destination.

The Channel Tunnel provides yet another link to the continent.

Planning your journey

If you're planning to take your car abroad, the major motoring organisations can help you to organise and plan the details of your trip.

They can

- save you time and money
- set up medical, travel and vehicle insurance
- provide equipment for minor repairs and breakdowns
- help you organise the correct documents for your car, trailer or caravan.

You can often make your trip much easier by using their facilities and experience.

Your route

Once you know which country you're going to visit you can begin to plan your route through the continent.

Again the motoring organisations can simplify this for you with

- computerised route guides
- summaries of motoring regulations
- details of tolls, etc.

They will recommend routes from continental ports or airports to specific destinations using motorway for speed and convenience or scenic routes for pleasure.

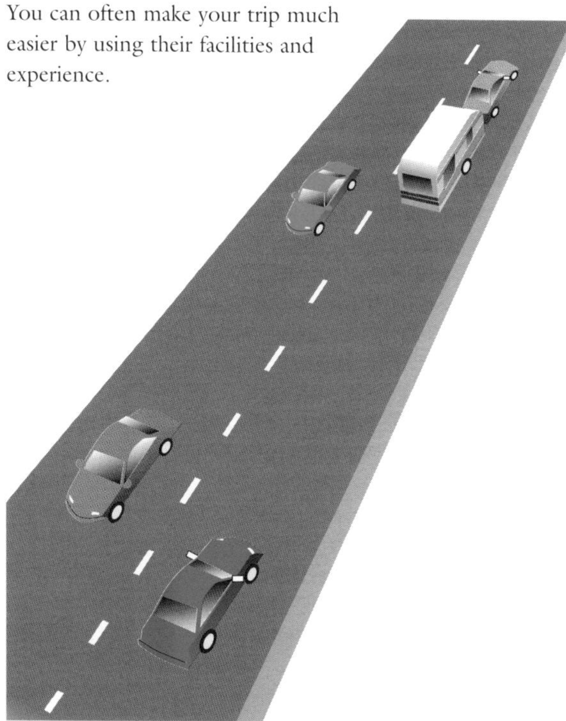

Your vehicle

Before you travel abroad have your car thoroughly checked and serviced. Checks to make include

- the spare tyre; make sure it's in good condition
- your tool kit and jack; make sure all items are complete and in working order
- make sure you have your spare car keys.

Lights

Your lights will need to be altered for driving on the right.

- Yellow tinted headlights are no longer required in most countries.
- Deflectors are required in most countries. These prevent your dipped beam dazzling drivers approaching on the left.

Carry a set of replacement bulbs.

Your mirrors

Check your mirrors. You must have clear all-round vision.

You will need to have exterior rear view mirrors especially on the left for driving on the right-hand side of the road.

If you're towing a caravan or trailer make sure you can see clearly behind, down both sides.

Seat belts

Check seat belts, and child safety belts. Make sure the fittings are secure.

Emergency equipment

In many countries emergency equipment must be carried. Check with motoring organisations to find out what is required in the countries you will be visiting. This equipment may include

- emergency repair kits
- spares kit
- emergency windscreen
- emergency warning triangle
- roof racks and roof boxes
- snow chains
- ski racks/boxes.

Precautions against breakdown

Dealing with breakdowns abroad can be especially time consuming and worrying without the help of one of the motoring organisations or breakdown services.

The best prevention is to have your car thoroughly serviced and to make regular checks on route.

You can also make sure you're prepared for minor breakdowns.

Driving documents

You must have all the necessary documents before leaving. Again, the motoring organisations will be able to tell you what's required for each country.

Insurance

Third party motor vehicle insurance is compulsory in most countries. It is strongly recommended you contact your insurer to make sure you're adequately covered.

Most insurance policies issued in the UK automatically provide third party cover in EC countries as well as in some others. They do not provide comprehensive cover unless you arrange this with your insurer, who may charge an extra premium.

Make sure you have the appropriate insurance certificate with you.

Certain countries require a bail bond as a security in the event of an accident. Consult your insurer.

Your driving licence

You must carry your national driving licence when motoring abroad. Even if you need an International Driving Permit (see below), take your national licence also.

If you want to drive a hired or borrowed vehicle in the country you're visiting ask about minimum age requirements, in case they apply to you.

Translation

In Italy, you must carry a translation with your licence. You can get this free of charge from the major motoring organisations. If you have a pink or pink and green EC type UK licence, this translation isn't required.

International Driving Permit (IDP)

Many non-EC countries still require an IDP.

To qualify for one, you must be 18.

To apply you'll need

- your driving licence
- a passport-sized photograph
- a fee.

The motoring organisations can issue your IDP.

Note. Seventeen-year-olds are not allowed to drive in most European countries.

Vehicle Registration Document

You must carry the original Vehicle Registration Document with you.

If you don't have your Vehicle Registration Document, apply to a Vehicle Registration Office for a temporary certificate of registration (V379). Apply through your local Post Office well in advance of your journey.

If you plan to hire, borrow or lease a vehicle you must also ensure you have all the relevant documents.

Personal documents

Passport/Visa

ALL persons travelling must either hold, or be named on, an up-to-date passport valid for all countries through which you intend to travel.

Carry your passport(s) at all times.

Keep a separate note of the number, date and place of issue of each passport, in case they are stolen or lost.

Travellers need a visa for some European countries. Check well in advance with the embassies or consulates concerned.

This is particularly important if you hold a UK passport not issued in this country, or the passport of any other nationality.

Note. You'll need a full UK passport in countries where the Visitor's Passport is not accepted. Check beforehand.

Medical expenses insurance

You're strongly advised to take out a comprehensive medical insurance cover for any trip abroad.

Most medical treatment can be obtained free of charge or at reduced cost from the health care schemes of countries with whom the UK has reciprocal health care arrangements.

Don't rely on these arrangements alone.

Department of Health leaflet E111

Details of the Department of Health leaflet E111 are available from any post office. It provides health advice for travellers.

Motoring regulations

Drink and driving

Don't drink and drive.

The laws and penalties abroad are often more severe than those in the UK.

Fire extinguisher

A fire extinguisher is compulsory in some countries and strongly recommended.

Advance warning triangle

The use of a warning triangle is compulsory in most countries for all vehicles with more than two wheels. Hazard warning lights should not be used instead of a triangle but to complement it. Some countries require two advance warning triangles.

Spare bulbs

Some countries require you to carry a spare set of bulbs.

First aid kit

Make sure your vehicle carries a first aid kit. It is compulsory in some countries and strongly recommended in many others.

Identification plate

If you're towing a caravan or trailer fit an identification plate.

Nationality plate

You must display a nationality plate of the approved size and design at the rear of your vehicle or caravan/trailer.

Passengers

Never take more passengers than your vehicle is built to carry.

Make sure you use your seat belts and everyone is secure before setting out on any journey.

Speed limits

There are speed limits in all countries which you must obey. A list of these limits can be obtained from the motoring organisations.

Remember, speed limits vary from country to country. Get to know them.

Obey speed limits. Many countries have severe on-the-spot fines for offenders. Others prosecute, and that could prove to be expensive.

Warning: police fines

On-the-spot fines are imposed for most minor motoring offences.

Make sure you

- know the regulations for each country you intend visiting
- obey them.

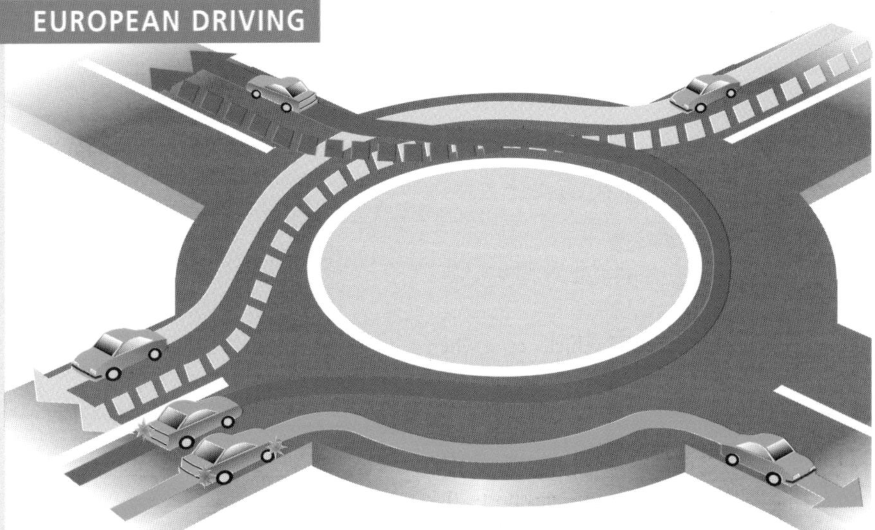

Driving in Europe

It can take time for you to adjust to driving on the right. Mistakes can lead to accidents.

Get into the habit of using all your mirrors before making any manoeuvre. This is particularly important before deciding to overtake. Remember to check the left exterior mirror where fitted.

Make certain you feel fit enough for your trip. Don't let your attention wander. It can be dangerous to forget where you are, even for a moment.

Each time you set out remember that you're in a foreign country where you must drive on the right.

Avoid driving for long periods and don't allow fatigue to set in.

Take special care after a rest when you drive out on to the road again.

Remember

Hire vehicles will normally be left-hand drive. These may feel unfamiliar at first.

Make sure you understand the controls before you drive.

After your trip

Don't forget to adjust to driving on the left again as soon as you return!

Defensive driving

- Take extra care at roundabouts. Be aware of the changed priority.
- Don't attempt to overtake until you're used to driving on the right.

Motorway tolls

Some countries charge motorway tolls. Find out about these and include them in your budget.

Security

Don't leave handbags, wallets or other attractive items within obvious view inside the vehicle, even when you're inside too.

Never leave valuables in an unattended parked vehicle overnight.

Loss of possessions, passports, tickets, cash and credit cards can be distressing and inconvenient when you're abroad.

Be on your guard against confidence tricksters.

Checklist

As part of your planning, make a checklist of equipment, documents and other items.

If you're travelling through several countries check against each item whether it's compulsory or strongly recommended.

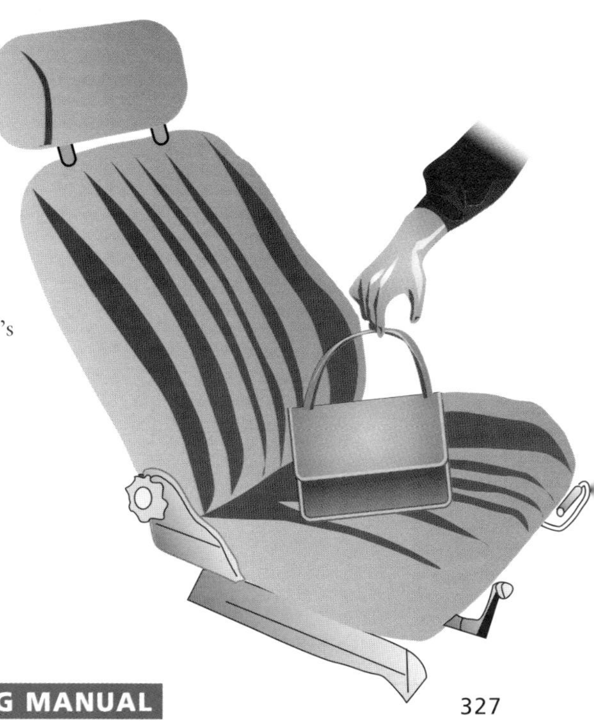

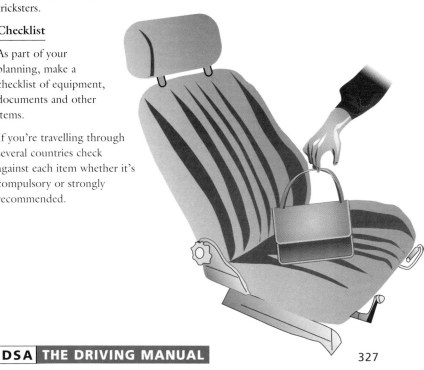

Vehicles with automatic transmission have always been a great help to drivers with physical disabilities, because there's less work for the feet and hands to do.

They've become increasingly popular with all drivers, not least because of the easier control and convenience they offer, particularly in congested urban conditions.

This section deals with the extra knowledge and skill required when driving vehicles with automatic transmission and four-wheel drive.

The topics covered

- Automatics
- Four-wheel drive

Automatics

Vehicles with automatic transmission have no clutch pedal. The transmission senses and selects the gear according to the road speed and load on the engine.

This not only makes the physical job of driving much easier but also allows you more time to concentrate on what's happening on the road.

Automatic transmission usually changes

- to a higher gear as the road speed increases
- to a lower gear as it falls.

It will also change down to a lower gear going uphill, as the load on the engine increases.

There are times, for example, going down a steep hill, when you need to keep in a low gear, even if the speed is constant, and the engine load is light.

The system normally tries to change to a higher gear in these situations. However, the driver is usually able to override the transmission by using the gear selector to remain in a suitable lower gear.

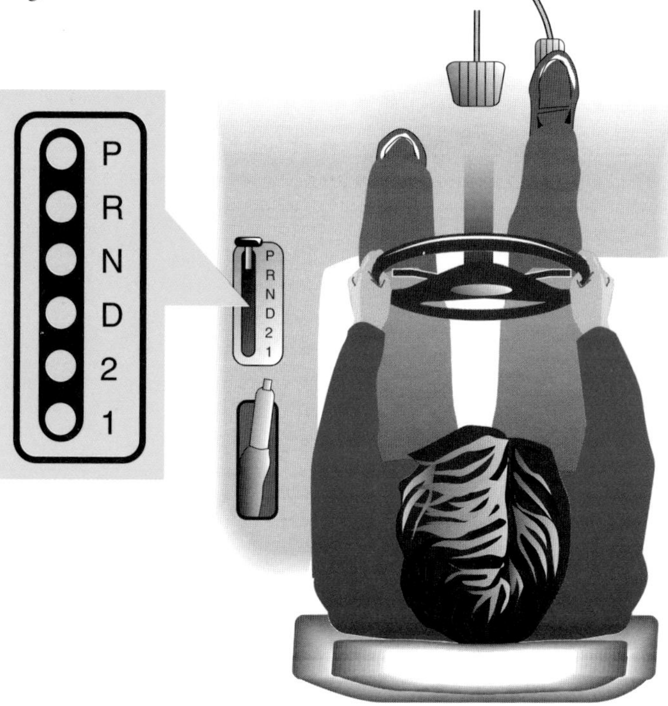

The gear selector

Virtually all automatics have a gear selector. There might be minor variations of the selector positions between different manufacturers.

With any automatic it's essential to study the handbook to understand the features of your particular model.

A typical gear selector layout includes

P (Park) which mechanically locks the transmission and should only be selected when the vehicle is stationary

R (Reverse)

N (Neutral) which is the same as neutral on a manual gearbox.

D (Drive) for driving forward

2 (second gear)

1 (first gear)

Some automatics with four forward gears have third gear as an additional position that comes after **D** (Drive).

These numbered gear positions enable you to prevent the transmission selecting a higher gear. This is particularly useful

- in heavy traffic
- when manoeuvring
- going down a steep hill.

Kick-down

This is a device that provides for quick acceleration when you need it, for example, to overtake.

Sharply pressing the accelerator pedal right down causes a quick change down to the next lower gear. To return to the higher gear, ease the pressure off the accelerator pedal.

The importance of the handbrake

Fully applying the handbrake whenever your vehicle is stationary is even more important on an automatic.

If the selector lever is in any position other than **P** or **N**, it will move off under power if the accelerator is pressed – accidentally or on purpose – unless the brakes are on.

If the choke (manual or automatic) is in use, an even lighter accelerator pressure can move the vehicle away.

Creep

Creep happens if the tick-over, or slow running of the engine creates enough power to move the vehicle. The brakes are necessary to prevent it moving.

Always check your vehicle for a tendency to creep excessively. Do this on the level (not uphill).

Never rely on creep to hold the vehicle on a hill – even though it doesn't move. The vehicle could roll back without warning if the engine stopped for any reason.

The safe rule is: *apply the handbrake fully whenever you pull up.*

Driving an automatic

Make sure you fully understand the procedure required before you attempt to drive a vehicle with automatic transmission.

- Never start the engine unless the selector is in the **P** (Park) or **N** (Neutral) position and the handbrake is fully applied.
- For normal forward driving move the selector lever to the **D** (Drive) position.

The transmission will then change gear as necessary if there's enough pressure on the accelerator.

Alternatively, selecting one of the numbered gears will give the same flexibility as a manual gearbox.

Controlled use of the accelerator is essential when driving an automatic as it has such a direct effect when the selector is in any position, other than **P** (Park) or **N** (Neutral).

Heavy acceleration should be avoided. It can

- cause the vehicle to surge forward (or backwards) out of control
- delay upward gear changes.

Control

When manoeuvring using hardly any accelerator and only light braking, one foot on each pedal is convenient and safe. When driving along, it's safer to use the right foot only for both accelerator and brake pedals, just as you do vehicles with a manual gearbox.

This develops anticipation by encouraging

- the early release of the accelerator pedal
- early and progressive braking.

It cuts out

- the instability and wear and tear brought about by braking against acceleration
- the need to learn a different method if you change from an automatic to a manual or vice versa.

Points to remember

Apart from avoiding the danger of excessive creep you should also

- make sure the tick-over is not set too fast. This can make your road speed more difficult to control and you could, for example, find yourself approaching a junction much too fast
- avoid over-confidence and driving too fast for the road and traffic conditions
- be aware of the reduced effect of engine braking on automatics. Use the gear selector to hold a lower gear when necessary
- control your speed as you approach a corner

Remember

Automatics sometimes change up as you approach a corner due to reduced pressure on the accelerator. To avoid this, slow down before you reach the corner, then accelerate gently as you turn.

Four-wheel drive

Four-wheel drive is normally engaged by a separate lever. This connects the second axle (usually the front wheels) into the transmission drive system.

Four-wheel drive has become much more widely available. There are three basic groups

- the original type
- the sport type
- the saloon.

The original four-wheel drive

The four-wheel drive vehicle was originally a military vehicle for use on rough terrain.

It was built to work in all weather and on difficult surfaces. It's now commonly used by farmers, contractors and public service authorities.

You don't need any extra skill to drive this type of four-wheel drive vehicle on the public road. However, if you drive off-road, you need to be wary on hilly terrain and soft surface.

Look out for rocks which could either damage the underside of vehicle or suddenly deflect the steering causing loss of control.

Defensive driving

When travelling diagonally downhill, always look for an escape route at right angles, down the slope if the vehicle strikes any object or the danger of overturning arises.

The 'sport' type off-road vehicle

These also date back to the military jeep but have been stylised to include the comforts of an ordinary saloon car.

The centre of gravity tends to be higher and the wheelbase shorter than those of ordinary vehicles.

Always keep to safe driving principles.

- Remember to take into account the nature of the terrain.
- Don't overstep your mark, even if your vehicle feels strong enough to handle any difficult contour or surface conditions.
- Take corners at a steady speed. Remember that all the wheels are generally locked into the transmission system and revolve at different speeds. This could affect the stability of the vehicle if driven recklessly.
- Don't expect the vehicle to do more than it's capable of. Don't drive through ordinary traffic on normal roads at high speed.

Saloon cars with four-wheel drive

A few saloon cars are now fitted with four-wheel drive. This can be

- an optional extra when buying a new vehicle
- part of the overall design so that sensors in the vehicle's drive system automatically engage four-wheel drive.

Benefits

The main benefit of four-wheel drive in a saloon car is greatly improved roadholding and cornering.

Limitations

Saloon cars with four-wheel drive can deal with some off-road conditions.

However, because of low ground clearance they will not deal with very soft surfaces. Special off-road vehicles have higher ground clearance and usually off-road tyres.

The same applies to snow. A four-wheel drive saloon will deal very well with snow up to a certain depth, but not with very deep snow.

A final word

Having studied this book, are YOU satisfied with your own standard of driving?

If you are satisfied, should you be?

Every one of us is capable of making mistakes on the road. However, not every driver is prepared to make allowances for those mistakes when they are committed by others.

Watch out for other people's mistakes and be ready to slow down or stop – even if you have the right of way. Never rely on other road users doing the right thing. It's dangerous.

Always be critical of your own standard of driving before you comment on that of another driver. Ask yourself if you always stick to the rules so that everyone else knows what to expect?

Remember, the perfect road user doesn't exist. Whatever stage you have reached as a driver, always aim for a higher standard.

Watch other drivers and copy the best of what you see. Be tolerant of the worst, and learn how to avoid such errors yourself.

There is no place on today's roads for impatience, intolerance, exhibitionism, aggression or selfishness. If you behave in any of those ways, you're well on your way to having an accident.

The ability to handle your vehicle and react quickly to road and traffic conditions doesn't necessarily make you either a good or a safe driver. Driving skill alone will not prevent accidents. Your attitude of mind is just as important, as is having a detailed knowledge of defensive driving techniques.

Developing the right attitude and behaviour is something you need to keep working at.

The good driver needs

- a sense of responsibility
- concentration on the job of driving
- good anticipation
- patience and confidence.

Above all, show courtesy and consideration to ALL road users.

Reducing the risk of accidents will make our roads safer for everyone. So make sure your aim is

'Safe driving for life'

Useful addresses

Driving Standards Agency
Stanley House
Talbot Street
NOTTINGHAM
NG1 5GU
Tel: 0115 901 2500

Guild of Experienced Motorists
Station Road
FOREST ROW
East Sussex
RH18 5EN
Tel: 01342 825676

Institute of Advanced Motorists
IAM House
359 Chiswick High Road
LONDON W4 4H5
Tel: 0181 994 4403

The Royal Society for the Prevention of Accidents (ROSPA)
Edgbaston Park
353 Bristol Rd.
BIRMINGHAM B5 7ST
Tel: 0121 248 2000
Fax: 0121 248 2001

Safe Driving – *for life*

The Official Theory Test for Car Drivers and Motorcyclists - new edition

It covers all aspects of the test, about 700 questions, together with their answers and explanations. It will help you to relate safe driving techniques to your daily driving, as well as prepare you for your theory test.

ISBN 0 11 551925 4 PRICE **£10.99**

NEW Making a Pass

A lively, informative video, aimed at learner drivers. Starring Anna Friel of *Brookside* and Steven Lord of *Common as Muck,* this 40 minute video is both entertaining and informative with a serious message about responsible driving.

ISBN 0 11 551877 0 PRICE **£14.99** (inc. VAT)

The Driving Test

Gives you the facts to pass your test and be a safe driver and contains the official syllabus. It tells you what to do before the test, about CBT for motorcyclists, the test requirements, skills, and faults to avoid, plus other useful information. For cars, motorcycles, and trailers.

ISBN 0 11 551778 2 PRICE **£4.99**

The Highway Code

The Highway Code defines the rules for all aspects of road safety, including signs and markings, hazards, other road users and traffic law. A video of The Highway Code is also available with drama and quiz sections.

Book ISBN 0 11 551843 6 PRICE **99 pence**
Video ISBN 0 11 551183 0 PRICE **£10.99** (inc. VAT)

Theory Test and Beyond CD-ROM version II

Driving brought to life in full colour, animation and MPEG video. Includes Theory Test questions, Driving Manual, Highway Code, Pass Plus and much more!

ISBN 0 11 312062 1 PRICE **£24.95** (inc.VAT)

Know Your Traffic Signs

An updated edition of the best-selling booklet which illustrates and explains the vast majority of traffic signs the road user is likely to encounter.

ISBN 0 11 551612 3 PRICE **£2.50**

NEW Audio Mock Theory Test

Devised to help new drivers prepare for the Theory Test. All you need to do is ring 0930 217 217. It takes approx. 30 minutes to complete the test, callers must be 18 or over and calls will be charged at 50p a minute.

Cyberdrive

Visit our new website for information about all the new books, CDs and videos to help you pass your test and advance your driving skills. And watch out for special promotions, competitions and the new on-line mock theory test, all on **http://www.cyberdrive.co.uk**

Books, CDs are available from The Stationery Office Bookshops and Agents (See Yellow Pages: Booksellers), and all good bookshops.

Order now on **0171 873 9090** or fax **0171 873 8200**

The Stationery Office

Printed in the United Kingdom for The Stationery Office
J24567, 10/97, C1000, 60860